Advanced Beginner to Intermediate Coursebook

Professor Mike Hainzinger

Caitlin -
Wish you all the
success in the future.
All the best,
Mike 龙老师
2018

First published in Great Britain in 2014 by Hodder and Stoughton.
An Hachette UK company.

British Library Cataloguing in Publication Data: a catalogue record for this title is available from the British Library.

Library of Congress Catalog Card Number: on file.

9781444198584

Typeset by Graphicraft Limited, Hong Kong.

Cover design by Mr B & Friends.

Printed and bound in Great Britain by CPI Group (UK) Ltd, Croydon CR0 4YY

John Murray Learning policy is to use papers that are natural, renewable and recyclable products made from wood grown in sustainable forests. The logging and manufacturing processes are expected to conform to the environmental regulations of the country of origin.

John Murray Learning
338 Euston Road
London NW1 3BH
www.hodder.co.uk

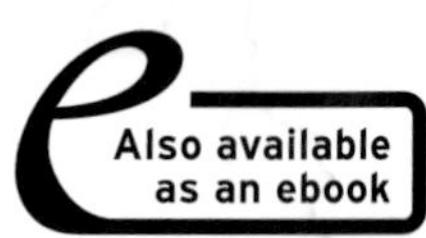

Contents

About the Author

Nǐ hǎo! I'd like to welcome you to *Chinese with Mike* and congratulate you on your decision to take on this fascinating language through this revolutionary course. I understand that you may be a bit skeptical about learning Chinese from a dude who lives and teaches in a one-car garage . . . How did the course come about? After college, I went to China to teach English and there began my love affair with the Chinese language. Returning to my home in Chicago, I settled into my garage and began teaching English and Chinese at a local college, where I have been an English and Chinese professor for several years now. However, I soon realized that my true calling in life was to share my passion for the Chinese language with the world, and it wasn't long before I found myself standing in front of my whiteboard in the garage sporting my coolest Hawaiian shirt, armed only with a marker pen and a profound desire to make learning Chinese fun. I set up a video camera and started filming. The course began to pick up a steady stream of learners on the Web and evolved into its current form.

About the Series

Here's how it works. Each level is composed of videos, a coursebook, and an activity book that together provide a comprehensive system for learning Chinese. The Absolute Beginner level contains Season 1 (Lessons 1–40) and Season 2 (Lessons 41–60) of *Chinese with Mike*. The Advanced Beginner to Intermediate level contains Seasons 3, 4, and 5 (Lessons 61–120). These videos are all on www.chinesewithmike.com as well. So, if you need to go back and review an earlier lesson not in this book, you can download it there. Each lesson comprises a 10–15 minute video; a corresponding lesson in both the Coursebook and Activity Book; lots of activities in a variety of types and supplemental audio with vocabulary and conversations spoken by native Chinese speakers. No matter what learning style works for you, I've got you covered.

Equally important, the lessons are organized from the ground up, beginning with the most basic sentence structures that are the easiest to learn. Each lesson smoothly builds on the previous ones, slowly building in complexity. Whereas other courses may present more frequent forms earlier, the aim of my course is to build up your language logically so you never feel overwhelmed. I can also assure you that you won't need to memorize random dialogues that you'll probably never use in real life. It's more important that you know how to ask and answer questions and generate your own sentences and conversations, and if you go through my series, you'll be able to do just that – and you'll understand exactly what you're saying and why you're saying it.

In **Season 1** (Lessons 1–40), a solid foundation in Chinese is laid. You'll start by learning **pīnyīn**, which is the name for the standard phonetic system that allows beginners to read, write and pronounce Chinese before learning to read and write actual characters. Then, I'll give you an overview on the four tones and the writing system. That'll bring us to Lesson 9, where you'll learn your first words, phrases, and conversation. The remainder of Season 1 is carefully organized around basic sentences with **shì**, the *be* verb in Chinese, and **hěn**. You'll be able to talk about yourself, your family, friends, job, home, and dogs and cats, and most importantly, you'll be ready for Season 2.

In **Season 2** (Lessons 41–60) you will be introduced to more verbs, vocabulary, and conversations that will help take your Chinese to the next level. Let me give you a few examples: If I didn't include Season 2 in the book, you wouldn't be able to tell people you can speak Chinese, you like to play basketball, or you want to eat beef fried rice. More importantly, you wouldn't even know how to ask permission to use the bathroom! Trust me, without Season 2 you wouldn't get very far in life. Like with any healthy addiction, it's important to have a daily dose, so keep up with it and good luck.

In **Season 3** (Lessons 61–80) you'll learn to tell people the milk is in the refrigerator and your dirty clothes are under the bed. You'll also learn about jobs, dreams and measure words so you can brag about how many *Chinese with Mike* episodes you've completed.

Season 4 (Lessons 81–100) takes all of the elements of the first three seasons and ties them together. You'll learn some new adjectives, adverbs, prepositions and conjunctions and best of all, you'll get to watch Mike Lǎoshī's ballet lesson and retirement press conference.

Season 5 (Lessons 101–120) was never meant to be, but Mike Lǎoshī was lured out of retirement. You'll learn how to make comparisons (*I am smarter than you*) and use superlatives (*This is the best Chinese book ever!*). Also, you'll be able to talk about the past and the future, ask your mom how she prepares her favorite recipe, and use transitions to put events in sequence.

How This Book Works

With all of these excellent materials at your disposal, you're probably wondering where to begin. If you are brand new to Mandarin Chinese, then you should start with Level 1, my Absolute Beginner course, which includes Seasons 1 and 2. If you have made a few false starts and have a good foundation, then it's OK to start here.

Here's how to use the book and video. I recommend you watch the video lesson first. Then open the Coursebook, which is an expansion of the video, and go through the corresponding lesson. Each lesson in the Coursebook begins with goals, summing up what you should know by the time you finish the lesson, and contains these sections: **Recap** highlights key points from previous lessons that you need to know to do the current lesson; **Words, Phrases and Stuff** presents vocabulary; **Patterns** highlights important sentence, word or vocabulary patterns in the lesson; **Get to Work** provides additional activities that help you practice and understand the lesson. Also included are frequent **Reviews**, varying in size (mini and extended) but each going back over the latest linguistic territory to help you find your way. Interspersed throughout the book are **Culture Points**, brief views into Chinese culture on topics related to the lessons, and **Challenges**, tasks that extend your understanding or help you practice the key points of a lesson. Last, in the back of the book are a **Pīnyīn Review Table**, which is a comprehensive table of initials and finals from additional notes on the **Writing System, Transcripts**, the **Answer Key**, and a **Chinese–English Glossary** for all of the Absolute Beginner level and the Advanced Beginner to Intermediate level of *Chinese with Mike*.

The Key to Vocabulary

As you can guess, the learning approach in *Chinese with Mike* is basically revolutionary: so carefully structured by me that it will feel less regimented and more spontaneous than that of traditional courses. This is especially true with vocabulary. Instead of giving you 10 or 15 cookie-cutter words every lesson, I mix it up; I vary the number of terms introduced, focus on the most useful language, add in oddball words, and in the videos will repeat words introduced in earlier units that are being used in a different way or definition. One of the most difficult aspects of learning any language is acquiring the vocabulary, so as the course progresses, some units focus only or mostly on acquisition, with exercises that will help you assimilate and practice terms already introduced.

The Key to Activities

The course includes listening, speaking, reading, writing, grammar and vocabulary exercises, in all four strands for comprehensive practice, with some activities based on information found only in the videos included in the Coursebook and most listening and more speaking activities found in the Activity Book. Activity types are designated by icons. Here is a list:

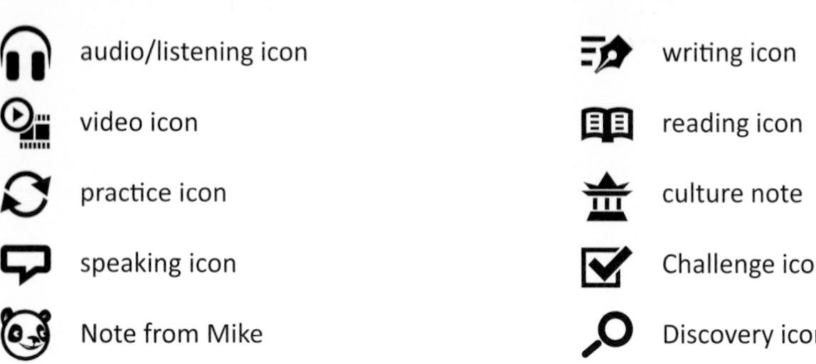

The Key to Success

I should warn you that my course is highly addictive, so if you have a family, career or social life, you may want to put those on hold for a little while. That said, remember that everyone learns at a different speed, so go at your own pace. You may need to review each lesson two or three times. Use your dictionary and the **Glossary**; check them for any words you don't know and to learn synonyms and antonyms not found in the book. The main thing is that as long as you're learning, you're making progress!

You probably have some of the same questions and concerns that I had when I was just starting out, so let's debunk a few myths.

MYTH: I have to know how to write characters if I want to learn to speak Chinese.

TRUTH: You will soon find out that there is a system called **pīnyīn** that allows you to read and speak perfect Chinese without knowing how to write a single character!

MYTH: I am too old to learn a new language.

TRUTH: You're never too old – and never too young! I was 22 years old when I learned my first Chinese word and plenty of older folks have succeeded in my classes; in fact, I've met several retirees who learned later in life and spoke completely fluent Chinese.

MYTH: Chinese is the hardest language in the world!

TRUTH: The Chinese language is not as complicated as people think. You may have heard it said that Chinese takes five years to learn well and a lifetime to master, but I can assure you that I'll cut that time in half because I know what you need to know to become proficient quickly. My philosophy in teaching Chinese is that this language is fun and easy to learn, and I cut through the academic jargon of most textbooks and explain it to you in the easiest and most logical way. I promise you this: If you stick with this course, I'll put the ease into learning Chinese. So sit back and follow my lead, and this revolutionary textbook and video series will have you speaking great Chinese before you can say "Chinese rocks!"

Acknowledgements

I would like to express my deepest gratitude to the following individuals who were instrumental in bringing this project to fruition. The good folks at John Murray Press Learning: Sarah Cole, Editorial Director, who found me in my garage and believed in my mission and ability to teach the world Chinese, Robert Williams, Commissioning Editor, David Swarbrick, Managing Director, Melissa Baker, Editorial Manager, Ross Fraser, Marketing Manager, and Rosie Gailer, Communications Director.

And a big thank you to everyone else:

Yen Hsin Wu, Lin Ting Fang, Jennifer Bunte, Shen Li, Geoff Rusch, Thomas R. Leavens, Justin Adams, Cristal Zheng, Yuxiang Liu, Licheng Gu, Marc L. Kaufman, Jack Haines, Bill Jordan, Tamara Brattoli, the Department of English and World Languages at Joliet Junior College, Dayna Crabb, Chi Zhang, Christina Liu, Neil Steinberg, Larry Potash, Tim Krosel, Mary Mroz, Seth Johnson, Ann Johnson, Ben and Charlotte Hainzinger, Cal and Marcia Hainzinger, Sarah and Amy Hainzinger, Han Yin, Alexandra Truman, Keith C. Chapman, Michael D. Clodfelter, Xiao Fen Yang, April Chou, Xiao Hong Yang, James and Nathan Harmon, David Stejkowski, Bratley Stone, Allison Wurtz, Taylor Smith, Andy Mollo, Danielle Tabaka, Chris Vicich, Beverly Galona, Keith Fink, Nicolai and Maria and Lukas Mandt, G. Jeffrey O'Malley, Benjamin Stech, Greg Stech, Michael Redman, Brian Kezele, Diana Rusch, Adam and Max Heidenreich, Sevan Loughran, Andrew Lenaghan, Justin Deverell, Bob McCauley, Terry Smith, Ursula Kallio, Wileen Hsing, Jin Hua, Paris and Jasmine Nissen, Charlotte Bucciarelli, Monica Wendt, Tim Cox, Kyle Fournier, Giovanni Zambrano, Carolyn Brinkerhoff, Amy and Ted Robinson, Brook Howard, Cleaver Brinkerhoff, Johnny and Kristin Wagner, Karen and Joel Hoobyar, Eric Tuntland, Christina Mastantuono, Peter Rizzo, Angela Myers, Eric Andrews, Paul Hanko, Neil O'Mara, Jeff Fisher, Eva Murdoch, Dave and Chrystal Burich, Michael Geraghty, Lilith Kalenderian, Maria Francia, and of course, my garage.

Additional credits and thanks to:

Producer CWM Seasons 1–2: Geoff Rusch

Producer CWM Seasons 3–5: Yen Hsin Wu

Supplemental Audio / Video editing / Consulting Season 5: Paul Hanko, Allison Wurtz

Webmaster for original CWM website: Jennifer Bunte

Chinese language consultants: Lin Ting Fang, Shen Li, Yen Hsin Wu, Han Yin, Chi Zhang

CWM intro music Seasons 3–5: Seth Johnson-Pointed www.sethjohnson-pointed.com

Additional CWM intro music episodes 103–4: Jackanapes www.jackanapesband.com

Pīnyīn

The Absolute Beginner level of *Chinese with Mike* introduces the **pīnyīn** that is used throughout this course. It also teaches all the tones. I have included them again here for your review. If you're not totally comfortable with this section, I recommend going to the Chinese with Mike website (www.chinesewithmike.com) and downloading Lessons 1–8 before moving forward.

Pīnyīn I

Here are the initials. Note that the first eleven initials, b–h, have the same consonant sound of the corresponding letters in English.

00.01 Listen to the sounds. Then listen again and repeat.

The Initials (21 total)				
b- (**b**all)	d- (**d**og)	g- (**g**um)	q-(i) (**chee**se)	sh-(i) (**shir**t)
p- (**p**oor)	t- (**t**on)	k- (**k**ing)	x-(i) (**shee**p)	r-(i) (**grrr!**)
m- (**m**ore)	n- (**n**ut)	h- (**h**ut)	zh-(i) (**ger**m)	z-(i) (pi**zz**a)
f- (**f**all)	l- (**l**ove)	j-(i) (**jee**p)	ch-(i) (**chir**p)	c-(i) (ca**ts**)
				s-(i) (**s**ip)

Pīnyīn II

00.02 Listen to the sounds. Then listen again and repeat.

Finals: first set			
Single		**Double**	**Triple**
-a (f**a**ther)	-u (f**oo**d)	-ai (**eye**)	-ang (m**ong**rel)
-o (l**ow**)	-ü (b**eau**ty)	-ei (h**eyyy**!)	-eng (h**ung**)
-e (**u**p)		-ao (c**ow**)	
-i (t**ee**th)		-ou (bl**ow**)	
		-an (**on**)	
		-en (**un**der)	

Pīnyīn III

The pronunciation of the final **-er** sounds almost equivalent to the English word *are*.

00.03 **Listen to the sound. Then listen again and repeat.**

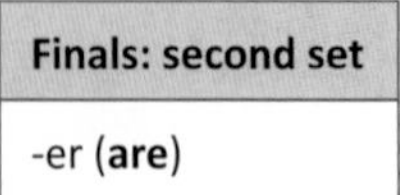

Finals: second set
-er (**are**)

Pīnyīn IV

These **finals** are combinations of the finals you have already learned.

00.04 **Listen to the sound. Then listen again and repeat.**

Finals: third set			
-ia (**ya**) (**yo**nder)	-ie (**ye**) (**yea**h)	-iu (**you**) (**yo**gurt)	-iao (**yao**) (**yow**l)
-ian (**yan**) (**yen**)	-in (**yin**) (bean)	-ing (**ying**) (r**ing**)	

Finals: fourth set		
-ua (**wa**) (**wo**bble)	-uo (**wo**) (**wo**ah!)	-uai (**wai**) (**why**)
-ui (**wei**) (**way**)	-uan (**wan**) (**wan**der)	-un (**wen**)

Pīnyīn V

There are no English sounds that are close to these finals.

00.05 **Listen to the sound. Then listen again and repeat.**

Finals: fifth set	
-iang (**yang**)	-ün (**yun**)
-uang (**wang**)	-iong (**yong**)
-ong (**weng**)	
-üe (**yue**)	
-üan (**yuan**)	

Tones

Before we get into pronunciation, here are a few facts about the tones. Mark the ones you know.

____________ There are four main tones: first, second, third, fourth.

____________ There is also a neutral tone.

____________ Neutral tones don't have tone marks.

____________ Some words have the same tone but different meanings.

In Chinese, pronunciation indicates the meaning of a word, and in **pīnyīn** tone marks are used to indicate **shēng** 声 (*tones*), or how a word should be pronounced.

00.06 Look at the tone as you listen. Then listen again and repeat.

First tone	¯	high and flat
Second tone	ˊ	rises
Third tone	ˇ	falls then rises
Fourth tone	ˋ	falls

Patterns

Here are a couple of rules regarding changes in tone: (1) When there are two third-tones in a row, the first one becomes second tone. (2) When more than two third-tone words are strung together, change them according to context.

Pattern 1: ˇ ˇ > ˊ ˇ

Pattern 2: ˇ ˇ ˇ > ˊ ˊ ˇ or ˇ ˊ ˇ

Examples:

1 Nǐ hǎo > Ní hǎo **2** Wǒ hěn hǎo > Wó hén hǎo or Wǒ hén hǎo

00.07 Listen to the words and identify the tones, 1–4.

1 _____ **2** _____ **3** _____ **4** _____ **5** _____

6 _____ **7** _____ **8** _____ **9** _____ **10** _____

Lesson 61

"Come one and all to my garage"

Yǒu 1

Welcome to Season 3! There's a lot to cover, so let's smash some coffee pots and start things off with a bang. It's time to:

- learn the verb **yǒu** to say *have / has*
- use **shénme** to ask what people have

There is no escaping the verb **yǒu**. In fact, you'll say it just about every time you're in a Chinese-speaking situation. While **yǒu** has a few definitions, the main definition (*to have*) is the most useful, so that's the definition we'll be focusing on over the next few lessons. We'll begin by making affirmative statements and questions.

Recap

In Seasons 1 and 2, we learned several important verbs, especially **shì**, **yào** and **xihuān**.

A Complete the sentences with the verb that corresponds with the English translation. Notice where we put the verb in affirmative statements.

1 Nà _________ xiāngjiāo. (*That **is** a banana.*)

2 Wǒ _________ chī xiāngjiāo. (*I **want** to eat a banana.*)

3 Wǒ _________ chī xiāngjiāo. (*I **like** to eat bananas.*)

B Review the three main patterns used to form a question.

1 Question word: Nà **shì** shénme? (*What **is** that?*)

2 With **ma**: Nǐ **yào** chī xiāngjiāo ma? (*Do you **want** to eat a banana?*)

3 With affirmative-negative: Nǐ **xǐ** bù **xǐhuān** chī xiāngjiāo? (*Do you **like** to eat bananas?*)

Words, phrases and stuff

A note on vocabulary: Despite my international fame and reputation as the most influential Chinese teacher since Confucius, I do happen to live and teach in a one-car garage. Well, as you can imagine, I don't have a lot of possessions, so I use the random objects in my garage as the vocabulary in many of the example sentences I write on the board. These words are then carefully defined and repeated throughout the course. The benefit for you is that you can learn new patterns without having to learn a lot of new vocabulary at the same time. (Genius, I know.) However, it's important that you expand your vocabulary, so in the lessons where I don't introduce too many new words in the videos, I include supplemental vocabulary sets for you to learn and then practice using in my amazing exercises.

61.01 Listen to the words. Then listen again and repeat.

Two Verbs, School Supplies, etc.

huānyíng	欢迎	*to welcome*	**bǐjìběn diànnǎo**	笔记本电脑	*laptop computer*
yǒu	有	*to have*	**píngbǎn diànnǎo**	平板电脑	*tablet (computer)*
bǐjìběn	笔记本	*notebook*	**yōupán**	优盘	*USB flash drive*
kèběn	课本	*textbook*	**zìdiǎn**	字典	*dictionary*
liànxíběn	练习本	*workbook*	**diànzishū**	电子书	*eBook*
			diànzishū yuèdúqì	电子书阅读器	*eBook reader*
			huā	花	*flowers*

If you take a look at the vocabulary list, you'll notice several of our new terms include the same **zì** (individual words / characters). These **zì** should give you a clue to the meanings of the new vocabulary in which they appear. Now you already know that the general word for book is **shū** (书) but can you figure out which **zì** refers to book-like objects?

Patterns

You can use **yǒu** in many different sentence patterns you've already learned. Basically, **yǒu** works the way it does in English, followed by a noun that names what the subject "has". Remember that questions with **shénme** (*what*), like other question words we've studied, put the subject first and the question word last.

Pattern 1: Subject + **yǒu** + noun.

Pattern 2: Subject + **yǒu** + shénme?

Examples:

1 **Wǒ yǒu huā.** (*I have a flower.*)

2 **Tāmen yǒu shénme?** (*What do they have?*)

Grammar tip: Just to be clear, a noun names people, places, or things.

Get to work

A Match the words and definitions.

1 ___ huānyíng
2 ___ yǒu
3 ___ kèběn
4 ___ diànzishū yuèdúqì
5 ___ bǐjìběn diànnǎo
6 ___ píngbǎn diànnǎo
7 ___ liànxíběn
8 ___ yōupán
9 ___ zìdiǎn
10 ___ bǐjìběn
11 ___ diànzishū
12 ___ huā

a tablet (computer)
b USB flash drive
c dictionary
d laptop computer
e flowers
f to welcome
g textbook
h to have
i notebook
j workbook
k eBook reader
l eBook

B Choose the correct verb to complete the sentence.

1 Wǒde māma (shì / yǒu) bǐjìběn diànnǎo.
2 Tāde érzi (xǐhuān / yǒu) yòng píngbǎn diànnǎo.
3 Nǐde péngyǒu (shì / yǒu) Zhōngwén kèběn.
4 Míngtiān māma (yào / yǒu) mǎi huā.

C Unscramble the words to make sentences with "yǒu".

1 yǒu / zìdiǎn / tā ______
2 yǒu / ma / kèběn / xīnde / lǎoshī ______
3 Zhōngwén / nǐde / liànxíběn / nán / nán / bù ______
4 shéide / zhèxiē / shì / huā ______

D Put the sentences into Chinese. Then say them out loud.

1 He has an expensive laptop computer. ______
2 What is a (USB) flash drive? ______
3 We have tablets (computers). ______
4 What does Bill have? ______

E Read the answers and give the questions using "shénme".

Example: Q: Nǐde nánpéngyǒu yǒu shénme? **A:** Wǒde nánpéngyǒu yǒu zìxíngchē.

1 **Q:** ______________________ **A:** Tā yǒu chēzi.

2 **Q:** ______________________ **A:** Tāde māma yǒu gǒu.

3 **Q:** ______________________ **A:** Wǒ yǒu mótuōchē.

4 **Q:** ______________________ **A:** Tāmen yǒu yú.

F Use the words in parentheses to write long answers to the following questions.

Ex: Q: Nǐ dìdi yǒu shénme? (an English dictionary) **A:** Wǒ dìdi yǒu Yīngwén zìdiǎn.

1 Lín Xiānshēng yǒu shénme? (a new tablet)

____

2 Tā bàbade péngyǒu xǐhuān zuò shénme? (read his Chinese textbook)

____

3 Nǐmende jiàoshòu yào zuò shénme? (buy an eBook reader)

____

4 Wáng Tàitai yǒu shénme? (beautiful flowers)

____

5 Zhè shì shéide yōupán? (my son's)

____

Lesson 62

"No or no?"

Méi Yǒu

AS*: Mike Lǎoshī, Mike Lǎoshī, can we learn *I don't have* something? I think you forgot to teach us that last time, and I really, really wanna know!

ML: OK, sit down, listen up and get ready to:

- learn the word **méi** to negate the verb **yǒu**
- use the particle **ma** to make *yes / no* questions with **yǒu**

You now know how to make affirmative statements and questions with **yǒu**. (It's pretty easy stuff!) In the past, when I introduced a new verb, the usual method was to show how to negate the verb along with how to do affirmative statements. That didn't happen in Lesson 61 as AS (*Annoying Student) noted. So we'll do it now. But if you're thinking you can say **Wǒ bù yǒu . . .** to mean *I don't have . . .*, I'm afraid you're wrong. WE DO NOT USE the word **bù** to negate the verb **yǒu**!

Recap

You've learned to add "bù" ("bú") before a verb to make it negative. Take a look at the example for *I am / am not Chinese*. Then brush up by changing the affirmative sentences to negative.

Ex: Wǒ **shì** Zhōngguórén. > Wǒ **bú shì** Zhōngguórén.

1 Wǒ yào. ________________

2 Wǒ huì. ________________

3 Wǒ xǐhuān. ________________

4 Wǒ néng. ________________

Words, phrases and stuff

62.01 **Listen to the words. Then listen again and repeat.**

To not have, Writing Utensils and more.

méi	没	*not*	**máobǐ**	毛笔	*brush pen*
yǒu	有	*to have*	**qiānbǐ**	铅笔	*pencil*
gāngbǐ	钢笔	*fountain pen*	______	笔	*pen*
làbǐ	蜡笔	*crayon*	**(zhào)xiàngjī**	(照)相机	*a camera*
mǎkèbǐ	马克笔	*marker, marker pen*			

A See if you can complete the rule: The general word for *pen*, ____________, often combines with other "zì" (*characters*) to indicate a specific type of pen, such as "yuánzhūbǐ" (*ballpoint pen*). Hint: Look at the endings of the words in the vocabulary list. Then, check the answer key and complete the list.

62.02 **Chinese speakers often use this general word for pen to describe most types of pens.**

B 62.03 **Listen to the following "yīnwèi . . . suǒyǐ" sentences and write the sentences in Chinese. Then translate.**

1 ____________________

2 ____________________

3 ____________________

4 ____________________

5 ____________________

Patterns

The verb **yǒu** is negated differently from the method with **bù** (**bú**) that you learned previously. Here's the rule: NEVER use **bù** with **yǒu**. Instead, use the negater **méi**. Here are patterns showing how to do it and how to answer *yes / no* questions with **yǒu / méi yǒu**.

Pattern 1a:	Subject + **yǒu** + noun (d.o.).	(affirmative)
1b:	Subject + **méi** + **yǒu** + noun (d.o.).	(negative)
Pattern 2a:	**Q:** Subject + **yǒu** + noun + **ma**?	(Yes/No question)
2b:	**A:** Yǒu / Méi yǒu. Subject + (méi) yǒu + noun.	(Yes/No answer)

The negater **méi** can be used with other verbs, but not in the present tense as it can be used with **yǒu**. We'll get into this further down the road.

Examples:

1a Wǒ **yǒu** qián. (*I have money.*)

1b Nǐ **méi yǒu** qián. (*You don't have money.*)

2a **Q:** Nǐ **yǒu** zìdiǎn **ma**? (*Do you have a dictionary?*)

2b **A: Yǒu**. Wǒ **yǒu** zìdiǎn. (*Yes* (lit. *have*). *I have a dictionary.*)

A Notice how we answer *yes / no* questions in Chinese. How would you answer: "Nǐ yǒu bǐ ma?" Give both the affirmative and negative answers here:

1 Yes: ______________________________

2 No: ______________________________

B Now, do you remember how to answer a question with "shénme"? Use the word in parentheses to answer the following question: "Nǐ gēge yǒu shénme?"

______________________________ (*a camera*)

Get to work

A Negate these statements with "méi". Then say the sentences out loud.

Ex: Tā yǒu fángzi. Tā méi yǒu fángzi.

1 Wǒ yǒu làbǐ. ____________________

2 Tāmen yǒu (zhào)xiàngjī. ____________________

3 Xuéshēng yǒu qiānbǐ. ____________________

4 Wǒmende yéye yǒu máobǐ. ____________________

B Choose "bù" (bú) or "méi" to complete the sentence.

1 Wǒde péngyǒu (bú / méi) huì shuō Yīngwén.

2 Tā (bù / méi) yǒu bǐjìběn diànnǎo.

3 Wǒmende jiàoshòu (bù / méi) yǒu fěnbǐ.

4 Tāde xiōngdì (bù / méi) xǐhuān xué gāngqín.

C Complete the conversations with appropriate questions and answers.

Ex: Q: Nǐ yǒu xīguā ma? **A:** Yǒu. Wǒ yǒu xīguā.

	Q	A
1	**Q:** Xiǎopéngyǒu yǒu làbǐ ma?	**A:** ________. Xiǎopéngyǒu méi yǒu làbǐ.
2	**Q:** Nǐde érzi yǒu qiānbǐ ma?	**A:** ________. Wǒde érzi yǒu qiānbǐ.
3	**Q:** ____________________?	**A:** Méi yǒu. Tāde nǚ'ér méi yǒu mǎkèbǐ.
4	**Q:** Nǐde lǎogōng yǒu píngbǎn diànnǎo ma?	**A:** Méi yǒu. ____________________.

Yǒu méi yǒu máobǐ?

"What do you use **máobǐ** for? Brush painting, or **guóhuà** 国画, an ancient form of Chinese painting based on the strokes and styles of calligraphy. Seven or so basic strokes are used to create blunt, solid, sharp, detailed, or delicate shapes. When you see traditional landscapes or flowers, birds, or goldfish painted on silk or paper, that is brush painting with **máobǐ**."

Lesson 63

"To have and have not"

Review of Yǒu and Méi Yǒu

You've probably heard people say that kids these days are lazy and would rather play with their cell phones, tablets, and other electronic devices than go outside or hang out with friends. Well, by the end of this lesson, you should know how to say just about all of that in Chinese! Get ready to:

- review everything about the verb **yǒu**
- learn to make questions with **yǒu méi yǒu**
- review the verb form **yǒu / méi yǒu** and **bù / bú** vs. **méi**

In this lesson, you'll learn how to ask about possessions or availability with the affirmative-negative form **yǒu méi yǒu**. Once you nail this form, you will have mastered the verb **yǒu**, and I will sleep better at night knowing that I've done my job (perfectly) as always. But just to make sure, we'll also review the use of **yǒu** and **méi yǒu** as well as **bù / bú** vs. **méi**.

Recap

Before we get going, try to remember: what do you know about using "yǒu"? Are these sentences correct? Correct the sentences with errors.

1 Wǒ méi xǐhuān tāmen. ____________________

2 Tāde māma méi huì zhǔfàn. ________________

3 Nǐ bú yǒu huā. ______________________

4 Nǐmen méi yǒu qiānbǐ. ________________

Words, phrases and stuff

Now, check out the new vocabulary. A few words to go with **yǒu** . . .

63.01 Listen to the words. Then listen again and repeat.

Phones

diànhuà	电话	*telephone*
shǒujī	手机	*cell phone / mobile*
shǒujīké	手机壳	*cell phone case*
zhìnéng shǒujī	智能手机	*smartphone*
zhìnéng kǎ	智能卡	*SIM card*
chōngdiànqì	充电器	*battery charger (for phones, computers, etc.)*

A Choose the correct definitions of the words from the video.

1 A word for *park* is **gōngkè / yáshuā / wánjù / gōngyuán**.

2 A word for *homework* is **gōngkè / yáshuā / wánjù / gōngyuán**.

3 To say *toy(s)* you should say **gōngkè / yáshuā / wánjù / gōngyuán**.

4 A *toothbrush* is a **gōngkè / yáshuā / wánjù / gōngyuán**.

B Cover the new vocabulary and complete the sentences with the correct word.

1 A **diànhuà** is a *cell phone / telephone*.

2 A **shǒujīké** is a *battery / cell phone case*.

3 The term for *battery charger* is **shǒujīké / chōngdiànqì**.

C Did you notice similarities in the new words? Look at the list again. What do these words have in common? Choose the word parts ("zì") they have in common. What do they mean?

diànhuà chōngdiànqì shǒujī shǒujīké

Patterns

Here is the pattern for the new question form. This is an affirmative-negative form used to ask *do / don't . . . ?* Notice that you answer an affirmative-negative type question the same way you answer a **ma** question.

Pattern 1: **Q:** Subject + **yǒu méi yǒu** + noun?

Pattern 2: **A: Yǒu / Méi yǒu.** Subject + (**méi**) **yǒu** + noun.

Examples:

1 Nǐ **yǒu méi yǒu** shǒujī? (*Do you (or don't you) have a cell phone?*)

2 **Méi yǒu**. Wǒ **méi yǒu** shǒujī. (*No* (lit. *don't have*). *I don't have a cell phone.*)

Try to unscramble this sentence. Is it a statement or a question?

méi / nǐmen / yǒu / shǒujī / yǒu ______________________

Review

Answer these questions to review "yǒu / méi yǒu" and "bù / bú" vs. "méi".

A What method(s) can you use to ask a question with "yǒu"?

1 __________ with **bù** (**bú**)

2 __________ with a question word

3 __________ with **méi**

4 __________ with **ma**

B Change the "ma" questions to affirmative-negative questions.

Ex: Tā yǒu shǒujī ma? Tā yǒu méi yǒu shǒujī.

1 Nǐ yǒu chōngdiànqì ma? ______________________

2 Tāmen yǒu Zhōngwén zìdiǎn ma? ______________________

3 Tāde mèimei yǒu hēisède shǒujīké ma? ______________________

4 Nǐmen yǒu máobǐ ma? ______________________

C Change the affirmative-negative questions to "ma" questions.

Ex: Tāmende fángzi yǒu méi yǒu chēkù? Tāmende fángzi yǒu chēkù ma?

1 Nǐ yǒu méi yǒu xīnde píngbǎn diànnǎo? ______________________

2 Chúshī yǒu méi yǒu hěn chángde dāozi? ______________________

3 Tā yǒu méi yǒu hěn guìde bǐjìběn diànnǎo? ______________________

4 Nǐde nǚ'ér yǒu méi yǒu gōngzuò? ______________________

D Match the patterns and sentences.

1 ____ subject + **yǒu** + noun + ma?
2 ____ subject + **yǒu** + noun. (d.o.)
3 ____ subject + **yǒu** + question word?
4 ____ subject + **méi** + **yǒu** + noun. (d.o.)
5 ____ subject + **yǒu méi yǒu** + noun?

a Wǒ yǒu chōngdiànqì.
b Tāmen yǒu méi yǒu zhìnéng shǒujī?
c Nǐ méi yǒu qián.
d Nǐ yǒu shǒujī ma?
e Tā yǒu shénme?

E Choose "bù" ("bú") or "méi" to complete the sentences.

1 Wǒ kě ____ kěyì yòng nǐde chōngdiànqì?
2 Yīshēng yǒu ____ yǒu bǐjìběn diànnǎo?
3 Nǐde wàipó ____ huì yòng píngbǎn diànnǎo ma?
4 Wǒde jiějie ____ yǒu hēisède bǐ.

F 63.02 Say the following in Chinese. Then listen and compare your answers to the native speakers.

1 Do you guys want a smartphone?
2 Do you guys have cell phones?
3 Do you (sing.) have a cell phone case?
4 This is a battery charger.

Lesson 64

"I have a lot of pandas"

Hěn duō

Do you have a lot of dogs? Cats? Books? Friends? Stick around and you can answer in Chinese. We're about to:

- learn the phrase **hěn duō** to say *much / many / a lot of*
- talk about what you have / don't have a lot of
- find out names of common tools

So far in *Chinese with Mike*, you've learned how to say *I want . . .* or *I have . . .* But we haven't covered how to specify how much of something we want or have. That's about to change. Why? Because, as I said, in this lesson we are focusing on **hěn duō**. Keep up!

Recap

By now you should be rock stars when it comes to asking and answering questions with the verb **yǒu**. (**Nǐ yǒu shuǐ ma? Yǒu. Wǒ** _________ _________.) You should also be up to speed on terms for the latest technological devices. (**Nǐ yào bú yào kàn wǒde píngbǎn diànnǎo?** ______ **Wǒ yào kàn nǐde píngbǎn diànnǎo.**) We're about to take it one step further.

Words, phrases and stuff

If you're not too techy but more of a handyman like me, then you'll want to know the names of some common tools. So here's some additional vocabulary for you.

64.01 Listen to the words. Then listen again and repeat.

How much and Tools

duō	多	*many, much, a lot of*	**chuízi**	锤子	*hammer*
hěn duō	很多	*a lot*	**luósīdāo**	螺丝刀	*screwdriver*
jìgōng	技工	*mechanic*	**jùzi**	锯子	*saw*
mùgōng	木工	*carpenter*	**diànzuān**	电钻	*drill*
gōngjùxiāng	工具箱	*toolbox*	**bānshǒu**	扳手	*wrench / spanner (UK)*
gōngjù	工具	*tools*	**qiánzi**	钳子	*pliers*

A Take a look at the following words: "jìgōng", "mùgōng" and "gōngjù". What do you think the word part "gōng" means? 1 metal, 2 wood, 3 strong, 4 work

B Choose the correct meaning for "hěn duō" for these words from the video.

1 qián many / much

2 shū many / much

3 péngyǒu much / a lot of

4 huā much / a lot of

Patterns

Here are some patterns to review. These will show you how to use **hěn duō** with what you already know. Note the patterns for asking and answering questions in the affirmative-negative form. When you use **bù/bú** to negate, remember to include the correct tone mark, depending on the tone(s) of the word(s) that follow it.

Pattern 1a: Subject + verb + **hěn duō** + noun.

1b: Subject + verb + **hěn duō** + noun + ma?

Pattern 2a: Subject + verb + (méi) + verb + **hěn duō** + noun?

2b: (Méi) yǒu. Subject + (méi) yǒu + **hěn duō** + noun.

Examples:

1a Wǒ yǒu **hěn duō** wánjù. (*I have a lot of toys.*)

1b Nǐ yǒu **hěn duō** bǐ ma? (*Do you have a lot of pens?*)

2a Nǐ yǒu méi yǒu **hěn duō** gōngjù? (*Do you (or don't you) have a lot of tools?*)

2b (Méi) yǒu. Wǒ (méi) yǒu **hěn duō** gōngjù. (*Yes / No. I (don't) have a lot of tools.*)

The opposite of **duō** (*much; many*) is **shǎo** (*less; few; little*). As you know, we use **duō** to express how *much / many* of something we have (**Wǒ yǒu hěn duō kāfēi/Wǒ yǒu hěn duō péngyǒu**); however, the word **shǎo** is rarely used to express just a *little / few* of something. To express a *few / little*, people usually just negate the verb **yǒu** and say **Wǒ méi yǒu hěn duō . . .** More commonly, **shǎo** is used to express frequency, like **Wǒ hěn shǎo kàn diànyǐng** (*I* (lit.) *very little watch movies (I seldom watch movies)*). We will get into adverbs of frequency later in the course, so let's deal with them then. For now, just understand the basics about **duō**.

Get to work

A Look at the English words in parentheses. Complete the sentences with the correct words in Chinese.

Ex: (My dad) yǒu hěn duō (tools). Wǒ(de) bàba yǒu hěn duō gōngjù.

1 (The carpenter) yǒu hěn duō (hammers.) ____________

2 (The mechanic) yǒu hěn duō (wrenches.) ____________

3 (Screwdrivers) zài nǎ lǐ? ____________

4 Nǐ yǒu (drill) ma? ____________

B Unscramble the sentences. Which one is a question?

1 wèishénme / Yīngwén / yǒu / hěn / nǐ / duō / zìdiǎn ____________

2 tāmen / ròu / chī / bù / néng / tài / duō ____________

3 jìgōng / wǒde / shì / lǎogōng ____________

4 chuízi / xīnde / yào / mǎi / mùgōng ____________

C 64.02 Answer these yes / no questions out loud with long answers. Then listen to the native speakers and compare your answers.

1 **Q:** Nǐde yéye yǒu hěn duō gōngjù ma? (yes)

2 **Q:** Tāmende fùqīn yǒu méi yǒu diànzuān? (no)

3 **Q:** Nǐde gēge shì bú shì hěn bàngde mùgōng? (yes)

4 **Q:** Nǐ huì bú huì yòng jùzi? (no)

D Contrast things your family and friends have and don't have a lot of. You can use the words in the box or make up your own.

bǐ	gōngjù	gǒu	huā	māo	qián	shǒujī	shū	wánjù	xiézi

1 Write four sentences about what your friends / family have a lot of.

Bàba yǒu hěn duō gōngjù. ______

______

2 Write four sentences about what your friends / family don't have much of.

Bàba méi yǒu hěn duō shū. ______

______

3 Use **dànshì** to create five contrasting sentences using the information given.

Ex: Teacher (markers / crayons) Lǎoshī yǒu hěn duō mǎkèbǐ dànshì tā méi yǒu hěn duō làbǐ.

a Mechanic (wrenches / computers) ______

b Chef (knives / telephones) ______

c Professor (books / magazines) ______

d Secretary (telephones / hammers) ______

e Carpenter (saws / forks) ______

Lesson 65

"Big lesson!"

Measure Words

At last: ways to give exact numbers. Now when you're asked how many siblings you have, you won't have to answer *a lot* instead of two or three or whatever. You won't get as many strange looks either. So let's get going and:

- master **gè**, our first measure word
- use **gè** to give numbers of people

When you say things like *I drank 16 cups of coffee this morning* or *I bought four packs of gum*, you are using measure words (i.e., cups / packs) to specify the exact amount or number of something. Measure words are more commonly used in Chinese than in English since they are required in more grammatical structures, and learning them can be a little intimidating at first. We're going to take it step by step and start with the most common measure word in Chinese – **gè**. In this lesson, you'll practice the use of **gè** to provide numbers of people.

Recap

To do this lesson, you'll need to remember your numbers in Chinese.

Complete the English translations. Then say the numbers out loud in order 1–10.

wǔ 五 ______	bā 八 ______	jiǔ 九 ______	sì 四 ______
èr 二 ______	liù 六 ______	yī 一 ______	sān 三 ______
qī 七 ______	shí 十 ______		

Words, phrases and stuff

Here is your introduction to measure words (MW).

65.01 **Listen to the words. Then listen again and repeat.**

A Basic Measure Word

gè	个	MW mainly for people and general objects
yīgè	一个	*one (of them); a / an*

Yīgè (1 gè) means *one* as a quantity but also may translate as *a / an*. For example, **Wǒ shì yīgè xuéshēng** translates into English as *I am a student*, not *I am one student.*

A Notice the two words for the number *two*: "èr", "liǎng". Which do you use for counting? Which for giving the number of people / objects?

B What is the difference between these two statements?

Wǒ yǒu mèimei. vs. **Wǒ yǒu yīgè mèimei.**

In addition to **gè**, the measure words **wèi** and **kǒu** can also be used as classifiers for people, but they are more often used in formal situations and when talking with people whom you don't know personally.

Patterns

Here is how to use **gè** to give an exact number:

Pattern 1: number + **gè** + noun

Pattern 2: **yīgè** + noun

Examples:

1 sān**gè** rén (*three people*)

2 **yīgè** yīshēng (*one / a doctor*)

Do you remember how to create numbers over ten? Here are three examples that show the three patterns:

Examples:

1 sìshí (40)

2 shíbā (18)

3 qīshíwǔ (75)

Now, use "gè" to say *10 people, 37 people, 14 people, 100 people*

Get to work

A Talk about your parents' families. How many brothers and sisters does your mother have? Your father? Complete the blanks with what is true for you and say the sentences out loud.

Ex: Tā yǒu liǎnggè gēge. OR Tā méi yǒu gēge.

Wǒ(de) bàba

1 Tā ___________ gēge.

2 Tā ___________ dìdi.

3 Tā ___________ jiějie.

4 Tā ___________ mèimei.

Wǒ(de) mama

5 Tā ___________ gēge

6 Tā ___________ dìdi.

7 Tā ___________ jiějie.

8 Tā ___________ mèimei.

When you want to say you do NOT have something (e.g. a brother / sister, a dog, a pencil, etc.), you do not include **yīgè** in the negated statement. Saying **Wǒ méi yǒu** (object) is enough.

B Use the words in the box to put these sentences in Chinese.

Ex: We have three children. Wǒmen yǒu sāngè háizi.
We don't have children. Wǒmen méi yǒu háizi.

yīshēng	xuéshēng	jǐngchá	jiàoshòu
péngyǒu	nánpéngyǒu	dìdi	shāngrén

1 She has two doctors. __________
2 He doesn't have friends. __________
3 The teacher has 23 students. __________
4 They have four professors. __________
5 Five police officers want coffee. __________
6 Ten businessmen / women are going to play golf. __________
7 She doesn't have a boyfriend. __________
8 He has a younger brother. __________

C 65.02 Listen to the conversation. Then answer the following questions.

1 Who is Yán Xīn?
2 Does Dàwèi have any older brothers? If so, how many?
3 Does Dàwèi have any younger brothers? If so, how many?
4 Does Dàwèi have any older / younger sisters?
5 What does Dàwèi's sister do?

"A new question word"

Jǐgè

Wow, you must be gettin' your kicks if you've made it all the way to Lesson 66! Awesome! Anyway, keep following the route because you're about to:

- review the question word **jǐ**
- use the new question word **jǐgè**

jǐ (*how many*) is an important question word that was first introduced in Season 1. It was used to ask *how many* but in situations where a measure word was not required. However, in Chinese you do need a measure word (**gè**) to state specific numbers of people. In this lesson, we will use **jǐ** combined with **gè** to ask *how many (people) are there . . . ?*

Recap

A Choose the items that are true about the uses of "jǐ".

____ ask date of the month ____ ask day of the week ____ ask time of day

____ use for small numbers ____ use with *ma* ____ ask age

B Match the Chinese and English translations for questions with "jǐ".

1 ____ Jīntiān shì jǐyuè jǐhào?	a What time is it?
2 ____ Xiànzài (shì) jǐ diǎn?	b What's the date today?
3 ____ Xiànzài shì jǐyuè?	c How old are you?
4 ____ Jīntiān shì xīngqījǐ?	d What month is it?
5 ____ Nǐ jǐ suì?	e What day (of the week) is today?

Words, phrases and stuff

66.01 Listen to the words. Then listen again and repeat.

A Question Word for Counting and Step Families

Now, on to your new question word. **Jǐgè** 几个 *how many (people)* is a common question and can be used for different purposes. In this lesson, we're using it for counting people.

jǐgè 几个 *how many (people)*

Jìfù 继父 *stepfather*

Jìmǔ 继母 *stepmother*

You can ask about the number of people in many ways, especially depending on the level of formality you want to use. To ask more formally, use **jǐ wèi**.

When you hear "jǐ" with "gè" in a question, what is the key thing it tells you?

a you should answer with *yes* or *no*

b you should answer with a number

You should know the names of family members already, but as there are so many blended families in today's world, I thought I'd give all you "steps" out there a shout-out.

Patterns

You need measure words in Chinese to count people, to ask *how many (of them) are there?* One easy way to ask about a number of people is to use **jǐgè**. Take a look at the patterns. Remember: do not use the particle **ma** when asking questions with **jǐgè**.

Pattern 1a: **Q:** Subject + yǒu + **jǐgè** + noun (d.o.)?

1b: **A:** Subject + yǒu + **(number) gè** + noun (d.o.).

Examples:

1a Nǐ yǒu **jǐgè** péngyǒu?

1b Wǒ yǒu **sìgè** péngyǒu.

Get to work

A Give the English translation of these questions. The first one has been done for you.

1 Nǐ yǒu jǐgè xiōngdì jiěmèi? How many brothers and sisters do you have?

2 Nǐ yǒu jǐgè xiōngdì? ______________________________

3 Nǐ yǒu jǐgè jiěmèi? ______________________________

B Match the phrases in Chinese and English. Use the numbers or nouns as clues. Then complete the answers.

Ex: sāngè yǎnyuán (three actors)

1 liùgè nóngmín	a one ____________
2 sìgè mùgōng	b five ____________
3 jiǔgè jìgōng	c ____________ lawyers
4 yīgè hùshì	d six ____________
5 wǔgè chúshī	e ____________ mechanics
6 liǎnggè lǜshī	f four ____________

C Given the answer, write the question.

1 **Q:** ______________________________

A: Wǒmen yǒu sāngè jiàoshòu.

2 **Q:** ______________________________

A: Tāmen yǒu yīgè háizi.

3 **Q:** ______________________________

A: Wǒde lǎoshī yǒu wǔgè xuéshēng.

4 **Q:** ______________________________

A: Wǒ méi yǒu xiōngdì jiěmèi.

D Your local government wants to know about your family. Complete this census with answers that are true for you.

Ex: Nǐ yǒu jǐgè āyí? Wǒ yǒu liùgè āyí.

CITY CENSUS

B Immediate family

1 Nǐ yǒu xiōngdì jiěmèi ma? ______________________

2 Nǐ yǒu jǐgè xiōngdì? ______________________

3 Nǐ yǒu jǐgè gēge? ______________________

4 Nǐ yǒu jǐgè dìdi? ______________________

5 Nǐ yǒu jǐgè jiěmèi? ______________________

6 Nǐ yǒu jǐgè jiějie? ______________________

7 Nǐ yǒu jǐgè mèimei? ______________________

E **66.02 Go back to D and listen to the census questions on the audio. Say the questions out loud and listen again to check your pronunciation.**

F **Read the pairs of sentences and insert the missing words. Then translate.**

1 Zhè shì shéi? ____________________

Zhè shì wǒde (stepmother) ____________________

2 Tā shì nǐmende (son) ma? ____________________

Shì. Tā shì wǒmende (son). ____________________

3 Tāmen shì bú shì nǐmende (daughters)? ____________________

Shì. Tāmen shì wǒmende (daughters). ____________________

4 Nà shì shéide (stepfather)? ____________________

Nà shì wǒde (stepfather). ____________________

Conduct a survey in Chinese. Don't be shy! Get out and practice speaking. Survey some Chinese people you know: friends, co-workers, classmates, online buddies. Ask about family. You can use the questions in D or make up your own.

Lesson 67

"How many markers can I juggle?"

More Measure Words

OK, so you can ask how many brothers and sisters people have, but is any conversation complete if you can't ask how many dogs, elephants and books they have too? I think not. So I guess I'd better show you how to:

- use **zhī** to talk about numbers of animals
- use **běn** to talk about numbers of books

So far you learned one measure word: **gè**. In this lesson, though, you are about to discover a couple more useful measure words: **zhī** and **běn**.

Recap

In the last lesson we worked with **jǐgè** to ask for a number (of people, specifically.)

Put an X next to the words that you'd use "jǐgè" to ask about.

______ nǚrén ______ shū ______ zázhì ______ bǐ ______ nǚháizi

______ xiōngdì ______ diànnǎo ______ jiěmèi ______ shǒujī ______ xuéshēng

______ lǎoshī ______ yīshēng ______ chúshī ______ péngyǒu ______ bǐjìběn

The most common measure word is **gè**, and an important fact about **gè** is that it is a default measure word you can use when you don't know the specific one.

Words, phrases and stuff

67.01 Listen to the words. Then listen again and repeat.

Measure Words and More

jǐ	几	*how many*
gè	个	MW for people, general objects
zhī	只	MW for animals
běn	本	MW for books, magazines, book-like objects
nóngchǎng	农场	*a farm*
chǒngwùdiàn	宠物店	*a pet store*
chǒngwù	宠物	*a house pet*

You'll soon discover that many nouns in Chinese can have more than one corresponding measure word, so do not be alarmed if you hear someone use a measure word other than what you've learned here. You're safe with these, but gradually you'll pick up alternates.

Patterns

The patterns for asking "how many?" questions using your new measure words are the same as they were for using **jǐgè**. To form the question, add **jǐ** to the measure word so that **jǐ** + **zhī**, or **běn** becomes **jǐzhī**, or **jǐběn**. To answer, simply replace **jǐ** with a number, and attach the MW.

Pattern 1a: **Q:** Subject + verb + **jǐ with MW** + noun (d.o.)?

Pattern 1b: **A:** Subject + verb + **(number) MW** + noun (d.o.).

Examples:

1a Dòngwùyuán yǒu **jǐzhī** lǎohǔ? (*How many tigers does the zoo have?*)

1b Dòngwùyuán yǒu **sānzhī** lǎohǔ. (*The zoo has three tigers.*)

Get to work

A Choose the correct definition for the words in bold.

1 The word **nóngchǎng** means (a farm / a pet store / a house pet).

2 The word **chǒngwùdiàn** means (a farm / a pet store / a house pet).

3 The word **chǒngwù** means (a farm / a pet store / a house pet).

4 The measure word **zhī** is for (people / animals / books).

5 The measure word **běn** is for (people / animals / books).

B Translate the following by giving the correct number, measure word, and noun in Chinese.

1 four cats ______________________________

2 six books ______________________________

3 five bears ______________________________

4 one professor ___________________________

5 ten magazines ___________________________

6 two Canadians ___________________________

C Look at the pictures and give the number of items in Chinese. Be sure to use the correct measure word. Write a complete sentence.

1 ____

2 ____

3 ____

D Choose the word that does not belong with the corresponding measure word.

1 zhī (háizi, lǎohǔ, niǎo, gǒu)
2 gè (háizi, jiàoshòu, dàxiàng, xuéshēng)
3 běn (zázhì, shū, gēge, kèběn)
4 gè (jìgōng, nǚrén, shīzi, xiǎopéngyǒu)
5 gè (nóngmín, mùgōng, māo, nánrén)

E Fill in the blanks with the correct translations and measure words.

Ex: Wǒ yǒu (five monkeys). Wǒ yǒu wǔzhī hóuzi. (*I have five monkeys.*)

1 Wǒde nǚpéngyǒu yǒu (one mouse).
2 Wǒ yǒu (three dogs).
3 Wǒde mèimei yǒu (four cows).
4 Wǒde gēge yǒu (two notebooks).
5 Wǒde dìdi yǒu (a dictionary).
6 Wǒ(de) māma yǒu (eleven birds).
7 Wǒ(de) bàba yǒu (eight frogs).
8 Wǒ(de) wàipó yǒu (nine magazines).
9 Wǒ(de) wàigōng yǒu (five books).

"Wǒ yǒu sānpíng shuǐ"

Even More Measure Words

Are you sick of measure words yet? Do you need about five cups of coffee to stay awake? How about a cold bottle of a tasty beverage to celebrate your progress thus far? Well, guess what? You're not going to know how to ask for either of those beverages – let alone a glass of water – if we don't get through this lesson. It's time to:

- learn measure words **zhāng**, **bēi** and **píng**
- use **gěi** to tell people to give you things

We're still plowing through an important part of Chinese grammar – measure words. Soon you will know how to ask for cups, bottles, and glasses of water, tea, beer and wine.

Recap

Complete these sentences to be sure you've gotten the basics so far.

1 Using ____________, you can talk about specific numbers of people.

2 Using ____________, you can talk about specific numbers of most animals.

3 Using ____________, you can brag about how many books you own!

4 Using ____________, you can ask *How many people . . . ?*

Words, phrases and stuff

As you know, a "zì" can combine with other "zì" to form "cí" (compound words). Take a look at these compounds. Cover up the vocabulary list and work out the meanings. Use the glossary if necessary.

Chá (TEA)

cháhú (*pot*) ___________

chábēi ________________

chábāo (*bag*) __________

lǜchá _________________

nǎichá (*milk*) __________

68.01 Listen to the words. Then listen again and repeat.

Measure Words and Beverages, etc.

zhāng	张	MW for flat objects
bēi	杯	MW for cups, glasses, drinks, beverages
píng	瓶	MW for bottles
bēizi	杯子	*a cup, a glass*
píngzi	瓶子	*a bottle*
píjiǔ	啤酒	*beer*
lǜchá	绿茶	*green tea*
hóngchá	红茶	*black tea*
pútáojiǔ	葡萄酒	*wine*
hóngpútáojiǔ	红葡萄酒	*red wine*
báipútáojiǔ	白葡萄酒	*white wine*
xiāngbīnjiǔ	香槟酒	*champagne*
qǐng	请	*please (do something)*
jiǔbā	酒吧	*pub*

Some Chinese measure words can stand alone as actual words but may require an additional **zì** as in **bēi / bēizi** and **píng / píngzi**. For example, we say **Wǒ yǒu sānbēi chá** (*I have three cups of tea*) but **Nà shì wǒde bēizi** (*That is my cup*). In the first sentence, **bēi** is a measure word used for counting the number of cups of tea; in the second, **bēizi** is a noun, the cup itself.

The measure word zhāng is used for flat objects. Can you write the English equivalents of the following words?

1 chuáng ____________ **2** zhǐ ____________ **3** zhuōzi ____________

Patterns

Use your new measure words in the same pattern you've learned for asking questions with MWs. Use the second pattern to tell people to give you things. Add **qǐng** to be polite.

Pattern 1a: Subject + verb + **jǐ** + MW + noun (d.o.)?

1b: Subject + verb + **(number) MW** + noun (d.o.).

Pattern 2: **(Qǐng) Gěi** + noun / pronoun + noun phrase (d.o.).

Examples:

1a Nǐ yào jǐ**píng** shuǐ? (*How many bottles of water do you want?*)

1b Wǒ yào liǎng**píng** shuǐ. (*I want two bottles of water.*)

2 **Qǐng gěi** wǒ yìbēi chá. (*Please give me a cup of tea.*)

Get to work

A Match the words in the box with the translations.

qǐng	lǜchá	zhāng	hóngchá	píngzi
bēi	hóngpútáojiǔ	píng	báipútáojiǔ	píjiǔ

1 red wine ______________________

2 a bottle ______________________

3 please ______________________

4 black tea ______________________

5 MW for cups, glasses ____________

6 green tea ______________________

7 MW for flat objects ____________

8 beer ______________________

9 white wine ______________________

10 MW for bottles ______________

B Read the shopping list and put it in Chinese.

1 ______________________ (3 bottles of water)

2 ______________________ (2 German books)

3 ______________________ (50 sheets of paper)

4 ______________________ (4 rabbits)

5 ______________________ (4 cups of coffee)

C Go back to B and tell someone to give you each item on the list. Say *please*.

D 68.02 Answer this mix of questions using long answers. Say them out loud then listen and compare your answers.

1 Nǐ xǐhuān Fǎguó pútáojiǔ ma? (Yes)

2 Tāde xīnde gōngjùxiāng hěn dà ma? (Yes)

3 Nǐde xiǎoháizi yǒu méi yǒu hěn duō wánjù? (No)

4 Nǐ yào bú yào hē yībēi lǜchá? (No)

5 Nàxiē mùgōng hěn qínláo ma? (Yes)

Tea: The Experience

If you go to China, you'll find that drinking tea can be an experience. Tea drinking is a ceremony that requires a special tea, special table, tea towel, teaspoons, and teapot (**Yíxīng zǐshā hú** purple sand clay pots are a favorite). Connoisseurs often prefer **pǔ'ěr chá** and **hēi chá** teas and may pay tens of thousands of dollars a pound for their tea and treasure the subtle fragrances as much as the taste: Is it like spring grass? A wood fire in autumn? For friends and family, on the other hand, tea is an occasion to talk and enjoy each other's company. Offering tea can be a sign of respect, apology, gratitude, or celebration. So, how do you take your tea? **Yào jiā niúnǎi** 要加牛奶 *with milk* or **Bú yào jiā niúnǎi** 不要加牛奶 *without milk*?

Lesson 69

"This one and that one"

Zhègè vs. Nàgè

It's hard to find time for a swim these days. The demand for my Chinese-teaching services is just too high. Oh, well, I guess I'd better dry my hair, throw on my bandana, and show you how to:

- use measure words in a different way
- use **zhègè** and **nàgè**

So far, we have used measure words exclusively with numbers to say how many people / objects we are talking about. In this lesson, we are getting into another use of measure words. Some words such as **zhè** and **nà** do not always require a measure word as in **Zhè shì píngguǒ** (*This is an apple*), but they do when they precede a noun as in **Zhègè píngguǒ hěn dà** (*This apple is big*). That is, to say *this apple* or *that chair* in Chinese, you need a measure word for **zhè** and **nà**. Got it? Let's dive in.

Recap

For this lesson you'll need to remember a few things we have covered before: (1) the meanings of **zhè** (*this*) and **nà** (*that*) (Lesson 19); (2) how to make adjective-noun combos with the particle **de** (Lesson 32); (3) the reason we use the measure word **gè** (Lesson 65).

Let's start by translating the following sentences. Then note if it requires a measure word or not.

1 Say: This is water. That is meat. ______________________

2 Say: This is a good book. That is a fast car. ______________________

3 Say: One teacher. Five students. ______________________

Words, phrases and stuff

69.01 Listen to the words. Then listen again and repeat.

This one and *That one*; Men and Women

zhègè	这个	*this, this one*
nàgè	那个	*that, that one*
nánrén	男人	*man*
nǚrén	女人	*woman*
(xiǎo)háizi	(小)孩子	*child; children*
nǚhái(zi)	女孩(子)	*little girl*
nánhái(zi)	男孩(子)	*little boy*
gāozhōng	高中	*high school*
gāozhōngshēng	高中生	*high school student*
dàxué	大学	*college, university*
dàxuéshēng	大学生	*college / university student*
nánshēng	男生	*a young man*
nǚshēng	女生	*a young woman*

Sometimes you can omit the nouns following **zhègè** and **nàgè**. For example, instead of saying **Wǒ yào chī zhègè píngguǒ** (*I want to eat this apple*), you can say **Wǒ yào chī zhègè** if it's clear which apple you are referring to. In such cases, **zhègè** and **nàgè** would translate as *this one* and *that one* respectively.

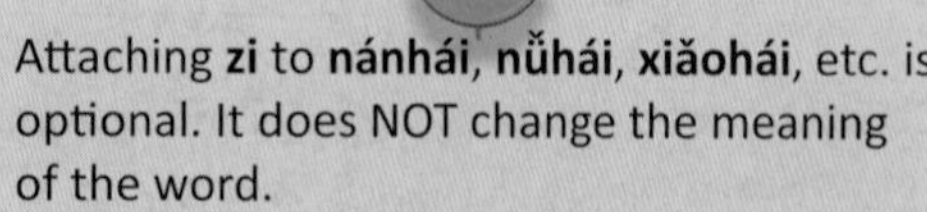

Attaching **zi** to **nánhái**, **nǚhái**, **xiǎohái**, etc. is optional. It does NOT change the meaning of the word.

Patterns

When we are talking about people and other nouns that take the measure word **gè**, our main pattern is **zhè /nà** + **gè** + noun to say *this . . .* or *that . . .* Since I'm sure you'll master that one in no time, let's take it one step further by including adjectives between **zhègè / nàgè** and the noun as well. Awesome!

Pattern 1a: **zhè** + **gè** + noun

1b: **nà** + **gè** + noun

Pattern 2: **Zhègè / Nàgè** + (**hěn**) adjective + de + noun

Examples:

1a **Zhègè** nǚhái(zi) (*this girl*)

1b **Nàgè** nánrén (*that man*)

2 Nàgè **hěn** gāode nánhái(zi) (*that tall boy*)

Look at the two sentences. Which one is correct? Why?

1 Zhè rén shì wǒde māma.

2 Zhègè rén shì wǒde māma.

Get to work

A Match the words in the box with the translations.

zhègè	dàxuéshēng	nàgè
gāozhōng	dàxué	gāozhōngshēng

1 college, university ______________
2 high school student ______________
3 college student ______________
4 that, that one ______________
5 high school ______________
6 this, this one ______________

B Put these phrases into Chinese.

1 this nurse ______________
2 that carpenter ______________
3 this teacher ______________
4 that college student ______________
5 that boy ______________
6 this high school student ______________

C Complete the sentences with the missing phrase in parentheses in Chinese. Then translate the sentences.

Ex: (This intelligent young woman) → Zhègè hěn cōngmíngde nǚshēng shì dàxuéshēng.
This intelligent young woman is a college student.

1 (That handsome man) jiào Mike Lǎoshī.

____

____

2 (That lazy high school student) bù xǐhuān zuò tāde zuòyè.

____

____

3 (This old professor) yǒu shíwǔběn Zhōngwén kèběn.

____

____

4 (That cute child) yào qù mǎi xīnde làbǐ.

____

____

D Use the clues to make long answers for the following questions. Say them out loud.

1 Nàgè rén shì shéi? (Joe's dad)

2 Zhègè nǚháizi shì nǐde nǚ'ér ma? (Yes)

3 Nàgè xiāofángyuán xǐ bù xǐhuān zuò yùndòng? (No)

4 Nàgè nǚrén jiào shénme míngzi? (Lily)

E 69.02 Listen to the people Dàwèi likes and dislikes and complete the sentences.

1 Dàwèi xǐhuān ____________ hěn piàoliàngde nǚrén.

2 Tā bù xǐhuān nàgè hěn ____________.

3 Tā hěn xǐhuān ____________ hěn bàngde yīshēng.

4 Tā bú tài xǐhuān zhègè ____________.

Lesson 70

"This panda needs to get a life!"

Zhè / Nà + Other Measure Words

I'm sorry to inform you that this will be our last lesson on measure words; I know you're disappointed, but don't worry, we'll be starting prepositions in our next lesson. Now that usually gets my students dancing on their chairs. But first, let's:

- combine other measure words with **zhè** and **nà**
- use **zhè / nà** to compliment and complain

Now that you've got the hang of using **zhègè** and **nàgè**, you should be able to combine **zhè / nà** with other measure words you know. So, let's plug in old measure words with *this / that* so you can say things like *This cup of coffee is too hot* and *That dog is so cute!*

Recap

Do the following to review and prepare for this lesson. If you have trouble, review lessons 65–9.

1 **Say:** I have two younger sisters. Ask: How many older brothers do you have?

2 **Say:** They want to buy 20 books. She wants a cup of coffee.

Words, phrases and stuff

70.01 **Listen to the words. Then listen again and repeat.**

Words to Describe Objects

tàng	烫	*hot, burning* (for objects)	**cháng**	长	*long*
bīng	冰	*ice, cold* (for objects)	**zhòng**	重	*heavy*
yìng	硬	*hard, firm*	**wǎn**	碗	MW for bowls
ruǎn	软	*soft*	**xiǎoxīn!**	小心	*to be careful; Be careful!*

A Remember "hǎo"? What does it mean in "Zhèzhī zhū hǎo dà"? Choose the correct translation.

1 ____________ This is a good pig.

2 ____________ This good pig is big.

3 ____________ This big pig is good.

4 ____________ This pig is so big.

B Remember that some adverbs intensify your speech. That is, they pump it up so you can compliment someone, complain, or just express strong feelings. Take a look at the list and try to match the intensifiers and definitions.

1 ____________ too

2 ____________ really

3 ____________ super

4 ____________ pretty (quite)

5 ____________ still, yet

6 ____________ so

7 ____________ extremely

a zhēn(de)

b fēicháng

c tài

d hǎo

e chāo

f hái

g mán

Patterns

Use the same pattern for **zhè / nà** with other measure words that you use with **gè**. Check out the way to use them with an intensifying adverb.

Pattern 1a: **zhè** + **MW** + noun

1b: **nà** + **MW** + noun

Pattern 2: **Zhè / Nà** + **MW** + noun + intensifying adverb + adjective.

Examples:

1a **zhè**běn shū (*this book*)

1b **nà**zhī lǎohǔ (*that tiger*)

2 **Nà**bēi kāfēi fēicháng tàng. (*That cup of coffee is extremely hot.*)

Get to work

A Match the words and English translations. Then check your answers.

wǎn	bīng	zhè	tàng	cháng
ruǎn	zhòng	yìng	xiǎoxīn	nà

1 heavy ______________________
2 ice; cold ______________________
3 long ______________________
4 this ______________________
5 to be careful ______________________
6 hot, burning ______________________
7 MW for bowls ______________________
8 soft ______________________
9 that ______________________
10 hard ______________________

B Use the words in parentheses to provide long answers to the following questions.

Ex: Q: Nàzhī māo shì shéide? (tāde) **A:** Nàzhī māo shì tāde.

1 **Q:** Nǐ kěyǐ gěi wǒ nàzhāng zhǐ ma? (Yes)
A: ______________________

2 **Q:** Nín yào bú yào mǎi nàpíng pútáojiǔ? (No)
A: ______________________

3 **Q:** Nàbēi lǜchá tài tàng ma? (Yes)
A: ______________________

4 **Q:** Nàzhī gǒu yǒu méi yǒu hěn duō wánjù? (No)
A: ______________________

5 **Q:** Nàzhāng chuáng hěn yìng ma? (Yes)
A: ______________________

C Let's review to be sure you remember the measure words (MW) we have covered so far and the reasons why we use them. Match each MW with the correct objects.

1 ____ gè
2 ____ běn
3 ____ zhī
4 ____ bēi
5 ____ píng
6 ____ zhāng

a book-like objects
b cups; glasses
c people; general objects
d flat objects
e most animals
f bottles

D Now use each of the measure words above in a sentence. Don't worry, I'll get you started.

Ex: This Chinese textbook **A:** Zhèběn Zhōngwén kèběn

1 This short man ______________________________

2 That English book ______________________________

3 That ugly dog ______________________________

4 This cup of green tea ______________________________

5 This bottle of milk ______________________________

6 That soft bed ______________________________

Lesson 71

"Nǐ zài nă lǐ? (again)"

Prepositions 1

Where's Dad? Where's my money? Locating people and things is a daily job, and to do it you have to use a preposition. So, how about we:

- review **zài** to tell where things are
- learn new prepositions and locations
- use **zài** with more prepositions to give other locations

The word **zài**, which is the most fundamental preposition in Chinese, was introduced in Lesson 29. We have since learned the important question **Nǐ zài nă lǐ?** (*Where are you?*) as well as common statements like **Wǒ zài jiā** (*I am at home*) and **Mike Lǎoshī zài chēkù** (*Mike Lǎoshī is in the garage*). When **zài** is used by itself (like the examples above), it means *at* or *in*, but it takes on more meanings (e.g. *on*) when it is used in combination with other prepositions. You'll see what I mean very soon, so be patient.

Recap

Watch the review of "zài". Then put "zài" in the correct place to complete these sentences.

1 Nǐ ____ yě ____ nǐde ____ chēkù ma?

2 Nǐ ____ nǐde ____ wòshì ____ ma?

3 Nǐ ____ túshūguǎn ____ ma?

4 Nǐ ____ cèsuǒ ____ ma?

Words, phrases and stuff

71.01 **Listen to the words. Then listen again and repeat.**

Locators and More

zài	在	*at, in, on*
lǐmiàn	里面	*inside, within*
wàimiàn	外面	*outside, on the outer side of*
lóushàng	楼上	*upstairs*
lóuxià	楼下	*downstairs*
wàiguórén	外国人	*foreigner*
fángjiān	房间	*a room*

A “Lǐmiàn” and “wàimiàn” are occasionally replaced by another ending, depending on the region of China. Is the other ending “-jiān” or “-biān”?

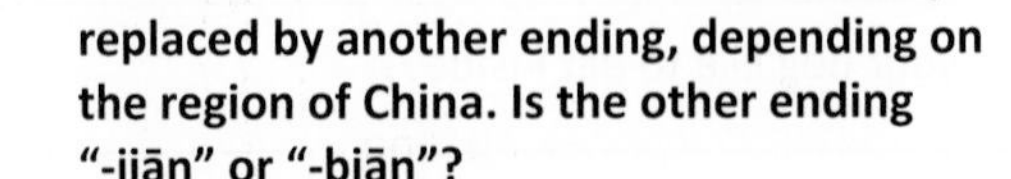

The same ending (**-biān**) can also be used for other prepositions ending in **-miàn** that we will cover soon.

B Mike Lǎoshī's devious pet panda has escaped again! Read and translate the following sentences with “zài” + preposition to help your favorite teacher find him. Where is he?

1. Tā bú zài lóushàng. ______________________
2. Tā bú zài tāde fángjiān. ______________________
3. Tā bú zài wàimiàn. ______________________
4. Tā zài lóuxià. ______________________

Patterns

The following question + answer patterns should be a review from Season 1 when we used **zài** to talk about everyday places (e.g., the supermarket, movie theater, park, etc.), so you shouldn't find these very complicated. The only difference is we are combining **zài** with another preposition (*inside*, *outside*, etc.) instead of a specific location.

Pattern 1: Subject + **zài** + **nǎ lǐ**?

Pattern 2a: Subject + **zài** + location / preposition.

2b: Subject + **bú zài** + location / preposition.

Examples:

1 Nǐde shū **zài** nǎ lǐ? (*Where is your book?*)

2a Tāmen **zài** lóushàng. (*They are upstairs.*) / Lily **zài** wàimiàn. (*Lily is outside.*)

2b Wǒmen **bú zài** lóuxià. (*We are not downstairs.*) / Wǒ **bú zài** jiā. (*I am not at home.*)

71.02 **Practice the old and new patterns with “zài”. Say in Chinese:**

1. Where are you?
2. I am at home.
3. You are at school.
4. Mom is at the bank.
5. They are downstairs.

yínháng 银行 bank

Get to work

A Match the words and meanings.

1 ____ lǐmiàn
2 ____ lóushàng
3 ____ wàiguórén
4 ____ lóuxià

a foreigner
b inside
c downstairs
d upstairs

B Write "Correct" or fix the incorrect English translations.

Ex: Wǒ dìdide fángjiān zài lóushàng. (My younger brother's room is downstairs.)
→ My younger brother's room is upstairs.

1 Chúfáng zài lóuxià. (The kitchen is downstairs.) ____________________

2 Nǐmende gǒu xǐhuān qù wàimiàn wán ma? (Does your dog like to eat inside?)
____

3 Nǐde xiǎohái zài jiā ma? (Are your children home?) ____________________

4 Wǒde mǔqīn hěn xǐhuān jiāo wàiguórén Yīngwén. (My mother really likes dancing with foreigners.) ____________________

C Look at the house and label the places. Use the words in the box to say where everyone in the family is. Use complete sentences, such as "Māma zài lóuxià". There may be more than one possible answer.

Bàba	Māma	Gēge	Mèimei	Gǒu	lǐmiàn
lóushàng	wàimiàn	lóuxià	fángjiān		

____

____

____

____

____

D **Construct sentences using "zài". Tell where things are around your home. Use any of the following things or make up your own.**

diànshì (*television*), **bīngxiāng** (*refrigerator*), **chēzi** (*car*), **chúfáng** (*kitchen*), **yīfú** (*clothes*), **kèběn** (*textbooks*), **zìdiǎn** (*dictionary*), **gōngjùxiāng** (*toolbox*), **qiú** (*ball*)

Ex: Wǒ mèimeide diànnǎo zài lóushàng. (*My little sister's computer is upstairs.*)

1 ______________________________

2 ______________________________

3 ______________________________

4 ______________________________

Lesson 72

"How did you get inside the garage?"

Prepositions 2

You know what the best thing is about having pandas living in your backyard? They make great props for teaching grammar lessons in Chinese! Watch and you can:

- bulk up your collection of prepositions
- form more specific prepositional phrases of location
- ask and say where people and things are more exactly

After you watch a strange man hunt for precious metals in Mike Lǎoshī's garage and see the panda in the tree, you may ask yourself what the purpose of this lesson is. This time we are taking our studies of prepositions to the next level. Instead of just saying *I am upstairs* or *I am outside*, we'll provide a specific reference point as well. After this lesson, you'll be able to say *The bird is above me* and *My cell phone is on the table* or *Some dude is inside my garage*. Let's do this!

Recap

Last time you learned to say that *my dad is upstairs*, *my mom is downstairs*, *my cat is inside*, and *my dog is outside*. Yes, it's the same pattern we've been using since Lesson 29 (subject + **zài** + location), so I don't think you need much more of a recap.

72.01 But just in case, say those things now, in Chinese. Then listen and compare your answers to the native speakers.

1. My dad is upstairs.
2. My mom is downstairs.
3. My cat is inside.
4. My dog is outside.

Words, phrases and stuff

72.02 Listen to the words. Then listen again and repeat.

Locators and Things

zài	在	*at, in, on*	**xióngmāo**	熊猫	*panda*
lǐmiàn	里面	*inside*	**báibǎn(bǐ)**	白板（笔）	*whiteboard (marker)*
wàimiàn	外面	*outside*	**hēibǎn**	黑板	*blackboard, chalkboard*
shàngmiàn	上面	*on top of, above*	**tiānhuābǎn**	天花板	*the ceiling*
xiàmiàn	下面	*under, below*	**dìbǎn**	地板	*the floor*
qiánmiàn	前面	*in front of*	**dìtǎn**	地毯	*the carpet / rug*
hòumiàn	后面	*behind, in back of*	**qiángbì**	墙壁	*wall*
			bīngxiāng	冰箱	*refrigerator*

Four of the new words share the word part "-bǎn". What does "-bǎn" probably mean?

1 a writing utensil   **2** a board

Patterns

The first two patterns (**1** and **2a**) are the same ones we used last time, so you shouldn't have any trouble. The third pattern (**2b**) is brand new this time, so pay closer attention. Let's rock it!

Pattern 1: Subject + **zài** + **nǎ lǐ**?

Pattern 2a: Subject + **zài** + **location / preposition**.

2b: Subject + **zài** + **noun(de)** + **location / preposition**.

Examples:

1 Nǐde chènshān **zài nǎ lǐ**? (*Where is your shirt?*)

2a Wǒde chènshān **zài lóuxià /xuéxiào**. (*My shirt is downstairs / at school.*)

2b Chēzi **zài wǒde péngyǒu(de) jiā**. (*The car is at my friend's house.*) / Báibǎn **zài wǒde hòumiàn**. (*The whiteboard is behind me.*)

In the video, I taught you the more formal way of constructing sentences with prepositions, so we've been saying things like **Niúnài zài bīngxiāngde lǐmiàn**, but you're more likely to hear **Niúnài zài bīngxiāng lǐ** omitting the **de** after **bīngxiāng** and the **miàn** after **lǐ**. Similarly, you'll hear people say **Nǐde bǐjìběn diànnǎo zài zhuōzi shàng** instead of the more formal **Nǐde bǐjìběn diànnǎo zài zhuōzide shàngmiàn**. It never hurts to know both ways – trust me.

Using the sentences that are provided, convert the following sentences to their longer / shorter forms.

1 Jīròu zài kǎoxiāngde lǐmiàn. ______________________________

2 Nǐde Zhōngwén kèběn zài chuáng shàng. ______________________

Get to work

A Complete the sentences with the correct word from the list.

dìbǎn	hēibǎn	báibǎn(bǐ)	tiānhuābǎn	xióngmāo	dìtǎn

1 (The ceiling) __________ zài wǒmende shàngmiàn.

2 (The floor) __________ zài (the rug) __________ de xiàmiàn.

3 (The panda) __________ hěn zhòng.

4 Lǎoshīde (whiteboard marker) __________ zài nǎ lǐ?

5 (The blackboard) __________ zài xuéshēngde qiánmiàn.

B Write the opposite of the following sentences.

Ex: Tāmen zài jiàoshòude hòumiàn. → Jiàoshòu zài tāmende qiánmiàn.

1 Shǒujī zài bǐjìběn diànnǎode shàngmiàn. ______________________

2 Wǒ jiějie zài wǒ māmade qiánmiàn. ______________________

3 Zhōngwén shū zài píngbǎn diànnǎode shàngmiàn. ______________________

4 Qiángbì zài wǒmende hòumiàn. ______________________

C Answer the followings questions about where these objects are in relation to the refrigerator.

1 Xiāngjiāo zài nǎ lǐ?
2 Chéngzhī zài nǎ lǐ?
3 Píngguǒ zài nǎ lǐ?
4 Kělè zài nǎ lǐ?
5 Lǎoshǔ zài nǎ lǐ?
6 Chǎofàn zài nǎ lǐ?

Lesson 73

"Practicing the hokey pokey dance"

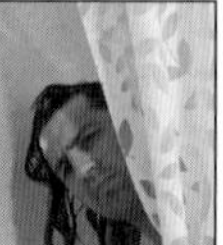

Prepositions 3

By the time you finish this lesson, you'll be able to tell people whether you're right or left-handed, but more importantly, you'll know that Mike Lǎoshī is a master on the barbecue. You'll get hungry just watching the episode – trust me. But try to control your appetite, for you must first:

- learn left from right
- use more prepositions
- talk more about where people and things are

This is our third and final lesson on prepositions, so when you need to provide the location or spatial relationships for people and / or objects, you should be in pretty good shape. If not, go work out. Ha ha ha. Get it? ☺

Recap

Last time we learned how to use prepositions to show the spatial relationship between two objects. To check that you understand, try unscrambling these sentences.

1 shàngmiàn / nǐde / zhuōzide / zài / kèběn (Your textbook is on the table.)

2 wǒde / jǐngchá / hòumiàn / zài (The police officer is behind me.)

3 shū / zài / wǒde / wǒde / lǐmiàn / shūbāode (My books are in my book bag.)

Words, phrases and stuff

73.01 **Listen to the words. Then listen again and repeat.**

More Locators and More Things

zài	在	*in, at, on*	**lóutī**	楼梯	*stairs*
pángbiān	旁边	*next to, beside*	**mén**	门	*door*
zuǒbiān	左边	*left, to the left of*	**chuānghu**	窗户	*window*
yòubiān	右边	*right, to the right of*	**huā**	花	*flower*
duìmiàn	对面	*across from, opposite of; face to face*	**qiú**	球	*ball*
zhōngjiān	中间	*in the middle of, between*	**shūcài**	蔬菜	*vegetables*

Unlike most of the prepositions you've already learned, this lesson's prepositions largely end with **-biān** instead of **-miàn**. Although in some regions **-miàn** is an acceptable ending for some of these, **-biān** is the more commonly used ending for these prepositions.

A Try to match the word part with the meaning.

1 -biān 边 a middle

2 -miàn 面 b edge, side

3 -zhōng 中 c surface

B How would we translate the following sentences in English?

1 Wǒde péngyǒu zài wǒde pángbiān.

2 Wǒ zài chēzide zhōngjiān.

C Put L or R for *on my left / right*:

1 _________ zài wǒde yòubiān 2 _________ zài wǒde zuǒbiān

Patterns

You can use the new prepositions in the same patterns that you have practiced in the last two lessons. To be sure that you have learned these patterns, use this method to bring them to life.

Instructions:

Step 1: Watch the video several more times.

Step 2: At home, notice where your books, furniture, clothes, etc. are situated: Is your cell phone charger next to your bed? Is your teddy bear on your bed? Are your dirty clothes under your bed?

Step 3: Now make sentences using the patterns.

To check your mastery, match the patterns and the sentences.

a Subject + **zài** + **noun(de)** + **preposition / location**.

b Subject + **zài** + **nă lĭ**?

c Subject + **zài** + **preposition / location**.

1 ______ Chuānghu zài ménde yòubiān.

2 ______ Wŏde gōngjùxiāng zài wàimiàn.

3 ______ Bĭjìbĕn diànnăo zài wŏde bàngōngshì.

4 ______ Wŏde chēzi zài jiā.

5 ______ Nàzhī niăo zài shùde lĭmiàn.

6 ______ Nĭde yōupán zài nă lĭ?

Get to work

A Match the words with their opposites.

1 ______ qiánmiàn

2 ______ lóushàng

3 ______ yòubiān

4 ______ shàngmiàn

a xiàmiàn

b zuŏbiān

c lóuxià

d hòumiàn

B 73.02 Add "bú" to negate the sentences. Say the sentences out loud. Listen and compare your answers. Then translate them into English.

1 Wŏde shŏujī zài wŏde shūbāode pángbiān.

2 Tāde bĭjìbĕn diànnăo zài nĭde bĭjìbĕn diànnăode yòubiān.

3 Yīshēng zài hùshìde zuŏbiān.

4 Yínháng zài túshūguănde duìmiàn.

yínháng 银行 bank

C Unscramble the sentences. More than one answer may be possible.

1 nàzhī / zài / yĭzide / gŏu / zhōngjian. ______

2 zài / shízhōngde / xiàmiàn / chuānghu. ______

3 nàgè / yòubiān / jĭngchá / zài / xiāofángyuánde. ______

4 pánzi / nĭde / zài / wŏde / zuŏbiān / pánzide. ______

D Look at the picture and label the objects in Chinese. Then write sentences using your prepositions to describe the objects' spatial relationships to each other. More than one answer may be possible.

Ex: Shāfā zài dìtǎn de shàngmiàn.
(*The sofa is on top of the carpet.*)

1 carpet / table ______________________

2 panda / sofa ______________________

3 chair / sofa ______________________

4 a glass of wine / laptop ______________________

5 laptop / dictionary ______________________

6 laptop / table ______________________

7 ceiling / panda ______________________

Barbecue: Chinese style

I love a good BBQ, especially mandarin ribs, which is a very popular spicy barbecue dish originating in northern China. Here's how you can make them yourself. Use five pounds of pork spare-ribs. Mix one cup of soy sauce, one cup of orange marmalade, three minced cloves of garlic, one teaspoon of ground pepper, and one half teaspoon of black pepper. Put the ribs in a baking pan and pour the sauce over them. Turn the ribs over to completely cover with sauce. Marinate them in the refrigerator for at least 12 hours. Barbecue them on the grill or put them in the oven. To roast, cook at 325° F (165° C) for 1½ hours. Baste frequently. Separate the ribs into servings and serve hot. Please make extra for Mike Lǎoshī.

*Stay tuned to www.chinesewithmike.com if you are interested in entering Mike Lǎoshī's annual rib cook-off (where I will be the judge).

Lesson 74

"Wǒ yào xǐ tóufǎ"

Yào vs. Xiǎng 1

It's not every day I let my fans get a sneak peek at some of my more private moments, but my producer thought it was a good idea. Don't get too distracted, though, because we're about to:

- review the verb **yào** and meet the verb **xiǎng**
- use **yào** to talk about what grooming tasks you must do
- understand the differences between **yào** and **xiǎng (qù)**

In Season 2, I introduced the three key definitions of the verb **yào**, a very important word. In this lesson, you'll practice using **yào**, but I'll also introduce **xiǎng**, a verb with several meanings, and we'll begin taking a look at some similarities and important differences between the two verbs.

Review

Yào

A What are three definitions of "yào"?

1 ______ to want (something immediately available)
2 ______ must
3 ______ to be going to
4 ______ might like to go

B Look at the situations in parentheses. Then match them to the correct use of "yào".

1 ______ Wǒde bóbo yào chī chǎofàn.
2 ______ Wǒmen yào qù túshūguǎn.
3 ______ Tā yào hē tāng.
4 ______ Nǐmen yào zuò hěn duō dōngxī.
5 ______ Wǒmen yào qù Màngǔ.

a (wants (something immediately available))
b (intention / plan)
c (necessity)

Words, phrases and stuff

Now, for a few new words about things you have to do!

74.01 Listen to the words. Then listen again and repeat.

Want vs. Want and Another Word

yào	要	*to want, be going to, must*
xiǎng	想	*to want, would like to, to think about, to miss*
shì	事	*things, matters, items, work*

Grooming

xǐ (zǎo)	洗（澡）	*to wash (to take a shower)*	**tóufǎ/tóufa**	头发	*hair*
shuā (yá)	刷（牙）	*to brush (teeth)*	**liǎn**	脸	*face*
guā (húzi)	刮（胡子）	*to shave (beard)*	**shǒu**	手	*hand(s)*
shū (tóufa/tóufǎ)	梳（头发）	*to comb (hair)*	**zāng**	脏	*dirty, filthy*
jiǎn (tóufa/tóufǎ)	剪（头发）	*to cut / trim (hair)*	**cháng**	长	*long (length)*

Tóufǎ often ends in the third tone when spoken in Taiwan and is neutral in mainland.

A What is a major difference in meaning between "yào" and "xiǎng"?

B What is a synonym for your new word "shì"?

1 tāng **2** dōngxī **3** shí

C Answer true or false.

1 Wǒ yào xǐ tóufǎ means *I must comb my hair.*

2 Wǒ xiǎng qù Xiānggǎng means *I have a plan to go to Hong Kong.*

Patterns

Here are basic patterns for using the two key verbs in this lesson. The first is for **yào** as *must*, known in English grammar as a modal. Modals add to the meaning of a second verb that follows.

Pattern 1: Subject + **yào** + **verb 2** + . . .

Example:

1 Wǒ **yào** xǐ yīfú. (lit. *I must wash clothes.*)

The next are for **yào** vs. **xiǎng** with **qù** (*to go*). In this sense, **yào** usually means *be going to* but can sometimes mean *must* depending on context. And if you answered the video question in "Words, phrases and stuff" correctly, you know that **xiǎng qù** means you are only thinking about going somewhere, i.e., you do not have a plan to do it, whereas **yào qù** means you intend to do it and you have a plan.

Pattern 2a: Subject + **yào / xiǎng qù** + **nǎ lǐ**?

2b: Subject + **yào / xiǎng qù** + place.

Examples:

2a Nǐ **yào qù nǎ lǐ**? (*Where are you going to go?*) /
Nǐ **xiǎng qù nǎ lǐ**? (*Where would you like to go?*)

2b Wǒ **yào qù** hǎitān. (*I'm going to / must go to the beach.*) /
Wǒ **xiǎng qù** kāfēitīng. (*I'd like to go to the coffee shop.*)

In Chinese, you don't need to add possessive adjectives like *my* or *his / her* for clarification to talk about reflexive actions. The reflexive is understood. For example, I can say **Wǒ yào xǐ shǒu** to mean *I must wash my hands*. I don't need to include **wǒde** to specify I'm washing MY own hands.

Get to work

A Use the clue to complete the sentences with the correct word.

1 Wǒde érzi hěn (zāng / shì). (dirty)
2 Tā yào (xǐ shǒu / xǐ zǎo). (take a shower)
3 Tāde (shǒu / tóufǎ) tài (liǎn / cháng). (hair) (long)
4 Bàba bù xǐhuan (guā / shū) húzi. (shave)

B Use the words in parentheses to say what grooming tasks you must do.

Ex: (comb hair) Jīntiān wǒ yào shū tóufǎ.

1 (wash my hands) Wǒ yào ____________________.
2 (cut my hair) Xīngqīsān wǒ yào ____________________.
3 (brush my teeth) Jīntiān zǎoshàng wǒ yào ____________________.
4 (wash my hair) Jīntiān wǎnshàng wǒ yào ____________________.

C Look at the situation and choose "yào" or "xiǎng"

1 going to wash my hair today (yào / xiǎng)
2 think I might like to go to the park (yào / xiǎng)
3 definitely going to study this afternoon (yào / xiǎng)
4 would like to go to Rome next year (yào / xiǎng)

"On with xiǎng"

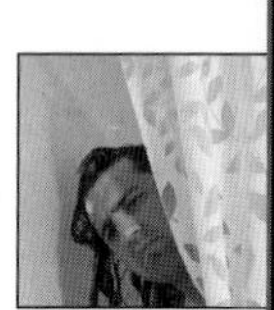

Yào vs. Xiǎng 2

Yes, I am shamelessly rocking a mullet, and no, I have not been caught in a time warp. I guess I just took the last lesson a little too far when I demonstrated some of your new vocabulary words, including "cut my hair". So if this doesn't prove I'm your fearless leader, I don't know what will. Anyway, let's:

- review **yào** vs. **xiǎng**
- learn the root meaning of **xiǎng**
- use **xiǎng** in its different meanings

You may have noticed that most of the previous lesson reviewed the major definitions of the verb **yào** and largely ignored our new verb – **xiǎng**, apart from my sweet overview of **xiǎng**'s major definitions. We're about to remedy that and take a closer look at the differences between the two verbs.

Recap

A What are the four meanings of "xiǎng"? Put them here. If you don't remember, watch the second half of lesson 74 for an overview.

1 ____________________

2 ____________________

3 ____________________

4 ____________________

Words, phrases and stuff

75.01 Listen to the words. Then listen again and repeat.

Things You Often "Xiǎng" and Food

xiǎng	想	*to want, would like to, to think about, to miss*
wèilái	未来	*the future*
bù	部	MW for movies, films
tái	台	MW for vehicles, machines, electronic objects
chǎofàn	炒饭	*fried rice*
báifàn	白饭	*white rice*
chūnjuǎn	春卷	*spring roll*
diǎn (cài)	点（菜）	*to order (food)*
fèn	分	*a portion, a share, an order of something*
wǎn	碗	*bowl;* MW for bowls

Watch the video and answer these questions about "xiǎng" vs. "yào".

A Which of the following are possible definitions of "xiǎng"?

1 to want; would like to

2 must

3 to think about

4 to miss

B Do these statements mean the same thing?: "Wǒ yào diǎn chǎofàn" and "Wǒ xiǎng diǎn chǎofàn".

1 Yes, they basically mean the same, but **xiǎng** is a little more polite.

2 No, **xiǎng** means you are thinking about fried rice, while **yào** means you are ordering it or saying you definitely want fried rice.

C How is "yào qù" different from "xiǎng qù"? (both: *want / would like to go*)

Patterns

Here are some of the major ways we use **xiǎng**.

Pattern 1a: Subject + **xiǎng** + noun. (*to think of / miss somebody or something*)

1b: Subject + **xiǎng** + noun + ma? (*to think of / miss somebody or something*)

Pattern 2a: Subject + **xiǎng** + verb 2 . . . (*would like to*)

2b: Subject + **xiǎng** + verb 2 + ma? (*would like to*)

2c: (Bù) **Xiǎng**. Subject + (bù) **xiǎng** + verb 2. (*would like / not like to*)

Examples:

1a Wǒ **xiǎng** wǒde gǒu. (*I miss my dog.*)

1b Nǐ **xiǎng** nǐde jiārén ma? (*Do you miss your family?*)

2a Míngtiān wǒ **xiǎng** kàn yībù diànyǐng. (*Tomorrow I would like to watch a movie.*)

2b Míngtiān nǐ **xiǎng** kàn yībù diànyǐng ma? (*Would you like to watch a movie tomorrow?*)

2c (Bù) **xiǎng** / **Xiǎng**. Wǒ (bù) **xiǎng** kàn (yībù) diànyǐng. (*No / Yes. I would not / would like to watch a movie.*)

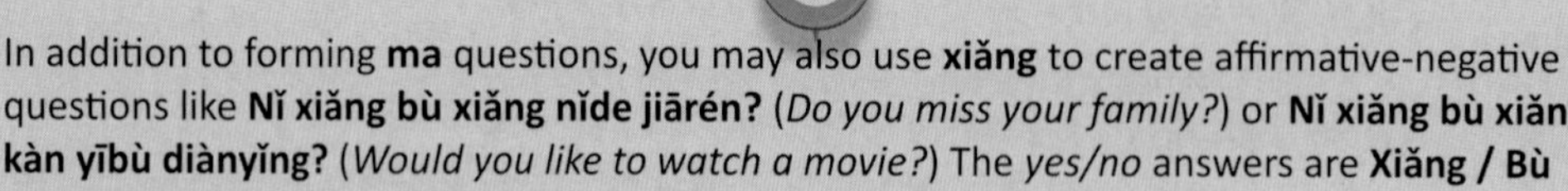

In addition to forming **ma** questions, you may also use **xiǎng** to create affirmative-negative questions like **Nǐ xiǎng bù xiǎng nǐde jiārén?** (*Do you miss your family?*) or **Nǐ xiǎng bù xiǎng kàn yībù diànyǐng?** (*Would you like to watch a movie?*) The *yes/no* answers are **Xiǎng / Bù xiǎng**, respectively.

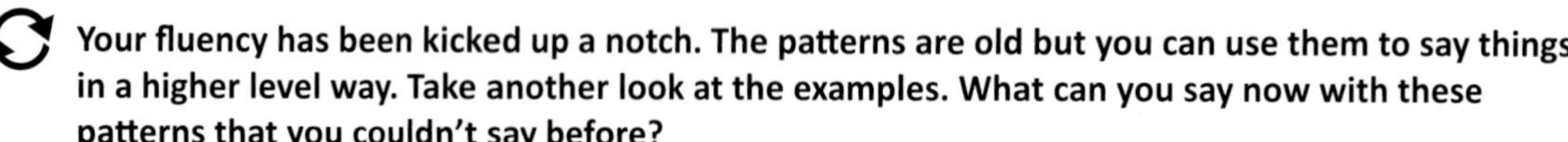

Your fluency has been kicked up a notch. The patterns are old but you can use them to say things in a higher level way. Take another look at the examples. What can you say now with these patterns that you couldn't say before?

Get to work

A Put C next to the phrases that have the correct measure words and fix the phrases that do not use the correct measure words. Then translate the phrases.

Ex: C sānbù diànyǐng three movies

1 ____________ sìwǎn báifàn ____________________
2 ____________ liǎngbù diànyǐng __________________
3 ____________ yīběn bǐjìběn diànnǎo ____________
4 ____________ yīpíng píjiǔ _____________________
5 ____________ yīgè xióng _______________________
6 ____________ wǔběn Fǎwén liànxíběn ___________
7 ____________ sānfèn chūnjuǎn __________________

B Read the sentences and choose the correct definition of "xiǎng" (a–d).

a want / would like (now)
b to think about
c would like to (at some point in the future)
d to miss something / someone

1 ____ Xiànzài wǒ xiǎng chī niúròu chǎofàn.
2 ____ Hòunián wǒmen xiǎng mǎi xīnde fángzi.
3 ____ Tā hěn xiǎng tāde nǚpéngyǒu.
4 ____ Nǐ xiǎng bù xiǎng jiā?
5 ____ Nǐmen xiǎng diǎn shénme cài?
6 ____ Zhèxiē dàxuéshēng zài xiǎng tāmende wèilái.

C Match the questions to the answers and say them out loud.

a Mike Lǎoshī xiǎng tāde bàbamāma ma?
b Tā xiǎng qù nǎ lǐ xuéxí Zhōngwén?
c Nǐ xiǎng diǎn shénme (cài?)
d Nǐ xiǎng qù nǎ lǐ?
e Nǐmen xiǎng kàn nàbù diànyǐng ma?

1 **Q:** ______________________ **A:** Wǒ xiǎng qù wǒde wàipó jiā.
2 **Q:** ______________________ **A:** Bù xiǎng. Wǒmen bù xiǎng kàn nàbù diànyǐng.
3 **Q:** ______________________ **A:** Xiǎng. Mike Lǎoshī xiǎng tāde bàbamāma.
4 **Q:** ______________________ **A:** Tā xiǎng qù Běijīng Dàxué xuéxí Zhōngwén.
5 **Q:** ______________________ **A:** Wǒ xiǎng diǎn yīfèn chūnjuǎn.

Lesson 76

"Uh oh"

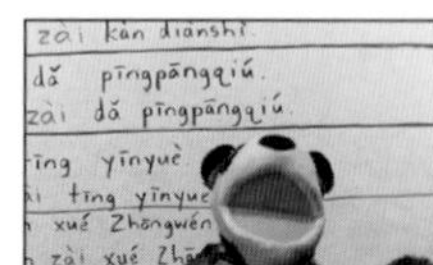

Yào vs. Xiǎng 3

Wow! I should have cut my hair a long time ago! Here I thought I was just bringing back a perfectly nice hairstyle and nothing more, but everywhere I go, people (especially the ladies) are complimenting me on it. I've even been asked to model! Anyway, you know I don't have time for this stuff. Let's:

- check your understanding of **yào** vs. **xiǎng**

We have covered the basic definitions of **xiǎng** and **yào**, looked at some overlapping uses and some differences in use between these two verbs. In this lesson, we'll keep practicing and do a quick review. Then we'll wrap this up. How 'bout it?

Recap

A Take a look at the following pairs of sentences. Is the translation correct (C) or incorrect (X)?

1 ____ Xiànzài wǒ xiǎng chī wǎncān. (*I would like to eat dinner now.*)

2 ____ Míngnián tā xiǎng qù Zhōngguó. (*Next year he / she is going to go to China.*)

3 ____ Wǒ mèimei hěn xiǎng tāde nánpéngyǒu. (*My older sister really misses her boyfriend.*)

B Which of the following definitions of "xiǎng" is interchangeable with the verb "yào"?

1 To think about

2 To miss

3 Want / would like something immediately available

4 Would like to (in future) but with no definite plan

Often, Chinese speakers will combine the verbs **xiǎng** + **yào** to mean *would like*. You already know that **Wǒ yào hē kāfēi** and **Wǒ xiǎng hē kāfēi** are both acceptable ways to say *I want / would like to drink coffee*, but it is very common to hear **Wǒ xiǎng yào hē kāfēi** as well. It's considered more polite or gentler than using **yào** by itself.

Words, phrases and stuff

Before we review, take a look at a few new words.

76.01 Listen to the words. Then listen again and repeat.

Fun and Places

pàiduì	派对	*a party*	**Jiùjīnshān**	旧金山	*San Francisco*
chūqù	出去	*to go out*	**Luòshānjī**	洛杉矶	*Los Angeles*
dàhòutiān	大后天	*three days from now* (lit. *the day after the day after tomorrow*)	**Jiāzhōu**	加州	*California*

Cover the vocabulary and match the words and definitions. Check you're right.

1 ____ pàiduì
2 ____ Jiùjīnshān
3 ____ chūqù
4 ____ Luòshānjī
5 ____ dàhòutiān
6 ____ Jiāzhōu

a San Francisco
b California
c a party
d Los Angeles
e to go out
f three days from now

Get to work

A Put these sentences in Chinese using "yào" or "xiǎng". If both are acceptable, put one of the verbs in parentheses.

Examples:
I'd like to go to the art museum tomorrow. → Míngtiān wǒ xiǎng qù měishùguǎn.
OR I want to eat dinner now. → Xiànzài wǒ yào (xiǎng) chī wǎncān.

1 Tomorrow you must go to the dentist. ____________________
2 The day after tomorrow he'd like to play tennis. ____________________
3 We are not going to the park today. ____________________
4 I want to order two portions of spring rolls. ____________________
5 What would you like to do tomorrow? ____________________
6 Is she going to do the laundry today? ____________________

B Use the words in parentheses to talk about David's plans and things he would like to do.

Examples:
(today / take a shower) → Jīntiān tā yào xǐzǎo.
(tomorrow / go to the beach to swim) → Míngtiān tā xiǎng qù hǎitān yóuyǒng.

1 (today / wash hair) ____________________

2 (next year / go to San Francisco) ____________________

3 (day after tomorrow / go to friend's house) ____________________

4 (Friday / go to party) ____________________

5 (today / play baseball) ____________________

6 (this year / go to Los Angeles) ____________________

Review

OK, ready? You're about to take a quiz to check your understanding of the two verbs **xiǎng** and **yào**. Do NOT look at the video again before you do the review. Instead, answer these questions first. Then go to the video or the Answer key and check your answers. If you have trouble you can also go back to Lessons 74 and 75.

Part 1: Basics

A Choose the correct definitions of "yào".

1 ______ would like to

2 ______ to want

3 ______ to miss

4 ______ must

5 ______ to think about

6 ______ be going to

B Choose the correct definitions of "xiǎng".

1 ______ would like to

2 ______ to want

3 ______ to miss

4 ______ must

5 ______ to think about

6 ______ be going to

Part 2: Patterns

A Match the patterns to the situations. Some patterns may be used more than once, and some items may have more than one possible answer. The "yào / xiǎng" pattern means that the two verbs can be used interchangeably.

a Subject + **yào** + verb.

b Subject + **xiǎng** + verb.

c Subject + **yào** + noun.

d Subject + **xiǎng** + noun.

1 ______ to tell the server you want to drink tea

2 ______ to say you think about your future

3 ______ to say you've got a plan to go to the beach

4 ______ to say you miss your dog

5 ______ to say you think you'd like to go to California

6 ______ to say you want milk

7 ______ to say you must wash your hands

B Read the sentences and choose the correct meaning of "yào" or "xiǎng." More than one answer may be possible.

a (yào) *want*	**b** (yào) *need / must*	**c** (xiǎng) *would like to*
d (xiǎng) *think about*	**e** (xiǎng) *miss*	**f** (yào) *going to (with a plan)*

1 ______ Nǐ yào bú yào qù kāfēitīng?

2 ______ Bú yào. Wǒ bú yào chūqù.

3 ______ Nǐ xiǎng bù xiǎng qù yóuyǒng?

4 ______ Nǐ yào qù Jiùjīnshān ma?

5 ______ Wǒ yào zhèzhī gǒu.

6 ______ Bù xiǎng. Wǒ bù xiǎng qù yóuyǒng.

7 ______ Nǐ yào yìbēi lǜchá ma?

8 ______ Nǐ xiǎng nǐde wèilái ma?

9 ______ Nǐ xiǎng mǎi fángzi ma?

10 ______ Xiǎng. Wǒ xiǎng wǒde péngyǒu.

C I want to know about YOUR life. What are two plans for today? What are you going to do? What two things would you like to do tomorrow (but have no plans for yet?)

Ex: 1: Jīntiān wǒ yào xǐzǎo. **Ex: 2:** Míngtiān wǒ xiǎng qù diànyǐngyuàn kàn diànyǐng.

____

____

____

____

Yǒu 2

How many markers are there in Mike Lǎoshī's garage? Guess the correct number and win a 30-minute lesson with Mike Lǎoshī, normally valued at $1000! Anyway, there are . . . Let's find out. Get ready ready to:

- use **yǒu** to say *there is / are*
- use **jǐ** and **duōshǎo** to ask *how many*

We spent a lot of time early in Season 3 going over the verb **yǒu**. Now that you are perfectly comfortable with one definition, it's time to move on to the second – but related – definition: *there is / there are*. These are the English translations of the other major definition of **yǒu**, which you are about to master when asking how many people or things are in a certain place. All set? Let's go!

Recap

To do this lesson, you'll need to check what you know about the verb **yǒu**.

A First, what does it mean? What was the definition you learned in Lesson 61?

1 to get **2** to have **3** to do

B Next, how do you negate "yǒu"?

1 with bù **2** with méi **3** with jǐ

C Last, try to say these sentences using "yǒu":

1 What do you have? **2** Do you have a cell phone? **3** How many sisters do you have?

Words, phrases and stuff

77.01 Listen to the words. Then listen again and repeat.

There is, There are

yǒu	有	*there is / are; (to have)*
jǐ	几	*how much, how many* (usually for smaller numbers up to 15 or 20)
duōshǎo	多少	*how much, how many* (for money and larger numbers)
kē	颗	MW for small, round objects
tái	台	MW for vehicles, machines, and electronic devices
zhōu	州	*a state* (part of a country)
zhī	支	MW for stick-like objects
bānjí	班级	*a class*
shěng	省	*a province* (part of a country)
shūjià	书架	*bookshelf*
shūguì	书柜	*bookcase*

In some cases, **yǒu** can be translated as both *there is / there are* and *to have*. Here's a very common example: **Nǐ jiā yǒu jǐgè rén?** may be translated as *How many people are in your family?* and *How many people does your family have?*

Which new measure word has the same pronunciation (but different character) as the measure word that we use for animals?

a kē **b** zhī **c** tái

Patterns

Look at the two sets of patterns, one for **jǐ** and one for **duōshǎo**. So far, we have used the question word **jǐ** to ask for the number of people or objects and **duōshǎo** exclusively for asking about money. However, like **jǐ**, **duōshǎo** is also used to ask about the number of people or things when dealing with larger numbers. Here are the rules:

What do you use to ask about . . . ?	jǐ	duōshǎo
a small number of people / things	x	
the number of people in a family	x	
the population of a town		x
the population of a country		x
15–20 people	x	x
Always uses a MW	x	

Unlike **jǐ**, you don't need to include a measure word in questions with **duōshǎo**. Occasionally, you will hear people use one, but it is usually omitted. HOWEVER, you must use a measure word after the number in your answer.

Notice in the following patterns that when you ask how many of something are located in a place, you use a reverse order from English for the sentence. In these patterns, the location comes first.

Part 1: "Jǐ" (for smaller numbers)

Pattern 1a: Subject / Location + **yǒu** + **jǐ** + **MW** + noun?

1b: Subject / Location + **yǒu** + **number** + **MW** + noun.

Part 2: "Duōshǎo" (for larger numbers)

Pattern 2a: Subject / Location + **yǒu** + **duōshǎo (MW)** + noun?

2b: Subject / Location + **yǒu** + **number** + **MW** + noun.

Examples:

1a Shūjiàde shàngmiàn **yǒu jǐběn** shū? (*How many books are on the bookshelf?*)

1b Shūjiàde shàngmiàn **yǒu shísìběn** shū. (*There are 14 books on the bookshelf.*)

2a Yīngguó **yǒu** duōshǎo(gè) rén? (*How many people are there in England?*)

2b Yīngguó **yǒu** 53,000,000 gè rén. (*There are 53,000,000 people in England.*)

If you're unsure of whether to use **jǐ** or **duōshǎo**, give it your best guess. When choosing between using **jǐ** and **duōshǎo** – like choosing the best measure word for something – you'll soon find that even Chinese people (and Mike Lǎoshī himself!) argue about which one is better to use in a certain context. So don't panic.

Get to work

A Choose the correct answer to complete the definition.

1 The word for a state (part of a country) is (kē / zhōu / tái / zhī).

2 The MW for small, round objects is (kē / zhōu / tái / zhī).

3 For stick-like objects use the MW (kē / zhōu / tái / zhī).

4 For vehicles, machines, and electronic devices use the MW (kē / zhōu / tái / zhī).

B Let's talk about books. Complete the sentences with "jǐběn" or "duōshǎo", depending on the approximate number of books in question.

Example: Shūguì yǒu duōshǎo shū?

1 Yǐzide shàngmiàn yǒu _________ shū?

2 Túshūguǎnde lǐmiàn yǒu _________ shū?

3 Shūdiànde lǐmiàn yǒu _________ shū?

4 Shūbāode lǐmiàn yǒu _________ shū?

C Match the "duōshǎo" questions with their answers. Then say the questions and answers out loud.

Ex: Dàxué yǒu duōshǎo xuéshēng? → 8,000 gè

1 ____ Nǐmende jiàoshì yǒu duōshǎo kèběn? a 150 tái

2 ____ Zhègè chéngshì yǒu duōshǎo rén? b 32 zhī

3 ____ Nǐde gāozhōng yǒu duōshǎo diànnǎo? c 25 běn

4 ____ Yéyede nóngchǎng yǒu duōshǎo jī? d 50,000 gè

Lesson 78

"Coming at you now!"

Present Progressive Tense

What are you doing right now? Are you driving? Are you texting? Are you watching *Chinese with Mike*? Well, hopefully you're not doing all three at the same time, as my videos require your undivided attention! Get ready to:

- learn to form the present progressive tense
- talk about what is happening now

We're nearing the end of Season 3. We've done new verbs, measure words, and prepositions, and you can say what you like, want, see, and the sorts of things you read, and so on. Now you're going to switch into a new mode. You'll take the language you've acquired and learn to express actions as they are happening, or in the present progressive tense. In English, we form present progressive by adding *-ing* to the main verb, as in, *I am writing, you are reading*. Got it? Good. Let's move on.

Recap

To talk about progressive actions you have to know some verbs. Look at the list. What do the following words mean? Do you know which ones are verbs?

______ kàn	______ chī	______ chàng(gē)	______ děng	______ xiàngjī
______ mài	______ hē	______ chuān	______ chéngshì	______ pǎo(bù)

Words, phrases and stuff

78.01 Listen to the words. Then listen again and repeat.

Present Progressive, Verbs, and Food

zài	在	indicates an action is in progress	**yīnyuè**	音乐	*music*
wán	玩	*to play*	**yóuxì**	游戏	*a game*
pàochá	泡茶	*to make tea*	**cài**	菜	*food; cuisine*

While **cài** is the primary word used to talk about food – especially Chinese food – here are a few more you might want to know:

fàn	饭	*food, a meal; lit. cooked rice*
shíwù	食物	*food; cuisine*
liàolǐ	料理	*food; cuisine* (esp. for Japanese cooking)

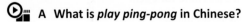

A What is *play ping-pong* in Chinese?

1 dǎ pīngpāngqiú **2** kàn pīngpāngqiú

B You could say "tán ______":

1 zúqiú (*football; Am. soccer*) **2** gāngqín (*piano*)

Patterns

So far you have learned to express yourself in Chinese in the simple present tense. You use the simple present tense to give general facts and talk about habits and routines. With progressive or continuous tenses you express action as it is happening. In English you add *-ing* to verbs to make them progressive, but in Chinese you form the progressive tense by placing **zài** before the verb.

Pattern 1: Subject + **zài** + **verb** + shénme?

Pattern 2: Subject + **zài** + **verb**.

Examples:

1. Nǐ **zài chī** shénme? (*What are you eating?*)
2. Wǒ **zài chī** chūnjuǎn. (*I'm eating spring rolls.*)

Get to work

A Match the words and definitions. One answer will be used twice.

1 ____ yóuxì
2 ____ cài
3 ____ pàochá
4 ____ zài
5 ____ wán
6 ____ yīnyuè

a indicates an action is in progress
b music
c to play
d a game
e to make tea
f food; cuisine

B Change the present tense statements into present progressive.

1 Tā xiě Rìwén zì. ____________________
2 Tāmen chī Zhōngguó cài. ____________________
3 Wǒmen hē lǜchá. ____________________
4 Tāde mèimei shuō Xībānyáwén. ____________________

C Read the answers and give the questions. Two questions are possible for each.

1 **Q:** ____________________ **A:** Nàzhī māo zài hē niúnǎi.
2 **Q:** ____________________ **A:** Zhègè nǚrén zài mài huā.
3 **Q:** ____________________ **A:** Tā zài tīng Yīngwén gē.
4 **Q:** ____________________ **A:** Wǒ nǎinai zài xǐwǎn.
5 **Q:** ____________________ **A:** Tāmen zài chī ròu.

D Use the words in the box to answer the questions.

gāo'ěrfūqiú	Yīngwén	pàochá	wǔcān

1 **Q:** Tā zài zuò shénme?
A: (studying English) ____________________
2 **Q:** Nàxiē yīshēng zài zuò shénme?
A: (playing golf) ____________________
3 **Q:** Zhèxiē xuéshēng zài zuò shénme?
A: (eating lunch) ____________________
4 **Q:** Tāmen zài zuò shénme?
A: (making tea) ____________________

E Look at the pictures and say what is happening.

a __________ b __________ c __________

Chinese Cuisines

You may have tried Chinese dumplings, Kung Pao Chicken and Mike Lǎoshī's favorite, stinky tofu. But did you know that each region of China has its own type of cuisine and varies greatly? Here are a few favorites of Mike Lǎoshī's. Cantonese: Sweet and sour dishes originated in the southern region of Canton. Beijing or Northern style (not entirely the same): When you order Peking duck, mandarin ribs, mongolian beef, pancakes or dishes with leeks and scallions, you're getting Beijing cuisine. Sichuan style is famous for hot and spicy and burn-your-mouth cuisine. These dishes spotlight pepper and chili as well as tofu along with beef, fish, pork, and poultry. Last, Jiangsu: This is a cuisine famous for its freshness, color and originality, and when you see those dishes of precision-cut vegetables in artful arrangements on plates, that'll be Jiangsu style.

Lesson 79

"More to do . . ."

More Present Progressive Tense

The two kids in the video won the right to introduce the lesson, but they also got to:

- learn that **zhèng** can intensify the progress of an action
- review the present progressive tense with some old verbs
- review the verb **zuò** (*to do; to make*)

Let's do a quick review and a few more examples with our new verb tense, the present progressive, which allows us to talk about actions that are happening or in progress at the moment. In this lesson you'll find out how to add emphasis to the fact that an action is in progress. On an extra note, you'll finally and formally meet the common and very useful verb **zuò**.

Recap

Answer these questions to review what you know about the present progressive tense in Chinese.

A Choose the statement that is true.

1 ____ Use subject + **zài** + noun to indicate that an action is in progress.

2 ____ Use **zài** + verb to indicate that an action is in progress.

B Match the verbs and definitions of these ordinary activities.

1	____ tiàowǔ	a	play soccer
2	____ kàn diànyǐng	b	walk
3	____ tī zúqiú	c	play a game
4	____ tīng yīnyuè	d	watch TV
5	____ pǎo(bù)	e	watch a movie
6	____ zǒu(lù)	f	run
7	____ kàn diànshì	g	dance
8	____ wán yóuxì	h	listen to music
9	____ shuā yá	i	read a newspaper
10	____ xǐ shǒu	j	brush teeth
11	____ dǎ bàngqiú	k	play baseball
12	____ kàn bàozhǐ	l	wash hands

C Go back to question B and make the phrases in Chinese present progressive.

Words, phrases and stuff

Ready for your new set of words? Take special note of **zhèng**, the intensifier, and of the common verb **zuò**.

79.01 **Listen to the words. Then listen again and repeat.**

More Present Progressive, Verbs, and Random Words

zài	在	*indicates an action is in progress*
zhèng zài	正在	*to be in the process of doing something (emphatic)*
zuò	做	*to make, to do*
fùxí	复习	*to review*
gōngxǐ	恭喜	*congratulations*
gōngzuò	工作	*a job; to work*
xīnwén	新闻	*the news*

Say: ***We are waiting for our friend.***

Patterns

Use **zhèng** before **zài** + verb to add emphasis to the fact that an action is in progress.

Pattern 1: Subject + **zài** + verb + shénme?
Pattern 2a: Subject + **zài** + verb.
2b: Subject + **zhèng zài** + verb.

Examples:

1 Nǐ **zài** zuò shénme? (*What are you doing?*)
2a Wǒ **zài** gōngzuò. (*I'm working.*)
2b Wǒmen **zhèng zài** pàochá. (*We are making tea right now.*)

What are two possible translations of "Wǒ zài gōngzuò"?

Get to work

A Match the words and definitions.

1 ____ zhèng zài
2 ____ zuò
3 ____ fùxí
4 ____ gōngxǐ
5 ____ gōngzuò
6 ____ xīnwén

a to be in the process of doing something
b a job; to work
c the news
d congratulations
e to review
f to make, to do

B Use "zhèng zài" and the words in parentheses to say what these people are doing right now.

1 Nàgè nánrén zài (running).
2 Nàgè nǚrén zhèng zài (playing tennis).
3 Tāmen zài (listening to music).
4 Nǐ érzi (brushing his teeth).

C Translate the following sentences from English to Chinese.

Ex: My mom is cooking. Wǒ māma (zhèng) zài zhǔfàn.

1 Her older brother is playing soccer.
2 I am drinking milk.
3 We are eating fried rice.
4 Your younger sister is sleeping.
5 They are watching the news.
6 She is washing her face.

Find out what people are doing right now. Walk around your house, go to a party, notice classmates, or go outside and scan the strangers nearby. Jot down notes in a notebook and then make complete sentences.

Example: shū tóufa → Wǒ mèimei zài shū tóufǎ. (*My little sister is combing her hair.*)

Lesson 80

"I set the gold standard!"

Yes / No Questions Review

Ah, freshly back from competing in my second Chinese-teaching Olympics. More importantly, though, is that we are closing out Season 3 with a stellar review of *yes / no* questions, so get ready to:

- answer *yes* and *no* in all the ways you should know
- learn more about how to answer no-verb questions

The headache you'll probably experience from trying to make sense of *yes / no* questions and answers in Chinese is natural, so don't worry – you're in good company. In some cases when an actual verb like **shì**, **yào**, **huì**, **xǐhuān** or **yǒu** is stated in the question, the answer is clear. However, questions such as **Nǐ máng ma?** state no verb yet still require a *yes / no* answer. Get prepared for an overview of all scenarios. And then we'll go one step further, and tackle the most acceptable answers to *yes / no* questions with no verb stated.

Recap

Most of the *yes / no* question and answer patterns should be pretty familiar to you at this point.

How would you provide short *yes / no* answers to the following questions where the verb is clearly stated? Give the *yes* and *no* answers.

1 Nǐ shì xuéshēng ma? ______________________________

2 Nǐ yào bú yào chī xiāngjiāo? ______________________________

3 Nǐ yǒu xiōngdì jiěmèi ma? ______________________________

4 Nǐ xǐ bù xǐhuān kàn diànyǐng? ______________________________

5 Nǐ huì tán jítā ma? ______________________________

Words, phrases and stuff

First, here are a few new words to work with.

80.01 Listen to the words. Then listen again and repeat.

Apartment Talk

fángdōng	房东	*a landlord*	**zū**	租	*to rent*
gōngyù	公寓	*an apartment building, a block of flats*	**fùqián**	付钱	*to pay money*
			zhuànqián	赚钱	*to earn money*

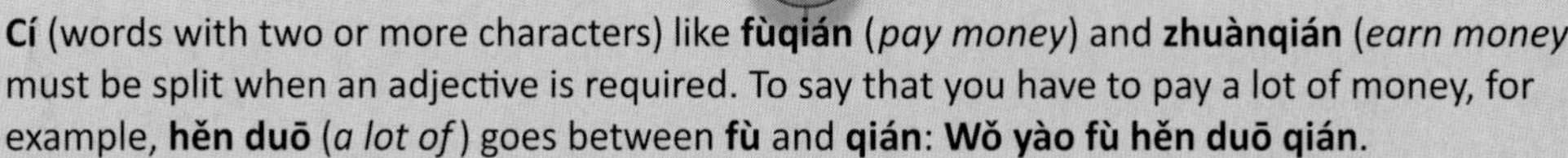

Cí (words with two or more characters) like **fùqián** (*pay money*) and **zhuànqián** (*earn money*) must be split when an adjective is required. To say that you have to pay a lot of money, for example, **hěn duō** (*a lot of*) goes between **fù** and **qián**: **Wǒ yào fù hěn duō qián**.

Cover up the new vocabulary and choose the correct meaning.

1 *A landlord* is a (fángdōng / gōngyù / zū).

2 *An apartment building* is a (fángdōng / gōngyù / zū).

3 The verb for *to rent* is (fùqián / zhuànqián / zū).

4 *To earn money* is (fùqián / zhuànqián).

Review of Yes / No Questions

I'm not going to do all the review work for you. So, to help you review, fill in the rules in the following explanations. Then check your answers.

Part 1: When verb is stated

As you recall from earlier lessons in Seasons 1–2, we usually answer **yes / no** by repeating the main verb. This is the case with some of the major verbs (e.g. **shì**, **yào**, **huì**, **xǐhuān**, and most recently, **yǒu**.)

Do you remember the rule with negating "yǒu"? Complete the rule.

Unlike the others, the verb **yǒu** takes ______ as a negater, not ______ / ______.

Here are the basic patterns:

Pattern 1a: Subject + verb + noun + **ma**?

1b: Subject + verb **bú / bù** verb + noun?

1c: Subject + **yǒu méi yǒu** + noun?

Pattern 2a: (**Bú / bù**) Verb. Subject + (**bú / bù**) **verb** + noun.

2b: **Yǒu / Méi yǒu**. Subject + (**méi**) **yǒu** + noun.

Two verbs

To form two-verb questions, either use "ma" (Pattern 1a) or repeat the first verb to make an affirmative-negative question (Pattern 1b).

Examples: patterns with **yào** and **huì**.

Pattern 1a: Subject + verb 1 + verb 2 + **ma**?

1b: Subject + verb 1 + **bú / bù** + verb 1 + verb 2?

Part 2: When verb is unstated

With **ma** questions such as **Nǐ hǎo ma?** or **Nǐ hěn lèi ma?** (see Lessons 18 and 26) we usually use ______ or ______ to answer *yes* or *no*, respectively. However, you will often hear the more common colloquial reply of simply repeating the adjective (**hěn hǎo / bù hǎo**) or (**hěn lèi / bú lèi**). Also note that you must answer by repeating the ____________ when you have an affirmative-negative question form such as **Nǐ è bú è?** or **Nǐ hǎo bù hǎo?**

Similarly, the verb is unstated when we ask questions with **zài** as preposition (Lesson 30). For example, if you are asked **Nǐ zài jiā ma?** you would answer *yes* with **Zài** and *no* with **Bú zài**.

Part 3: Present Progressive Tense

Now, back to where we started, wrapping up the present progressive. For *yes / no* questions with **zài** + verb to indicate the present progressive tense, you may be able to answer with ______ or ______, but it is impossible to establish a simple, firm rule. The form seems to depend on the region and the variation of Mandarin spoken there. Depending on the region, you'll hear answers to *yes / no* questions in multiple ways. Take a look:

Example:

Q: Nǐ zài kàn shū ma?

A: Shì / (Bù / Méi yǒu). Wǒ (méi yǒu) zài kàn shū.

Get to work

A Give two possible short answers to the following.

Ex: Nà shì nǐde gōngyù ma? → Shì. / Bú shì.

1 Tā máng bù máng? ______
2 Tāmen yào bīngqílín ma? ______
3 Tā yào zū zhègè fángzi ma? ______
4 Nǐde fùmǔ xǐ bù xǐhuān dǎ májiàng? ______
5 Tā (hěn) è ma? ______
6 Nǐ māma yǒu chēzi ma? ______
7 Nàgè mùgōng huì bú huì yòng diànzuān? ______
8 Lǎoshī yǒu méi yǒu fěnbǐ? ______
9 Nǐ nǚ'ér zài xuéxiào ma? ______
10 Wǒ kěyǐ qù cèsuǒ ma? ______
11 Māma (zhèng) zài xǐwǎn ma? ______

B Complete the sentences with the correct new vocabulary words.

1 Yīnwèi tā shì yīshēng, suǒyǐ tā (*earns a lot of money*). ______
2 Yīnwèi nàxiē yīfú hěn guì, suǒyǐ nǐ yào (*pay a lot of money*). ______
3 Yīnwèi tāmende (*apartment building*) yǒu lǎoshǔ, suǒyǐ tāmen xiǎng zhǎo xīnde.
______
4 Yīnwèi wǒ méi yǒu qián, suǒyǐ wǒ yào zhǎo (*a job*). ______

C 80.02 Answer the following questions using long answers. Say them out loud. Then compare your answers.

Ex: Nǐ shì xuéshēng ma? → Shì. Wǒ shì xuéshēng.

1 Nǐ huì shuō Zhōngwén ma? ______
2 Nǐ xiǎng qù Zhōngguó ma? ______
3 Míngtiān nǐ yào bú yào kàn nǐde Zhōngwén kèběn? ______
4 Nǐ hěn cōngmíng ma? ______
5 Nǐ xǐ bù xǐhuān xuéxí Zhōngwén? ______
6 Xiànzài nǐ zài jiā ma? ______

Lesson 81

"Check out my latest invention!"

Subject + Time + Action

How'd you like my dual marker swords? How about the new "Past, Present and Future" photo on the wall? Yeah, they're great and all, but what's even better is we're kicking off Season 4, which I'm calling "Stop! Grammar Time!" So, take a deep breath, and get ready to:

- talk about word order in Chinese sentences
- review "time words"
- understand where to place "time words" in Chinese sentences

Season 3 (Lessons 61–80) was a critical step in your journey to learn Mandarin Chinese. I'm glad you made it through, but hey, was there ever any doubt? Anyway, I'll do my best to keep measure words, prepositions, and all those other important concepts fresh in your mind as we tackle the rules for the word order in Chinese sentences. Let me welcome you to Season 4 of *Chinese with Mike*!

Recap

Here are some time words you should know already. What are their English equivalents?

1 Jīntiān ____________ **3** Míngnián ____________

2 Míngtiān ____________ **4** Zuótiān ____________

So far we've placed time words before the subjects of our sentences. For example, we've asked questions like "*Jīntiān* **nǐ** hǎo ma?" and "*Míngtiān* **nǐ** yào qù nǎ lǐ?" We've made statements, such as "*Zuótiān* **wǒ** hěn lèi" and "*Xīngqīsān* **wǒ** xiǎng chūqù." Notice the time words (in *italics*) come before the subjects (in **bold**) – just like in English.

Words, phrases and stuff

81.01 Listen to the words and phrases and repeat.

Time Words and New Places

chūguó	出国	*to leave the country; go abroad*	**yèdiàn**	夜店	*nightclub*
yóujú	邮局	*post office*	**yàofáng**	药房	*pharmacy*
miànbāodiàn	面包店	*bakery*	**jiàotáng**	教堂	*church*

81.02 Listen to Pèishān describe her busy week. When does she go to the following places? One word will be used twice.

míngtiān hòutiān jīntiān xīngqīrì

1 chūguó ____________
2 yóujú ______________
3 miànbāodiàn ________
4 yèdiàn _____________
5 yàofáng ____________

Patterns

You've learned to put time words before the subject – just like in English. While it's acceptable to put the time phrase before the subject, it's more common / convenient to place it after the subject, especially when you begin building more complex sentences.

Pattern 1: **Time** + subject + action.

Pattern 2: Subject + **time** + action.

Examples:

1 **Jīntiān** wǒmen yào qù dòngwùyuán. (*Today we are going (to go) to the zoo.*)
2 Wǒmen **jīntiān** yào qù dòngwùyuán. (*Today we are going (to go) to the zoo.*)

Get to work

A The following sentences follow the time + subject pattern. Convert them to the subject + time pattern.

Ex: Xiànzài wǒ yào chī wǎncān. → Wǒ xiànzài yào chī wǎncān.

1 Jīntiān nǐ máng ma? ______________________

2 Xīngqīrì wǒmen bù xiǎng qù nǐde pàiduì. ______________________

3 Wǔyuè wǒde fùmǔ yào chūguó. ______________________

4 Zuótiān tāde yáchǐ hěn tòng. ______________________

B The following sentences follow the subject + time pattern. Convert them to the time + subject pattern.

Ex: Wǒmen míngtiān yào qù túshūguǎn zuò zuòyè. →
Míngtiān wǒmen yào qù túshūguǎn zuò zuòyè.

1 Wǒ bàba xiànzài bú zài zhè lǐ. ______________________

2 Tāmen zuótiān hē lǜchá. ______________________

3 Māma qiántiān qù yóujú. ______________________

4 Nǐde yéye míngtiān yào qù miànbāodiàn ma? ______________________

C Complete with the two possible translations.

Ex: I can't go out right now. → Xiànzài wǒ bù néng chūqù. Wǒ xiànzài bù néng chūqù.

1 Our professor is going to go abroad in July. ______________________

____

2 She doesn't want to go to the nightclub tomorrow. ______________________

____

3 I have to work on Tuesday. ______________________

____

4 Yesterday my little brother ate fried rice. ______________________

____

5 We are going to go to church on Sunday. ______________________

____

6 Are you going to go to the pharmacy today? ______________________

____

D Find the errors in the following sentences. Correct the ones that have errors.

1 Hòutiān nǐ yào bú yào lái wǒ jiā ma? ______________________

2 Nǐ zuótiān yào qù kāfēitīng ma? ______________________

3 Wǒde nǚpéngyǒu xiǎng xuéxí Zhōngwén míngtiān. ______________________

4 Wǒmen liùdiǎn bàn shàng Zhōngwén kè. ______________________

Lesson 82

"Music calms me."

Subject + Time + Action 2

Hope I didn't turn your world upside down when I taught you about reversing the subject and time in the last lesson. It's something new to get used to, but it shouldn't be that painful, especially if I'm serenading you with my harmonica. Anyway, we'd better:

- form questions and answers using our new (subject + time) sentence structure
- learn some music words

Let's get more comfortable with the new grammar we learned in the last lesson. And if you're good, I'll let you move on to Lesson 83. Deal?

Recap

Keep in mind that in Chinese it is acceptable to put the time word(s) before the subject (like we do in English) or the subject before the time (unlike English). Thus, you'll hear statements like **Jīntiān wǒ hěn gāoxìng** (lit. *Today I very happy*) and **Wǒ jīntiān hěn gāoxìng** (lit. *I today very happy*). Let's take it one step further and create questions using our new subject + time + action pattern. Don't chicken out!

A First, spend five seconds matching the meanings of the following words.

1 ____ shénme — a a question particle
2 ____ nǎ lǐ — b what
3 ____ ma — c where

B Now, answer the following questions using the answers in parentheses.

1 Jīntiān nǐ yào qù nǎ lǐ? (the bakery) ____________________
2 Míngtiān nǐde péngyǒu xiǎng zuò shénme? (go to a nightclub) ____________________
3 Hòutiān tāmen yào qù kàn qiúsài ma? (Yes) ____________________

Words, phrases and stuff

82.01 **Listen to the words and phrases then listen again and repeat.**

Random Words and Music

yínháng	银行	*bank*
bānjiā	搬家	*to move (house)*
kǒuqín	口琴	*harmonica*
xiǎotíqín	小提琴	*violin*
lǎba	喇叭	*horn (trumpet)*
gǔ	鼓	*drum*
tán	弹	*to play (a stringed instrument like piano / guitar)*
lā	拉	*to pull; (to play a bowed instrument)*
tuī	推	*to push*
chuī	吹	*to blow; (to play a wind instrument)*
dǎ	打	*to hit; to beat; to strike (to play a percussion instrument)*

In Season 1 you learned how to say *play the guitar* (**tán jítā**) and *play the piano* (**tán gāngqín**) and for both, the verb **tán** (弹) was used. However, when it comes to playing musical instruments – like playing sports – there are many different verbs that translate to mean *play*, depending on the type of instrument. So even though you'll use **tán** with piano / guitar, you'll use **lā** (*pull*) with violin, **chuī** (*blow*) with horn / harmonica, and **dǎ** (*hit*) with drum.

Patterns

Pattern 1: Subject + **time** + action + question word?

Pattern 2: Subject+ **time** + action.

Pattern 3: Subject + **time** + action + ma?

Pattern 4: Yes / No. Subject + **time** + action.

Examples:

1 Tā **xiànzài** xiǎng zuò shénme? (*What does he / she want to do now?*)

2 Tā **xiànzài** xiǎng lā xiǎotíqín. (*He / She wants to play the violin (now).*)

3 Nǐ **míngnián** xiǎng bānjiā ma? (*Would you like to move next year?*)

4 Xiǎng. Wǒ **míngnián** xiǎng bānjiā. (*Yes, I would. I would like to move next year.*)

Get to work

A Match the picture with the new and old vocabulary words.

1 gāngqín ______ a

2 jítā ______ b

3 gǔ ______ c

4 xiǎotíqín ______ d

5 kǒuqín ______ e

6 lǎbā ______ f

B Think about how you play the instruments in Exercise A. Do you use your fingers? Your mouth? A bow? Fill in the correct verbs to complete the sentences and then say them out loud.

Ex: Tā hěn huì tán jítā.

1 Wǒ nǚ'ér huì ____ gāngqín dànshì wǒ érzi bú huì.

2 Tā jiějie bú huì ____ xiǎotíqín kěshì tā mèimei huì.

3 Nǐ dìdi huì bú huì ____ lǎba?

4 Nǐde nánpéngyǒude gēge huì ____ gǔ ma?

C Given the answers, write "ma"-question(s). There are two possibilities for each.

Ex: Bù kěyǐ. Nǐ xīngqīyī bù kěyǐ chūqù. → Wǒ xīngqīyī kěyǐ chūqù ma? / Wǒ xīngqīyī kě bù kěyǐ chūqù?

1 Bù xiǎng. Tā jīntiān bù xiǎng lā xiǎotíqín. ______

2 Xiǎng. Tāmen jīnnián xiǎng bānjiā. ______

3 Shì. Zuótiān wǒ lǎopó hěn shēngqì. ______

4 Yào. Dàwèi míngtiān yào qù yínháng. ______

"Alright, I want to teach you something about Chinese music, and I also want to find out who my real fans are – the ones who remember my very first episode when I taught you about the basics of Mandarin and Cantonese. Anyway, since my producer wouldn't let me include this interesting fact in my episode, I'll tell you now how these two well-known dialects influenced C-pop – the abbreviation for Chinese popular music. Even though C-pop originated in Shanghai, today we have divisions within the genre, primarily Cantopop (sung in Cantonese) and Mandopop (sung in Mandarin). The split within C-pop was brought on by a condemnation of pop music around 1949 when mainstream opinion of it was not favorable. Several prominent C-pop artists sought refuge in Hong Kong, which is predominantly Cantonese-speaking, and Taiwan, which is predominantly Mandarin-speaking, and Cantopop and Mandopop were born and still thrive today."

Lesson 83

"Get your signed photo while they last."

Subject + Time + Action 3

Well, you can see the new "Past, Present and Future" photo is a must-have. I knew it would be a hit with the younger crowd, but I must admit it was a humbling moment when I saw my ugly mug atop that old lady's **gāngqín**. Guess I have more fans than I thought. Anyway, let's:

- review important questions from Season 1
- make question-answer sets using our new structure and question words
- learn words to talk about holidays and time off from work

Ah, I must admit this is one of my favorite episodes. Why? Well, for one, we're really starting to talk like real Chinese people (not fake ones), and two, my hair looks great.

Recap

OK, so in Lesson 81, we flip-flopped time and subject and made statements using our new subject + time + action sentence pattern. In Lesson 82, we threw the corresponding questions into the mix, allowing you to create question-answer dialogues. Now we are plugging in actual question words that we learned a long time ago so you see how they fit into the bigger picture. It'll be painless – trust me.

A Let's revisit Season 1 and translate the following "jǐ" questions.

1 Xiànzài (shì) jǐdiǎn? ____________________

2 Xiànzài shì jǐyuè? ____________________

3 Jīntiān shì xīngqījǐ? ____________________

B What are two ways to say these sentences in Chinese?

1 I was extremely busy yesterday. ____________________

2 Tomorrow I am going to go to the bank. ____________________

3 Where would you like to go today? ____________________

Words, phrases and stuff

Listen to the words and phrases then listen again and repeat.

Holidays

chūmén	出门	*to leave the house; (lit. to go out the door)*
fàng	放	*to release; to let out; set off*
fàngjià	放假	*to have a vacation / holiday*
shǔjià	暑假	*summer vacation*
hánjià	寒假	*winter vacation*
jiàrì	假日	*a day off; a non-working day*
jiérì	节日	*holiday; a festival* (e.g. Christmas; New Year's Day)
zhōumò	周末	*the weekend*

The words **jiàrì** and **jiérì** look similar and have similar definitions. The difference is that **jiàrì** simply means *a day off from work / school* whereas **jiérì** refers to an official holiday like Christmas, Chinese New Year, Mike Lǎoshī's birthday, etc.

Patterns

We have established that you can switch the time + subject or subject + time and it won't make much difference in meaning. However, when you are using a time question word (e.g. **jǐdiǎn**, **jǐyuè**, **xīngqījǐ**), it's extremely uncommon to use it BEFORE the subject. So stick to placing time question words AFTER the subject.

Pattern 1: Subject + **(time) question word** + action?

Pattern 2: Subject + **time** + action.

Examples:

1 Tāmen **jǐdiǎn** yào chūqù? (*What time are they going (to go) out?*)

2 Tāmen **bādiǎn** yào chūqù. (*They are going (to go) out at 8:00.*)

Get to work

A Match the question word with the corresponding answer.

1 ____ jǐdiǎn

2 ____ xīngqījǐ

3 ____ jǐyuè

a shíyuè

b jiǔdiǎn

c xīngqīsān

B Look at the statements and form their corresponding questions.

Ex: Bù xiǎng. Wǒde xiānshēng xīngqītiān bù xiǎng qù bówùguǎn. →

Nǐde xiānshēng xīngqītiān xiǎng qù bówùguǎn ma? /

Xīngqītiān nǐde xiānshēng xiǎng qù bówùguǎn ma?

1 Tāmen liùdiǎn bàn yào chūmén. ____________________

2 Tā qī diǎn sìshíwǔ fēn chī zǎocān. ____________________

3 Wǒ bàbamāma bāyuè yào bānjiā. ____________________

4 Bù. Wǒ zuótiān bú lèi. ____________________

C List five activities that are part of your daily routine. Refer to Lesson 74 if you've forgotten some of your daily activities.

Ex: Wǒ bā diǎn shíwǔ fēn chī zǎocān.

Jīntiān

D Unscramble the sentences.

Ex: Tā zhǔfàn jǐdiǎn? → Tā jǐdiǎn zhǔfàn?

1 dàxuéshēng / jǐyuè / fàng / shǔjià / nàxiē? ____________________

2 háizi / nǐde / yào / chūmén / jǐdiǎn? ____________________

3 xīngqījǐ / fàngjià / lǎogōng / nǐ? ____________________

4 xiǎng / bù / jīntiān / xiǎng / nǐ / gōngzuò? ____________________

Shangri-La

“Living in a garage, I often dream of faraway places. When my surroundings get me down, I imagine escaping to a peaceful, green and grassy, earthly paradise tucked away among the snow-capped mountains, untouched by the world outside and whose inhabitants shun all violence and materialism. Apparently, another world-famous author imagined such a place, which he called Shangri-La. This mythical place, said to hold the world's cultural treasures, is described in a novel written by British author James Hilton in 1933 called *Lost Horizon*. Possibly based on the ancient Tibetan Buddhist theory of seven hidden cities, many people wonder if it was in fact set in a real place. At least many tourists hope so. In the twenty-first century people still search for the lost paradise, travelers coming from all parts of the world to the Kunlun Mountains where the city was said to exist. They may not find this hidden world, but they do find snow-capped mountains, grassy green valleys, fantastic hiking trails, the base for treks into Tibet and lots of souvenirs of Shangri-La. If you find it, let me know. And don't tell anyone else.”

Lesson 84

"Do you want my autograph?"

Subject + Time + Action 4

After this lesson, you'll be able to tell your parents that you don't like going to school. More importantly, you'll learn how to fake being sick so you can stay home from school / work and watch more CWM episodes! Sorry, just kidding – that advice isn't included here. But I will teach you:

- how to talk about your school / work schedule
- verbs to talk about school and work

We're rolling right along here in Season 4. Although we're not changing up our sentence structure this time, I've got some important new school / work vocabulary for you. Think about it: since most people spend the first part of their lives going to school, the second part working, and the third part telling stories about the first two parts, this lesson's vocabulary is never gonna get old!

Recap

Last time we brought back the question word **jǐ** and formed questions and answers using our new subject + time + action sentence patterns. For example, we asked **Nǐ érzi xīngqījǐ yào qù pàiduì?** (*What day is your son going to the party?*) and **Nǐ jǐdiǎn xiǎng chī wǔcān?** (*What time would you like to eat lunch?*) We'll keep the same sentence patterns going this time and incorporate our new vocabulary.

A Say the following time words in Chinese.

1. 4:30
2. November
3. 5:00
4. Monday
5. 6:45
6. Tomorrow

B If you want to succeed at school or work, then you'd better make sure you remember to eat and sleep. Think about your own routines and answer the following questions.

1 Nǐ jǐdiǎn chī zǎocān? ______________________________

2 Nǐ jǐdiǎn chī wǔcān? ______________________________

3 Nǐ jǐdiǎn chī wǎncān? ______________________________

4 Nǐ jǐdiàn qù shuìjiào? ______________________________

Words, phrases and stuff

84.01 Listen to the words and phrases then listen again and repeat.

Verbs for School and Work

kè	课	*class; course; lesson*
táng	堂	MW for classes; lessons
shàngkè	上课	*to go to / attend class*
shàngbān	上班	*to go to / start work / be at work*
xiàkè	下课	*to finish class / school*
xiàbān	下班	*to finish work; get off work*
kāishǐ	开始	*to begin; to start*

In Lesson 72, I introduced **shàng** (*on; above*) and **xià** (*under; below*) as prepositions that we can use to give locations of people and objects. However, **shàng** and **xià** have several other meanings in Chinese as well, and we will continue to cover additional definitions as we move along. In this lesson, **shàng** translates as *to go / attend* and **xià** translates as *to finish*. Most important of all, we can use this definition of **shàng** to indicate that we want to use the bathroom (**Wǒ yào shàng cèsuǒ**). So it's worth remembering!

Patterns

Pattern 1: Subject + **(time) question word** + action?

Pattern 2: Subject + **time** + action.

Examples:

1 Nǐ xiānshēng **jǐdiǎn** shàngbān? (*What time does your husband go to work?*)

2 Wǒ xiānshēng **qīdiǎn** shàngbān. (*My husband goes to work at 7:00.*)

In the past, we have primarily used the verb **qù** (not **shàng**) when talking about going to school (**qù xuéxiào**) or work (**qù gōngzuò**). In the previous tip, I've noted that **shàng / xià** have a similar meaning when you're talking about attending or finishing school or work. You'll also hear people often combine **qù** + **shàng** when you are talking about the process of going to school or work (**Wǒ xiànzài yào qù shàngkè / shàngbān**).

Get to work

A Translate the following sentences into Chinese.

1 I have to work tomorrow. ______

2 Do you have to work today? ______

3 What time does your wife finish work? ______

4 What time does your older sister finish class? ______

B Choose the answer choice that makes sense.

Ex: Yīnwèi míngtiān shì (<u>jiàrì</u> / shàngkè), suǒyǐ wǒ hěn gāoxìng.

1 Zhèxiē gāozhōngshēng jǐdiàn yào (kè / shàngkè).

2 Nàgè shāngrén jǐdiǎn (táng / kāishǐ) shàngbān.

3 Yīnwèi lǎoshī hěn lèi, suǒyǐ tā xiǎng (xiàkè / shàngkè).

4 Wǒ míngtiān yǒu sì (táng / kāishǐ) kè.

C Given the hint, provide long answers to the following questions.

Ex: Nǐ gēge jǐdiǎn xiàbān? (8:00) **A:** <u>Wǒ gēge bādiǎn xiàbān.</u>

1 Nàgè jiàoshòu xīngqījǐ shàngkè? (Wednesday) ______

2 Zhèxiē xuéshēng jǐdiǎn xiàkè? (3:30) ______

3 Dàxuéshēng jǐyuè fàng hánjià? (December) ______

4 Gāozhōngshēng jǐyuè fàng shǔjià? (June) ______

D Write a journal entry about what you do at school or work. For example, what time do you start? Eat lunch? Finish work? And, most importantly, what time do you read your *Chinese with Mike* book?

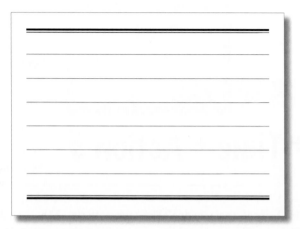

Interview as many (Chinese) people as you can to see what time they start and end work. Maybe you have a few friends online? Ask about their family and friends too. What's the average? Write a little report.

Lesson 85

"Even I get sick."

Subject + Time + Action 5

Can you tell me – in Chinese – that you don't like your math class? That you do like your English class? That you LOVE your Chinese class? I'm sure you'll be able to soon, for we're about to:

- learn the names of common school subjects
- review Chinese word order of subject + time + action
- use **shàngkè** / **xiàkè** to talk about classes you're attending.

In the last lesson you learned how to say you were starting / attending / finishing class using the verbs **shàngkè** / **xiàkè**. After this lesson you'll be able to specify which class(es) you are attending as well! Let's also learn the important prefix **dì**, which will allow us to form ordinal numbers, like *first*, *second* and *third*.

Recap

In Lesson 84 you learned two new definitions for the verbs **shàng** and **xià**. Awesome. You'll continue to learn ways to use these words as we move on. In this lesson, we're recycling an old rule we used many lessons ago: verb-object combos, such as **kànshū** (*reading*), **chànggē** (*singing*), and **kāichē** (*driving*). To specify the type of book you read, song you sang, or food you ate, you can split the verb and the direct object noun by inserting an adjective. So, you can say: **kàn Fǎwén shū**; **chàng Rìwén gē**; or **kāi Měiguó chē**.

A Try splitting the verb-object combos to translate the following:

Ex: Listen to German songs → tīng Déwén gē.

1 Sing English songs ______________________

2 Read Spanish books ______________________

3 Write Chinese characters ______________________

B Now take your translations from A and use each one in a sentence. Use verbs like "xǐhuān", "huì", "ài", etc.

Ex: Listen to German songs → Wǒ xǐhuān tīng Déwén gē.

1 ______________________

2 ______________________

3 ______________________

Words, phrases and stuff

85.01 **Listen to the words and phrases then listen again and repeat.**

School Subjects

dì	第	prefix for ordinal numbers
Zhōngwén kè	中文课	*Chinese class*
Yīngwén kè	英文课	*English class*
diànnǎo kè	电脑课	*computer class*
shùxué kè	数学课	*mathematics class*
lìshǐ kè	历史课	*history class*
tǐyù kè	体育课	*physical education class*

A 85.02 **Listen to Dàwèi's schedule. Put the classes in the correct order by writing each class next to the correct number.**

1 ______________________________

2 ______________________________

3 ______________________________

4 ______________________________

B **What time does David finish school today?**

Patterns

Pattern 1: Subject + time question word + action?

Pattern 2: Subject + time + action.

Examples:

1 Nǐmen jǐdiǎn shàng **Zhōngwén** kè? (*What time do you guys have Chinese class?*)

2 Wǒmen yīdiǎn shàng **Zhōngwén** kè. (*We have Chinese class at 1:00.*)

Get to work

A Write the following ordinal numbers in English.

Ex: dìjiǔ = ninth

1 dìwǔ ____________
2 dìsān ____________
3 dìqī ____________
4 dì'èr ____________
5 dìyī ____________
6 dìshíliù ____________
7 dìbāshísì ____________
8 dìjiǔ ____________
9 dìsì ____________
10 dìyībǎi ____________

B Finish the sentence by splitting the verb-object with an adjective.

Ex: Wǒ xǐhuān xiězì dànshì wǒ bù xǐhuān xiě Rìwén zì.

1 Wǒ xǐhuān kāichē dànshì ____________
2 Tā xǐhuān kànshū dànshì ____________
3 Tāmen xǐhuān tīnggē dànshì ____________
4 Wǒmen xǐhuān chànggē dànshì ____________

C Look at the table and write complete sentences answering the questions about Pèishān's school schedule.

Spring semester

8 am	Japanese
9 am	Chinese
12 pm	lunch
2 pm	Computer class

1 Pèishān jǐdiǎn shàng Rìwén kè? ____________
2 Pèishān jǐdiǎn shàng Zhōngwén kè? ____________
3 Pèishān jǐdiǎn chī wǔcān? ____________
4 Pèishān jǐdiǎn shàng diànnǎo kè? ____________

D Do you remember your measure words? Fill in the MW (if required) and answer the questions.

Ex: Nǐ jīntiān yào shàng jǐ ______ kè? (3) → Wǒ jīntiān yào shàng 3 táng kè.

1 Tāmen jiā lǐ yǒu jǐ ______ gǒu? (4)

2 Nǐmende Zhōngwén bānjí yǒu duōshǎo ______ xuéshēng? (19)

3 Nǐde shūbāo lǐ yǒu jǐ ______ shū? (5)

4 Nǐ yào gěi nǐde lǎoshī jǐ ______ píngguǒ? (2)

Lesson 86

"When are you going to come to my garage?"

Shénme Shíhòu

Does your mom hang up on you when you ask to borrow money? As you can see, mine does, and it's pretty rude if you ask me. Oh well, I'll get over it. I have more important things to do like:

- teach you a new question word (**shénme shíhòu**)
- review subject + time + action sentence structures

Recap

We talked about attending classes at school and learned the important prefix **di** so that we could turn cardinal numbers (*one*, *two* and *three*) into ordinal numbers (*first*, *second* and *third*). So, how would you say *I must attend Chinese class at 3:00*? Right: **Wǒ sāndiǎn yào shàng Zhōngwén kè.**

A It's never too early for an ordinal numbers review! Match the following ordinal number phrases to their translations.

1 ____ dìsānzhāng zhǐ	**a** fifth book
2 ____ dì'èrgè jiā	**b** third sheet of paper
3 ____ dìwǔběn shū	**c** fourth class
4 ____ dìjiǔbēi shuǐ	**d** second home
5 ____ dìqītái diànnǎo	**e** ninth cup of water
6 ____ dìsìtáng kè	**f** seventh computer

Even though you're learning the catch-all term for asking *when* this time, it's still important to remember our individual **jǐ** questions for time.

B Answer the following about Dàwèi's schedule using the answers in parentheses.

1. Dàwèi jǐyuè yào fàng shǔjià? (July)
2. Tā xīngqījǐ xǐhuān qù gōngyuán dǎ lánqiú? (Saturday)
3. Tā jǐdiǎn yào shàng Zhōngwén kè? (9 o'clock)

Words, phrases and stuff

86.01 Listen to the words and phrases then listen again and repeat.

Life and Entertainment

shénme shíhòu	什么时候	*When?*
bìyè	毕业	*to graduate*
jiéhūn	结婚	*to marry; to get married*
huí	回	*to return; to go back*
yǎnchànghuì	演唱会	*a concert*
yǎnzòuhuì	演奏会	*a classical music concert*
gējù	歌剧	*(Western) opera*

The word **yǎn** (演) means *to act; to perform*, which should help you remember the meanings of **yǎnchànghuì** and **yǎnzòuhuì**. And, of course, I'm sure you remember the word for *actor / actress* from Season 1. Write it here: ______________________________

Patterns

Shénme shíhòu is the general question word that means *when* in Chinese. Unlike the other time question words we've covered (**xīngqījǐ**, **jǐyuè**, **jǐdiǎn**), this one does not require the corresponding time word in the answer. For example, if I ask you **xīngqījǐ**, you're required to give me a day of the week as your answer; if I ask you **jǐyuè**, you're supposed to answer with a month, and similarly with **jǐdiǎn**, you're required to give a time of day. The cool thing about **shénme shíhòu** is that you can answer with any time word! Sweet!

Pattern 1: **Q:** Subject + **shénme shíhòu** + action?

Pattern 2: **A:** Subject + time + action.

Examples:

1 Nǐ **shénme shíhòu** xiǎng jiéhūn?

2 Wǒ 2016 nián xiǎng jiéhūn.

Get to work

A Answer the following questions using the time word in parentheses. Use complete sentences.

Ex: Tā shénme shíhòu yào (*go out*)? (xiànzài) → Tā xiànzài yào chūqù.

1 Nǐmen shénme shíhòu xiǎng qù (*watch the concert*)? (liù diǎn)

____

2 Tāmen shénme shíhòu yào (*get married*)? (xiàtiān)

____

3 Nǐde nánpéngyǒu shénme shíhòu yào qù (*see the opera*)? (hòutiān)

____

4 Nǐ shénme shíhòu yào qù (*watch the classical music concert*)? (xīngqīwǔ)

____

B Given the answer, write the question using shénme shíhòu.

Ex: Pèishān sānyuè huí Táiwān. → Pèishān shénme shíhòu huí Táiwān?

1 Dàwèi míngtiān yào qù kàn yǎnchànghuì. ______________________________

2 Wǒmen míngnián xiǎng bānjiā. ______________________________

3 Wǒměnde nǚ'ér hòunián bìyè. ______________________________

4 Wǒde péngyǒu xīngqīyī yào qù kàn gējù. ______________________________

C Unscramble the following sentences.

Ex: shíhòu / kàn / shénme / qù / yào / zúqiúsài / nǐ? → Nǐ shénme shíhòu yào qù kàn zúqiúsài?

1 shénme / shíhòu / mǎi / fángzi / xīnde / jiārén / nǐde / xiǎng ______________________________

2 xīngqīrì / bù / qù / wǒ / yǎnzòuhuì / néng / kàn ______________________________

3 wǔyuè / bìyè / tā / ma / yào ______________________________

4 shíhòu / tāmen / mài / xiǎng / nàbù / chēzi / hēisède / shénme ______________________________

"Don't sweat the small stuff."

Sequencing Periods of Time 1

I hope you guys are doing a lot better with forming subject + time + action sentences than I am with my new meditation routine. You know why? Because I'm about to shake things up on you a little bit! Better get ready to:

- take time expressions to the next level
- review prepositions to talk about location

We've done plenty with subject + time + action sentences. This time we're combining time expressions so that instead of simply saying *today* or *at 8:00* we can now say *today at 8:00 in the morning* all in a single sentence. Check out how the grammar works!

Recap

Last time we learned a very useful question word – **shénme shíhòu**. Its basic definition is *when*, so you may use it when asking for either a very general or specific time. For example, if I ask **Nǐ shénme shíhòu yào chūguó?** (*When are you going abroad?*), the answer could be *next year* or *tomorrow* or *today at 5:00*, depending on the situation. Let's continue using **shénme shíhòu** as our question word in this lesson, but let's give more specific times in our answers. Deal?

Let's make sure you remember some of the time words we'll be combining to make new, more specific time phrases. Match the following words with their meanings.

1 ____ qiūtiān	**a** 8 o'clock
2 ____ míngnián	**b** autumn; fall
3 ____ wǎnshàng	**c** last year
4 ____ xiàwǔ	**d** afternoon
5 ____ qùnián	**e** next year
6 ____ bādiǎn	**f** this year
7 ____ yīyuè	**g** evening
8 ____ jīnnián	**h** January

Words, phrases and stuff

87.01 Listen to the words and phrases then listen again and repeat.

Two Travel Words

chūfā 出发 *to start out; to begin a journey*

huíjiā 回家 *to return home; to go back home*

Patterns

In Mandarin, time words (e.g. **sānyuè**, **wǎnshàng**, **jīntiān**, **wǔdiǎn**, etc.) must be placed in a specific order beginning with the largest time period. For example, you would say **jīnnián** (*this year*) before **sìyuè** (*April*) because a year is a longer period of time than a month. Similarly, you would say **jīntiān** (*today*) before **xiàwǔ** (*afternoon*) because a full day is longer than just the afternoon.

Pattern 1: Time word 1 (longer period) + time word 2 (shorter period)

2: Subject + time word 1 (longer period) + time word 2 (shorter period) + action.

Examples:

1 jīntiān wǎnshàng (*(lit. today evening); this evening*)

2 Wǒ míngtiān zǎoshàng yào qù túshūguǎn. (*Tomorrow morning I am going to go / have to go to the library.*)

Watch the video again and create your own timeline to show how to order time expressions when you combine them. No cheating – you must use different time words than I use in the video lesson.

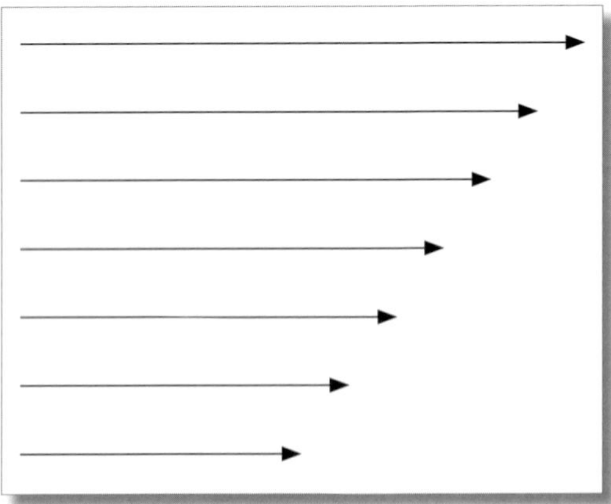

Get to work

A Write the following time expressions in Chinese.

Ex: This summer → jīnnián xiàtiān

1 Next winter (the winter of next year) ____________________
2 Last fall (the fall of last year) ____________________
3 Tomorrow afternoon ____________________
4 This morning ____________________
5 6:00 in the evening ____________________
6 7:00 in the morning ____________________
7 This October (October of this year) ____________________
8 Last June (June of last year) ____________________
9 On March 15 ____________________
10 Tomorrow morning ____________________

B Look at the chart and answer the questions.

	Today	Tomorrow
Morning	Play basketball	Attend math class
Afternoon	Review Chinese	Do history homework
Evening	Watch TV	Play the trumpet

Ex: Dàwèi shénme shíhòu yào liànxí xiǎotíqín? → Dàwèi míngtiān xiàwǔ yào liànxí xiǎotíqín.

1 Dàwèi shénme shíhòu yào dǎ lánqiú? ____________________
2 Dàwèi shénme shíhòu yào chuī lǎba? ____________________
3 Dàwèi shénme shíhòu yào fùxí Zhōngwén? ____________________
4 Dàwèi shénme shíhòu yào shàng shùxué kè? ____________________
5 Dàwèi shénme shíhòu yào kàn diànshì? ____________________
6 Dàwèi shénme shíhòu yào zuò lìshǐ zuòyè? ____________________

C Think about your own life and what you're going to do in the near future. Use our new time-word sequence to fill in the blanks to create questions and answers.

Ex: Nǐ shénme shíhòu yào xǐzǎo? → Wǒ jīntiān wǎnshàng yào xǐzǎo.

1 Nǐ shénme shíhòu yào _______? ______________________________

2 Nǐ shénme shíhòu yào _______? ______________________________

3 Nǐ shénme shíhòu yào _______? ______________________________

4 Nǐ shénme shíhòu yào _______? ______________________________

D Answer the questions using the words in parentheses.

Ex: Chén Xiānshēng shénme shíhòu yào qù shàngbān? (tomorrow afternoon) →
Chén Xiānshēng míngtiān xiàwǔ yào qù shàngbān.

1 Tāde érzi shénme shíhòu shàng tǐyù kè? (Tuesday morning)

____

2 Nàxiē xuéshēng shénme shíhòu xiàkè? (3:30 in the afternoon)

____

3 Nàgè xiǎoháizi jǐdiǎn yào huíjiā? (6:00 in the evening)

____

4 Nǐmen shénme shíhòu yào chūfā? (this evening)

____

"Come fly with me."

Sequencing Periods of Time 2

This chapter should have been called "Planes, Trains, and Automobiles". You'll have no excuse for missing your flight after this amazing chapter. And guess what? You won't need a ticket to:

- learn important vocabulary for traveling
- review sequential time phrases

If you've been looking through this book trying to find a chapter devoted to making airline and hotel reservations, this is probably the closest I come to it. Don't worry – you're gonna get some useful new vocabulary, but much more importantly, your understanding of word order in Chinese sentences is getting stronger, which will allow you to navigate your way through conversations.

Recap

Let's keep rockin' and rollin' by tying together the last lesson's sentence structure with this lesson's new vocabulary.

Let's make sure you remember some of the old transportation vocabulary. Write the English equivalents for the following words.

1 zìxíngchē / jiǎotàchē ______________________________

2 chēzi ______________________________

3 mótuōchē ______________________________

Words, phrases and stuff

Look at the words **fēi** and **piào** in the vocabulary list. Notice I left a blank space for you to write the definition using your deductive reasoning skills. Look at the other words that contain these two **zì** and try and figure out what these two words mean on their own. Hint: **fēi** is a verb, and **piào** is a noun.

88.01 Listen to the words and phrases then listen again and repeat.

Travel

fēi	飞	______________
fēijī	飞机	*airplane*
(fēi)jīchǎng	飞机场	*airport*
shàng	上	*to get on / in (a train, plane, bus, etc.)*
xià	下	*to get off / out of (a train, plane, bus, etc.)*
huǒchē	火车	*a train*
huǒchēzhàn	火车站	*train station*
gōnggòng qìchē / gōngchē	公共汽车/公车	*bus*
bāshì	巴士	*bus*
zuò	坐	*to sit; to take (a plane, a train, etc.)*
piào	票	______________
chēpiào	车票	*a bus / train ticket*
jīpiào	机票	*airplane ticket*
zhāng	张	MW for sheets of paper; tickets; flat objects

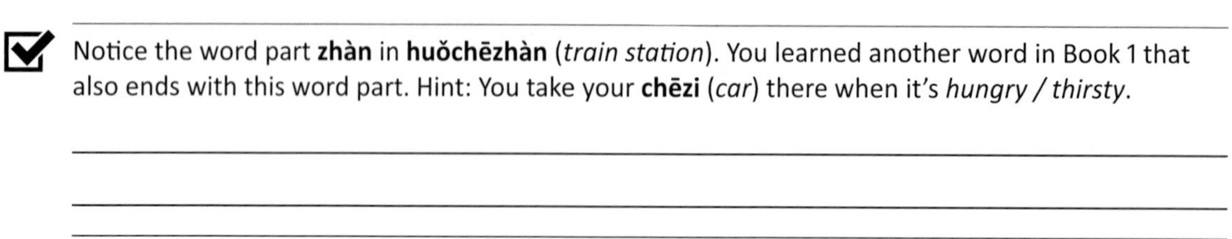

One of the major verbs we'll use in this lesson is **zuò** (坐) *to sit*. It has the same pronunciation (but different character) as another important verb we have learned recently: **zuò** (做) *to make; to do.*

Notice the word part **zhàn** in **huǒchēzhàn** (*train station*). You learned another word in Book 1 that also ends with this word part. Hint: You take your **chēzi** (*car*) there when it's *hungry / thirsty*.

____

____

____

Patterns

Alright, since I'm sure you've already mastered our basic pattern that we're using in this lesson (subject + time + action), I'll just throw some new examples at you so you can get more familiar with some of our new vocabulary.

Examples:

1 Nǐ shénme shíhòu yào qù huǒchēzhàn? (*When do you have to go to the train station?*)

2 Wǒ xīngqīyī wǎnshàng 7 diǎn yào qù huǒchēzhàn. (*I have to go to the train station on Monday evening at 7 o'clock.*)

3 Tā shénme shíhòu yào shàng fēijī? (*When is he / she going to board the plane?*)

4 Tā xiàgèxīngqīyī zǎoshàng yào shàng fēijī. (*He / She is going to board the plane next Monday morning.*)

5 Nǐmen jǐdiǎn yào xià gōngchē? (*What time are you guys going to get off the bus?*)

6 Wǒmen xiàwǔ liǎngdiǎn yào xià gōngchē. (*We are going to get off the bus at 2 o'clock in the afternoon.*)

Get to work

A Where are the following locations? Use prepositions we learned in Lessons 72–3 to answer the questions.

Ex: (The train) zài nǎ lǐ? (inside the train station) → Huǒchē zài huǒchēzhànde lǐmiàn. OR Huǒchē zài huǒchēzhàn lǐ.

1 (The airport) zài nǎ lǐ? (next to the casino)

2 (The bus) zài nǎ lǐ? (across from the park)

3 (His bus ticket) zài nǎ lǐ? (under his book)

4 (Your plane ticket) zài nǎ lǐ? (on the table)

B Match the questions and their abbreviated answers.

1 ____ Nǐ xiǎng mǎi shénme?

2 ____ Tā yào zuò huǒchē háishì fēijī?

3 ____ Nàgè rén yǒu méi yǒu piào?

4 ____ Nǐmen shénme shíhòu yào shàngchē?

5 ____ Liǎngzhāng chēpiào duōshǎo qián?

a 25 kuài 3 máo

b jīntiān wǎnshàng jiǔ diǎn bàn

c zuò fēijī

d Yǒu

e yīzhāng jīpiào

C Translate the following sentences into English.

Ex: Nǐmen jǐdiǎn yào chūfā? → What time are you guys setting off?

1 Nǐmen jīntiān xiàwǔ yào shàng fēijī ma? ____________________

2 Nǐde chēpiào pián bù piányí? ____________________

3 Tāmen shénme shíhòu yào zuò gōnggòng qìchē? ____________________

4 Nǐ māma jǐdiǎn xià fēijī? ____________________

5 Wǒmen míngtiān wǎnshàng bādiǎn yào zuò huǒchē. ____________________

6 Zhèxiē jīpiào tài guì! ____________________

D When's your next vacation? Write a few sentences about where you would like to go and what you are going to do. Give a detailed itinerary.

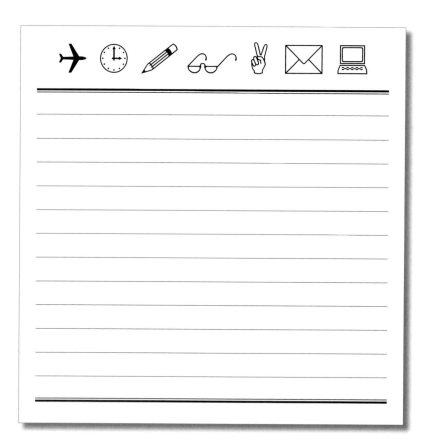

Lesson 89

"I'm too busy for this."

Gè for New Time Words

You know how to say **jīntiān**, **míngtiān** and **zuótiān**. You also know how to say **jīnnián**, **míngnián** and **qùnián**. Let's fill in the gaps by learning how to say *this week / month*, *next week / month* and *last week / month*. Without further ado, it's time to:

- learn more time expressions
- learn another definition for **shàng** and **xià**

Hope you haven't forgotten about our most important measure word **gè**!

Recap

A Let's make sure you know your basic time words, or you won't do too well with this lesson. Answer these true or false questions. If false, make the necessary corrections as well.

1. There are qī tiān in a yuè. ____________________
2. There are about sānshí tiān in a xīngqī. ____________________
3. There are sānbǎi liùshíwǔ tiān in a nián. ____________________
4. There are èrshísìgè xiǎoshí in a tiān. ____________________
5. Mike Lǎoshī is the greatest Chinese teacher ever. ____________________

B We will also be using "shàng" and "xià" again as well. Write three definitions for each.

1. shàng: __________ __________ __________
2. xià: __________ __________ __________

Words, phrases and stuff

89.01 Listen to the words and phrases then listen again and repeat.

Countries and Time Expressions for Months and Weeks

Yàzhōu	亚洲	*Asia*	**yuèlì**	月历	*monthly calendar*
Àozhōu	澳洲	*Australia*	**zhègèxīngqī**	这个星期	*this week*
Ōuzhōu	欧洲	*Europe*	**shànggèxīngqī**	上个星期	*last week*
Fēizhōu	非洲	*Africa*	**xiàgèxīngqī**	下个星期	*next week*
Běi Měizhōu	北美洲	*North America*	**zhègèyuè**	这个月	*this month*
Nán Měizhōu	南美洲	*South America*	**shànggèyuè**	上个月	*last month*
Bōlán	波兰	*Poland*	**xiàgèyuè**	下个月	*next month*

So you can see from the vocab that **běi** means *north* and **nán** means *south*. Can you recall the words for *east* and *west*? Hint: I taught you in Lesson 56 that the Chinese word for *things; stuff* is formed by combining the **zì** for *east* and the **zì** for *west*.

Patterns

Pattern 1: zhè / shàng / xià + gè + xīngqī / yuè.

Pattern 2a: Subject + time question word + action?

Pattern 2b: Subject + time + action.

Pattern 3a: Subject + time + action + question word?

Pattern 3b: Subject + time + action.

Examples:

1 shànggèyuè/xiàgèxīngqī (*last month / next week*)

2a Nǐ shénme shíhòu yào qù Fēizhōu? (*When are you going (to go) to Africa?*)

2b Wǒ xiàgèxīngqīliù yào qù Fēizhōu. (*I am going (to go) to Africa next Saturday.*)

3a Nǐ xiàgèxīngqī xiǎng zuò shénme? (*What would you like to do next week?*)

3b Wǒ xiàgèxīngqī xiǎng qù kàn gējù. (*I would like to see an opera next week.*)

Get to work

A Do you know the Seven Wonders of the Ancient World? Maybe not, but hopefully you at least know something about the seven continents. And sorry, I didn't include Antarctica – I don't like the desert. Use the words in the box to create sentences about where these people would like / are planning to go. Then translate them into English.

Yàzhōu	Àozhōu	Ōuzhōu	Fēizhōu	Běi Měizhōu	Nán Měizhōu

Ex: (xiǎng) My younger sister / Europe / next winter →
Wǒde mèimei míngnián dōngtiān xiǎng qù Ōuzhōu.

1 (xiǎng) Her older sister / Australia / next fall ____________________

2 (yào) His younger brother / South America / this year ____________________

3 (xiǎng) Our mom and dad / North America / next year ____________________

4 (yào) My sisters / Asia / next month ____________________

B 89.02 **How would you translate these sentences into Chinese? Write them, then say them out loud and compare your answers.**

Ex: Last week I was in Australia. → Shànggèxīngqī wǒ zài Àozhōu. OR
Wǒ shànggèxīngqī zài Àozhōu.

1 Last month (the weather) was cold. ____________________

2 I am super busy this week. ____________________

3 Next week I am going to Africa. ____________________

4 I start taking Chinese classes next month. ____________________

5 My girlfriend was extremely tired last week. ____________________

6 Professor Lin is in China this month. ____________________

C Write the questions to the following statements.

Ex: Tā xiàgèxīngqīliù wǎnshàng yào chūqù. → Tā shénme shíhòu yào chūqù?

1 Wǒ zhègèyuè kāishǐ wǒde xīnde gōngzuò. ____________________

2 Tāmen zhègèxīngqīwǔ yào zuò fēijī. ____________________

3 Wǒmen xiàgèyuè xiǎng qù Yàzhōu. ____________________

4 Wǒ jiějie shànggèxīngqī zài Běijīng. ____________________

Lesson 90

"I live for holidays."

Adverbs of Frequency

Trick or treat! Well, as usual you'll be getting another treat from me: a fabulous lesson on adverbs of frequency! If my strobe light didn't hypnotize you, you'd better get ready to:

- learn some adverbs of frequency
- practice new vocabulary to talk about routines
- review prepositions to talk about location

As you can imagine, my garage is a pretty popular destination on Halloween; it's the only day all of my fans have an excuse to trespass. Anyway, you're going to learn some adverbs of frequency so you'll be able to tell people all about your daily, weekly, monthly, and yearly routines!

Recap

The transition into this lesson shouldn't be too bad. The only difference is that we are not giving a specific point in time (like *last Wednesday* or *next week*); instead, we are talking about words to express ongoing routines, but the sentence pattern is the same. Simple!

Since you're going to be talking about your daily, weekly, monthly, and yearly routines, let's do a refresher on some of our basic vocabulary you'll need to remember before tackling this lesson.

Match some old vocabulary words with their translations.

1 ____ xīngqī	**a** month
2 ____ yuè	**b** day
3 ____ nián	**c** week
4 ____ tiān	**d** year

Words, phrases and stuff

90.01 Listen to the words and phrases then listen again and repeat.

Halloween and Adverbs of Frequency

Wànshèngjié	万圣节	*Halloween; All Saints' Day*
zhīzhū	蜘蛛	*spider*
nánguā	南瓜	*pumpkin*
nánguādēng	南瓜灯	*jack-o'-lantern*
měi	每	*each; every*
měitiān	每天	*every day*
měinián	每年	*every year*
měigèyuè	每个月	*every month*
měigèxīngqī	每个星期	*every week*
tōngcháng	通常	*usually*
qǐchuáng	起床	*to wake up; get out of bed*

Patterns

Pattern 1: time word (of frequency) + time word

Pattern 2: subject + time word (of frequency) + verb.

Examples:

1 měitiān xiàwǔ (*every afternoon*)

2 Wǒ měitiān xuéxí Xībānyáwén. (*I study Spanish every day.*)

Following the time expression in sentences with the word **měi** (*every*), it is also very common to add the word **dōu** (*all*) for emphasis, so instead of saying **Wǒ měitiān xuéxí Xībānyáwén** as you see in Example 2, you can say **Wǒ měitiān dōu xuéxí Xībānyáwén**. For now, include **dōu** in your sentences if you want, but I'm more concerned about practicing **měi**. We'll have a whole lesson on **dōu** in Lesson 98, so we can spice things up then.

Get to work

A 90.02 **Listen and fill in the time the following expressions you hear in Chinese. Then translate the sentence.**

Ex: Wǒ → (měitiān zǎoshàng) xǐ liǎn. → (I wash my face every morning.)

1 Wǒ ______________ liànxí xiě Zhōngwén zì. ______________________________

2 Nǐ ______________ dǎ lánqiú. ______________________________

3 Tā ______________ yào chūguó. ______________________________

4 Wǒmen ______________ xǐhuān qù lǚxíng. ______________________________

5 Nǐmen ______________ qù jiāyóuzhàn. ______________________________

6 Tāmen ______________ fàng shǔjià. ______________________________

B How often do you do the following activities? Use your new vocabulary to complete the sentences. Then translate them.

Ex: Wǒ ______________ xǐ liǎn. Wǒ měitiān zǎoshàng xǐ liǎn. →

(I wash my face every morning.)

1 Wǒ ______________ chī wǎncān. ______________________________

2 Wǒ ______________ shuā yá. ______________________________

3 Wǒ ______________ jiǎn tóufǎ. ______________________________

4 Wǒ ______________ qù kàn yīshēng. ______________________________

5 Wǒ ______________ qù chāojí shìchǎng. ______________________________

C Use the answers in parentheses to answer the following questions.

Ex: Nǐ tōngcháng jǐdiǎn qǐchuáng? (6:45 in the morning) →
Wǒ tōngcháng zǎoshàng liù diǎn sìshíwǔ fēn qǐchuáng.

1 Tā tōngcháng jǐdiǎn shuìjiào? (10:00 in the evening)

____

2 Nǐmen tōngcháng jǐdiǎn qù shàngbān? (8:00 in the morning)

____

3 Nǐ tōngcháng jǐdiǎn zuò gōnggòng qìchē? (3:00 in the afternoon)

____

4 Nǐ jiā tōngcháng jǐdiǎn chī wǎncān? (6:30 in the evening)

____

 D **Write about what you like to do every summer. Do you have any traditions? Or do you just hang out?**

Lesson 91

"Let's play hide-and-seek."

Subject + Place + Action 1

Ready or not, here I come! If you saw the video for this lesson, you already know that **Xiǎo Màikè** and I just played an intense game of hide-and-seek. I'm a little tired, but you know I've got enough left in me to:

- review the preposition **zài** and some random locations
- introduce the sentence pattern of subject + place + action

Congrats! You're more than halfway through Season 4 of CWM, so hopefully you've added a lot of good weapons to your Mandarin Chinese arsenal. Even though we've stuck mainly to the subject + time + action sentence structure, we've plugged in a number of variations for the time word / phrase. Let's see how we combine subject + place + action this time. Cool?

Recap

Before we combine a location and an action in the same sentence, let's make sure you remember how to use the preposition **zài** to say where someone / something is.

Answer with the words in parentheses.

1 Bàba zài nǎ lǐ? (at home) ____________________

2 Māma zài nǎ lǐ? (at work) ____________________

3 Gēge zài nǎ lǐ? (in the bathroom) ____________________

4 Jiějie zài nǎ lǐ? (at school) ____________________

5 Mèimei zài nǎ lǐ? (her friend's house) ____________________

6 Dìdi zài nǎ lǐ? (at the park) ____________________

Words, phrases and stuff

91.01 Listen to the words and phrases then listen again and repeat.

Rooms and Places

zài	在	*in; at; on*
zài	再	*again*
cì	次	*a time (in order)* (e.g. the first time to do something; I've done that ten times)
zhuō mí cáng	捉迷藏	*to play hide-and-seek*
fángjiān	房间	*a room*
kètīng	客厅	*living room*
shūfáng	书房	*the study (n)*
cèsuǒ	厕所	*bathroom*
wòshì	卧室	*bedroom*
shūdiàn	书店	*bookstore*
yóujú	邮局	*post office*

Zài (在) vs. **zài** (再): There are two vocabulary words this time that are spelled and pronounced the same, but notice, of course, that the characters are different. The first: **zài** 在 (*in; at; on*) is the preposition that we often combine with other prepositions (see Lessons 71–3) to provide location. The other **zài** 再 (*again*), helps form the word **zàijiàn** (再见), which literally means *see again* or *goodbye*.

Patterns

Most sentences that contain a subject, a place and an action follow Patterns 3 and 4. However, beware that a few – not many – verbs, such as **zhù** (*to live*) and **zuò** (*to sit*) do not follow this same sentence structure. For example, in the question **Nǐ zhù zài nǎ lǐ?** (*Where do you live?*), the place and action are reversed. Similarly, in the answer **Wǒ zhù zài Zhījiāgē** (*I live in Chicago.*) the place and action are reversed as well. However, aside from this extremely common question, you will rarely encounter this exception. Like all other question / answer patterns we've studied so far, the key is to pay attention to the question you're being asked so that your answer follows the same pattern.

Pattern 1:	Subject + **zài** + nǎ lǐ?
Pattern 2:	Subject+ **zài** + **place**.
Pattern 3:	Subject + **zài** + nǎ lǐ + action?
Pattern 4:	Subject + **zài** + **place** + action.

Examples:

1 Nǐ **zài** nǎ lǐ? (*Where are you?*)

2 Wǒ **zài cèsuǒ**. (*I am in the bathroom.*)

3 Nǐ **zài** nǎ lǐ mǎi shū? (*Where do you buy books?*)

4 Wǒ **zài shūdiàn** mǎi shū. (*I buy books at the bookstore.*)

Get to work

A **91.02 Listen to the sentences about some of Dàwèi's and Pèishān's routines. Write where they do each of the activities in the chart.**

	Dàwèi	**Pèishān**
Liànxí Zhōngwén		
Chīfàn		
Kàn diànshì		

B **Here's a mixed review of location (from Seasons 1 and 3). Use the words in parentheses to answer the questions about where these people / things are.**

Ex: Nǐde bǐjìběn diànnǎo zài nǎ lǐ? (on the floor) → Wǒde bǐjìběn zài dì(bǎn) shàng.

1 Yóujú zài nǎ lǐ? (to the left of the library) ____________________

2 Nǐ érzide dàxué zài nǎ lǐ? (in London) ____________________

3 Yínháng zài nǎ lǐ? (behind the restaurant) ____________________

4 Tāde shǒujī zài nǎ lǐ? (on his bed) ____________________

5 Lǎoshīde fěnbǐ zài nǎ lǐ? (in front of the blackboard) ____________________

6 Nǐde péngyǒu zài nǎ lǐ? (at the airport) ____________________

C **Match the English questions with Chinese answers.**

1 Where does he work?

2 Where do they drink beer?

3 Where do you work?

4 Where does Joe take Chinese (classes)?

5 Where do you guys play ping-pong?

6 Where do the students play hide-and-seek?

a Tā zài biànlì shāngdiàn gōngzuò.

b Wǒmen zài dìxiàshì dǎ pīngpāngqiú.

c Tāmen zài jiǔbā hē píjiǔ.

d Wǒ zài měishùguǎn shàngbān.

e Xuéshēng zài gōngyuán wán zhuō mí cáng.

f Tā zài gāozhōng shàng Zhōngwén kè.

D **Where do people you know do certain activities? Include a subject, place, and action.**

Ex: Wǒ māma zài chúfáng zuòfàn.

____

____

____

____

E **Xiǎo Màikè and I played hide-and-seek in the video. Write the different places that Xiǎo Màikè hides on me. In Chinese, of course.**

____

____

Lesson 92

"Doing the turkey dance."

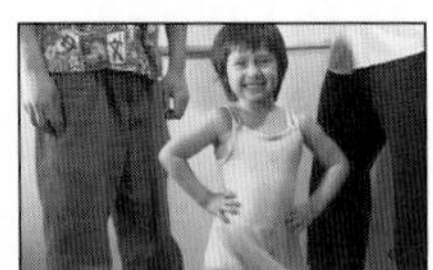

Subject + Place + Action 2

Last time I introduced an important new sentence structure that you'll use 24 / 7 in Chinese – seriously. I'm too busy enjoying the fall colors and watching football to teach you a lot more new stuff, so I've thrown in some new vocabulary and added an exciting twist to our subject + place + action pattern, but for the most part, we're reviewing. Get ready to:

- learn the names for new places
- review our subject + place + action pattern

In Lesson 91, I introduced the sentence structure for including a location and action in the same sentence. So, instead of just saying **Wǒ zài túshūguǎn** (*I am at the library*) like we did in Lesson 30, we're adding an action. Now you can make sentences like **Wǒ zài túshūguǎn qīn wǒde nǚpéngyǒu** (*I kiss my girlfriend at the library*). Nice!

Recap

First, prove to me that you remember the basic pattern from last time and answer the questions about some of your basic routines.

Ex: Nǐ zài nǎ lǐ kàn diànshì? **A:** Wǒ zài kètīng kàn diànshì.

1 Nǐ zài nǎ lǐ kàn shū? ____________________

2 Nǐ zài nǎ lǐ shàngkè / shàngbān? ____________________

3 Nǐ zài nǎ lǐ xǐ liǎn? ____________________

4 Nǐ zài nǎ lǐ shuìjiào? ____________________

5 Nǐ zài nǎ lǐ chī zǎocān? ____________________

Words, phrases and stuff

92.01 **Listen to the words and phrases then listen again and repeat.**

New Places

shìchǎng	市场	*market*	**cháguǎn**	茶馆	*teahouse*
mǎi cài	买菜	*buy groceries*	**bówùguǎn**	博物馆	*museum*
bàngqiúchǎng	棒球场	*baseball field*	**lǚguǎn**	旅馆	*motel*
tíngchēchǎng	停车场	*parking lot*	**cānguǎn**	餐馆	*restaurant*
dǔchǎng	赌场	*casino*	**túshūguǎn**	图书馆	library

1 **What are the other words for *hotel* and *restaurant*?** ____________________

2 **What does "guǎn" mean?** ____________________

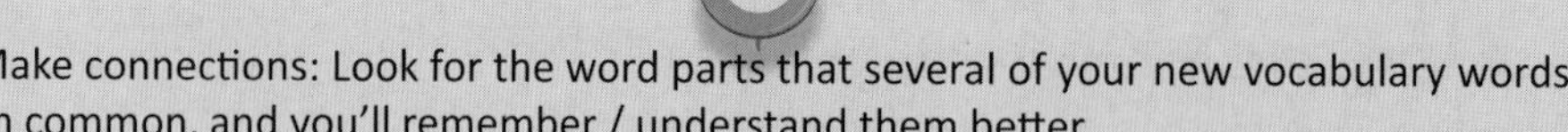

Tip: Make connections: Look for the word parts that several of your new vocabulary words have in common, and you'll remember / understand them better.

Patterns

Last time we talked about your normal routines (see Patterns 1–2). This time let's take it a step further and include a second verb (**xǐhuān** / **yào** / **xiǎng**) and talk about where you *like / want / would like* to do certain activities (see Patterns 3–4). Notice that when you include a place with (**zài** . . .), the first verb comes before the place, and then the second after it.

Pattern 1: Subject + zài + nǎ lǐ + **verb 1** (action)?

Pattern 2: Subject+ zài + place + **verb 1** (action)

Pattern 3: Subject + **verb 1** + zài nǎ lǐ + **verb 2**?

Pattern 4: Subject + **verb 1** + place + **verb 2**.

Examples:

1 Nǐ zài nǎ lǐ **shàngkè**? (*Where do you attend class?*)

2 Wǒ zài xuéxiào **shàngkè**. (*I attend class at school.*)

3 Nǐ xǐhuān zài nǎ lǐ **pǎobù**? (*Where do you like to run?*)

4 Wǒ xǐhuān zài gōngyuán **pǎobù**. (*I like to run in the park.*)

Get to work

A Test your vocabulary. The following sentences don't make sense. Replace the underlined word with one that makes sense.

Ex: Tā zài dǔchǎng mǎi cài. → Tā zài shìchǎng mǎi cài.

1 Tāmen zài tíngchēchǎng dǎ bàngqiú. ______

2 Wáng Lǎoshī zài bàngqiúchǎng shàngkè. ______

3 Shéi xiǎng qù dòngwùyuán hē chá? ______

4 Wǒmen zài jīchǎng shuìjiào. ______

B Unscramble the following sentences.

Ex: bàngqiúchǎng / kàn / Lǐ Yīshēng / qù / xǐhuān / bàngqiúsài. →
Lǐ Yīshēng xǐhuān qù bàngqiúchǎng kàn bàngqiúsài.

1 nǐmende / cháguǎn / zài / shàngbān / péngyǒu / ma? ______

2 tíngchēchǎng / nǎ lǐ / zài / lǚguǎnde? ______

3 shìchǎng / mǎi / hěn duō / měigèxīngqī / dōngxī / wǒ / zài ______

4 liànxí / túshūguǎn / xuéshēng / zài / Zhōngwén / nàxiē ______

C Given the answer, write the question. If you have two verbs, don't forget to split them with the place.

Ex: Tāmen yào zài tíngchēchǎng tíngchē. → Tāmen yào zài nǎ lǐ tíngchē?

1 Tāmen xiǎng zài lǚguǎn gōngzuò. ______

2 Wǒmen xǐhuān zài gōngyuán wán zhuō mí cáng. ______

3 Zhāng Yīshēng zài yīyuān shàngbān. ______

4 Wǒ yào zài cānguǎn chī zǎocān. ______

D Where do you like to spend your time? What do you like to do there? Write five sentences about where you enjoy doing certain activities.

Ex: Wǒ xǐhuān zài gōngyuán kànshū. (I like reading in the park.)

Wǒ xǐhuān zài dàxué shàng lìshǐ kè. (I like going to history class at the university.)

Wǒ xǐhuān zài jiā kàn diànshì. (I like watching TV at home.)

______

______

______

______

______

Lesson 93

"Meet my personal assistant."

Time and Place

OK, so you've met Justin. All famous people seem to have personal assistants, so I figured I might as well find one, too. Hopefully this won't be a decision I'll regret, but it's too early to tell. For now, let's:

- review subject + time + action
- review subject + place + action
- combine both sentence structures to create: subject + time + place + action

In this lesson, we won't worry about questions; let's just get used to including both time and place in a single sentence for the first time. Take my hand. I won't lead you astray.

Recap

A **93.01 Practice making statements with the subject + time + action pattern. Then say them out loud.**

1 I play golf on Saturdays. ______

2 She goes to the supermarket every Tuesday. ______

3 We go to the nightclub every Friday evening. ______

B **93.02 Now make statements with the subject + place + action pattern. Then say them out loud.**

1 They eat lunch in the dining room. ______

2 My dad works at the bank. ______

3 Her mom teaches at the university. ______

Words, phrases and stuff

93.03 Listen to the words and phrases then listen again and repeat.

Have a BBQ, then go to the Gym

niúpái	牛排	*steak*	**jiànshēn**	健身	*to work out*
kǎoròu	烤肉	*to grill; to barbecue*	**tǐyùguǎn**	体育馆	*gymnasium*
hòuyuàn	后院	*backyard*	**jiàoshì**	教室	*classroom*
jiànshēnfáng	健身房	*the gym*	**xiàngqí**	象棋	*chess*

Patterns

The sentence pattern for subject + time + place + action that we are covering in this lesson is very useful when you talk about your routines in life. For example, maybe you make breakfast in the kitchen every morning, buy groceries at the supermarket on Friday, get a haircut once a month, and sleep in a one-car garage every night. Oops! Now I'm talking about my own life. Anyway, think about when and where you do certain activities, and let's practice our new sentence pattern.

Pattern: Subject + time + place + action.
↓ ↓ ↓ ↓
Wǒ xīngqīwǔ zài gōngyuán dǎ lánqiú.

Examples:

1 Tā měigèxīngqīliù zài tǐyùguǎn dǎ yǔmáoqiú.

2 Tāmen měitiān zài jiā wán diàndòng yóuxì.

3 Wǒ bàba tōngcháng zài jiànshēnfáng jiànshēn.

Get to work

A Complete the sentences with the correct Chinese words. Then translate the sentences into English.

Ex: Tā měigèxīngqīliù wǎnshàng zài (backyard) kǎo niúpái. →
hòuyuàn – He / She grills steak in the backyard every Saturday evening.

1 Wǒmen (every summer) zài hǎitān yóuyǒng. ______

2 Tāmen zǎoshàng qī diǎn zài (the train station) děng huǒchē. ______

3 Gāo Tàitai měinián dōngtiān zài kāfēitīng hē (hot chocolate). ______

4 Nàgè shāngrén tōngcháng zài (motel) shuìjiào. ______

5 Pèishān měitiān xiàwǔ zài (the gym) zuò yùndòng. ______

B 93.04 Listen to following statements about Lili's routines and complete the sentences with the missing times, places, or actions.

1 Lili ______ zài yùshì xǐliǎn.

2 Lili ______ zài fàntīng chī wǔcān.

3 Tā měigèxīngqī zài ______ mǎi cài.

4 Tā měinián xiàtiān zài ______ kǎoròu.

5 Lili ______ zài Běijīng kàn yǎnchànghuì.

6 Lili měigèxīngqīyī wǎnshàng zài ______ shàng tǐyù kè.

C Talk about your weekly routine. Use our new sentence structure to provide the time, place, and action.

Ex: Wǒ měitiān zǎoshàng zài yùshì shuāyá. (Every morning I brush my teeth in the bathroom.)

______

______

______

______

D Some of the following sentences have incorrect word order. Fix the incorrect sentences.

Ex: Jack zài kètīng měitiān wǎnshàng wán xiàngqí. →
Jack měitiān wǎnshàng zài kètīng wán xiàngqí.

1 Wú Lǎoshī měigèxīngqīsān zài jiàoshì shàngkè. ______

2 Wáng Jiàoshòu zài xuéxiào wǎnshàng shàng Zhōngwén kè. ______

3 Wǒmen měinián xiàtiān chī bīngqílín zài gōngyuán. ______

4 Wǒde nánpéngyǒu zài dǔchǎng xīngqīyī dǎ májiàng. ______

Lesson 94

"Meet my ballet teacher."

Review of Time and Place

Do I look that out of shape? Well, my doctor apparently thinks so. He recommended that I get more exercise, so I've decided to hire a ballet teacher. In fact, Justin, my personal assistant, is out looking for one right now. Anyway, he's not back yet, so let's:

- practice our new pattern with two-verb combinations
- learn new verbs

I don't want to overwhelm with you with too much at once, so let's spend a little more time getting familiar with our new word order: subject + time + place + action. Just to keep you on your toes, though, I'll throw in some new vocabulary – how about that?

Recap

Let's make sure you were with me in the last lesson. Plug in the following time words and places to complete the statements below.

1 Wǒmen (every evening) (in the basement) dǎ pīngpāngqiú.

2 Nǐmen (every morning) (in the kitchen) pàochá.

3 Lín Xiānshēng (in the morning) (at the gym) zuò yùndòng.

4 Bill (Wednesday afternoon) (in his bedroom) liànxí xiǎotíqín.

5 Mike Lǎoshī (every day) (in the garage) jiāo Zhōngwén.

Words, phrases and stuff

94.01 Listen to the words and phrases then listen again and repeat.

Verbs and Places

chàng(gē)	唱歌	*to sing (a song)*
dǎ májiàng	打麻将	*to play mahjong*
jiāoshū	教书	*to teach*
yóuyǒng	游泳	*to swim*
jiànshēn	健身	*to work out*
huáxuě	滑雪	*to ski; skiing*
lǚxíng	旅行	*to travel*
zhòng huā	种花	*to plant; grow flowers*
yóuyǒngchí	游泳池	*swimming pool*
kāfēitīng	咖啡厅	*coffee shop; café*
huāyuán	花园	*garden*
tàijí	太极	*taiji (tai chi), the martial art*
dìlǐkè	地理课	*geography class*

Patterns

If you've been paying attention, you should remember we spent several lessons covering the sentence patterns (1) time + subject + action (**Jīntiān wǒ yào shàngbān.**) and (2) subject + time + action (**Wǒ jīntiān yào shàngbān**). We then covered the sentence patterns (3) subject + place + action (**Wǒ zài cānguǎn shàngbān.**) and (4) subject + verb 1 + place + verb 2 (**Wǒ xǐhuān zài cānguǎn shàngbān.**) Last time we combined these two sentence patterns so we had (5) subject + time + place + action (**Wǒ měigèxīngqīwǔ zài cānguǎn shàngbān.**) all in a single sentence! This time we will continue with the same pattern, but we will also get into working with two-verb combinations, which change the grammar. For example, when you include the verbs **xǐhuān** (*like*), **yào** (*want*), **xiǎng** (*would like*) in a sentence that also includes time and place, we must restructure the sentence. Once again, we'll split verbs around the place. Take a look at Pattern 2.

Pattern 1: Subject + time + place + action.

Pattern 2: Subject + time + **verb 1** + place + **verb 2**.

Examples:

1 Gāo Lǎoshī zǎoshàng liùdiǎn zài jiàoshì **jiāo** Zhōngwén. (*Teacher Gao teaches Chinese at 6:00 in the morning in the classroom.*)

2 Gāo Lǎoshī zǎoshàng liùdiǎn **yào** zài jiàoshì **jiāo** Zhōngwén. (*Teacher Gao is going to / must teach Chinese at 6:00 in the morning in the classroom.*)

Get to work

A Review the sentence patterns you've learned while practicing your new vocabulary. Complete the sentences with the correct translation; then choose the correct sentence pattern for each. Use the numbers given for each pattern above.

Ex: Wǒmen měinián chūntiān zài (garden) zhòng huā. →
(We plant flowers in the garden every spring. (Pattern 1))

1 (That woman) xǐ bù xǐhuān zài tǐyùguǎn dǎ tàijí? ____________________

2 Nǐ měinián shí'èryuè zài nǎ lǐ (ski)? ____________________

3 Wǒmen xiànzài yào zài (the swimming pool) yóuyǒng. ____________________

4 Wǒmen míngnián xiàtiān xiǎng zài Yìdàlì (travel). ____________________

B Complete the sentences with times and places that make sense.

Ex: Nàzhī māo __________ __________ shuìjiào. → Nàzhī māo měitiān zài shāfā shàng shuìjiào.

1 Wǒmen __________ __________ xuéxí Éwén.

2 Tāmen __________ __________ shàng dìlǐ kè.

3 Wǒ āyí __________ __________ jiāo Yīngwén.

4 Wǒde péngyǒu __________ __________ kǎoròu.

5 Tā bàba __________ __________ shū tóufǎ.

6 Nàgè jiàoshòu __________ __________ shàngbān.

C Let's try our new sentence pattern when we have two verbs. Split the time and place by adding "yào", "xiǎng" or "xǐhuān" in the following sentences. Then rewrite as complete sentences.

Ex: Tā jīntiān wǎnshàng zài diànyǐngyuàn kàn xīnde diànyǐng. →
Tā jīntiān wǎnshàng yào zài diànyǐngyuàn kàn xīnde diànyǐng.

1 (xiǎng) Wǒ míngtiān wǎnshàng zài bàngqiúchǎng kàn qiúsài.

____

2 (xiǎng) Tāmen míngnián chūntiān zài Běi Měizhōu lǚxíng.

____

3 (xǐhuān) Wǒ māma měitiān zǎoshàng zài gōngyuán dǎ tàijí.

____

4 (yào) Nǐmen jīntiān xiàwǔ cāntīng chīfàn ma?

____

D Write a few sentences about your evening to say what you do (and where) and what you would like to do that you don't currently do. For example: ***I watch television in my bedroom in the evening. I would like to work out at the gym.***

Ex: Wǒ wǎnshàng zài wòshì kàn diànshì. Wǒ wǎnshàng xiǎng zài jiànshēnfáng jiànshēn.

____

____

____

____

"We need to talk turkey."

Time and Place Questions

Maybe I spoke too soon about Justin's solid job performance thus far. Trust me – if he ever pulls an immature prank like that again (publicly, at least) I will have to fire him. In fact, if the turkey hadn't been so delicious, he'd have already been gone. Anyway, he's getting another chance, and YOU are getting the chance to:

- form questions using subject + time + place + action
- learn useful verb-noun combinations

The past couple of lessons we've worked with our more advanced word order: subject + time + place + action (STPA), but we have made statements only – no questions. That's about to change, as here I'll give you either the time or the place, and we'll use a question word to replace the other, unknown component.

Recap

A Choose the time words that make most sense in the following sentences.

1 Tā ____________ jiǎn tóufǎ.	**a** měitiān
2 Tāmen ____________ qù lǚxíng.	**b** měigèyuè
3 Wǒmen ____________ shuāyá.	**c** měinián

B Choose the place words that make the most sense in the following sentences.

1 Wǒmen ____________ pǎobù.	**a** zài shìchǎng
2 Wǒ ____________ mǎi cài.	**b** zài yǎnchànghuì
3 Dàwèi ____________ tīng yīnyuè.	**c** zài gōngyuán

Words, phrases and stuff

95.01 Listen to the words and phrases then listen again and repeat.

Places and Verb-Noun Combinations

Gǎnēnjié	感恩节	*Thanksgiving*
zúqiúchǎng	足球场	*soccer field*
bàngōngshì	办公室	*office*
gāozhōng	高中	*high school*
mǎi dōngxī	买东西	*go shopping*
(zuò) zuòyè	做作业	*(to do) homework*
xiě gōngkè	写功课	*(to write / do) homework*
kāihuì	开会	*(to attend) a meeting*
kǎoshì	考试	*to take a test; a test; an exam*

What's the word for "stuff" or "things" in Chinese? What is the translation?

Patterns

Pattern 1: Subject + **time-question word** + place + action?

Pattern 2: Subject + time + place + action.

Pattern 3: Subject + time + **place-question word** + action?

Pattern 4: Subject + time + place + action.

Pattern 5a **Q:** Subject + time-question word + verb 1 + place + verb 2?

Pattern 5b **Q:** Subject + time + verb 1 + place-question word + verb 2?

Pattern 5c **A:** Subject + time + verb 1 + place + verb 2.

Examples:

1 Nǐ měitiān zài nǎlǐ shàngbān?

2 Wǒ měitiān zài bàngōngshì shàngbān.

3 Nǐmen shénme shíhòu zài dàxué shàng shùxué kè?

4 Wǒmen xīngqīyī wǎnshàng zài dàxué shàng shùxué kè.

5a Nǐmen jǐdiǎn yào zài cāntīng chī wǎncān?

5b Nǐmen liùdiǎn yào zài nǎ lǐ chī wǎncān?

5c Wǒmen liùdiǎn yào zài cāntīng chī wǎncān.

This'll be our last word-order lesson for now; I need a little break to teach you some other cool stuff.

Get to work

A Answer the questions by adding a time word / phrase that makes sense.

Ex: Tāmen shénme shíhòu zài zúqiúchǎng tī zúqiú? → Tāmen xīngqīrì zài zúqiúchǎng tī zúqiú.

1 Nǐ fùqīn shénme shíhòu zài cāntīng chī wǔcān? ____________________

2 Nǐde mìshū jǐdiǎn zài bàngōngshì hē kāfēi? ____________________

3 Tā xīngqījǐ zài fàndiàn gōngzuò? ____________________

4 Tāmende nǚ'ér jǐyuè yào zài Yìdàlì kāishǐ gōngzuò? ____________________

B Answer the questions by adding a place word that makes sense.

Ex: Nǐ jīntiān zǎoshàng zài nǎ lǐ kāihuì? → Wǒ jīntiān zǎoshàng zài bàngōngshì kāihuì.

1 Tāmen míngtiān wǎnshàng yào zài nǎ lǐ dǎ wǎngqiú? ____________________

2 Nǐmen xiàgèxīngqī yào zài nǎ lǐ mǎi cài? ____________________

3 Tā érzi měitiān zài nǎ lǐ zuò zuòyè? ____________________

4 Lili tōngcháng xǐhuān zài nǎ lǐ mǎi dōngxī? ____________________

C Use "yào", "xiǎng" and "xǐhuān" to create sentences about what your family members, friends, and enemies would like to do. Don't forget to split the time and place with the first verb that is provided.

Ex: (yào) Wǒ bàba xiàgèxīngqī yào zài gāo'ěrfūqiúchǎng dǎ gāo'ěrfūqiú.

1 (xǐhuān) ____________________

2 (xiǎng) ____________________

3 (yào) ____________________

4 (xiǎng yào) ____________________

"Wèishénme huǒjī zài zhè lǐ?"

Yě and Hé

I'm bringing back one of the first ten Chinese words I ever taught you and introducing a new one, too! What more could you possibly ask for? Let's get going and . . .

- review the adverb **yě** (*also, too, and*)
- learn the conjunction **hé** (*and*)

In English, we use the word *and* constantly. In Chinese, on the other hand, there are several words to express the equivalent of the English *and*, but they are not as commonly used as they are in English. Excited to find out more? Thought so.

Recap

A Since "yě" (*too*; *also*; *and*) is the only word we've used to mean *and* so far, let's see if you remember how to use it. How would you translate these sentences into English?

1 Nǐ hěn cōngmíng, yě hěn qínláo. ______

2 Tā xǐhuān dǎ bàngqiú, yě xǐhuān dǎ wǎngqiú. ______

3 Wǒmen xiǎng qù Běijīng, yě xiǎng qù Dōngjīng. ______

B Now translate these sentences back to Chinese.

1 We are short. We are thin, too. ______

2 She likes to eat apples. She also likes to eat bananas. ______

3 I can play the piano. I can play the drums, too. ______

Words, phrases and stuff

96.01 Listen to the words and phrases then listen again and repeat.

Places, *Yě*, *Hé*, Food

yě	也	*also; too; and*	**tóngshì**	同事	*colleague; co-worker*
hé (hàn)	和	*and*	**dàn**	蛋	*egg*
Zhōngguóchéng	中国城	*Chinatown*	**péigēn**	培根	*bacon*
gāo'ěrfūqiúchǎng	高尔夫球场	*a golf course*	**pīsà**	披萨	*pizza*
chāojí shìchǎng	超级市场	*supermarket*	**règǒu**	热狗	*hot dog*
jiāyóuzhàn	加油站	*gas station*	**hànbǎo**	汉堡	*hamburger*
jiāyóu	加油	*to get gas; an expression meaning "Go for it!"*	**shǔtiáo**	薯条	*French fries*

Remember, hé is the common pronunciation for *and* in mainland China, while **hàn** is more common in Taiwan.

Patterns

In Lesson 9, I introduced the word **yě** to mean *also* or *too*, as in **Wǒ yě hěn hǎo**, but it can also be translated as *and* when it is used to join two adjectives sentences (**Wǒ yào kàn diànyǐng, yě yào kàn diànshì.**) However, the word **yě** cannot be used to join two subjects (*Bill and I are friends.*) or objects (*I ate apples and bananas.*) If we want to combine two subjects or objects, we use **hé**. Let's check it out.

Pattern 1a: Subject + hěn + adjective 1 + **yě** + hěn + adjective 2.

Pattern 1b: Subject + action 1 + **yě** + action 2.

Pattern 2: Subject 1 + **hé** + subject 2 + hěn + adjective.

Pattern 2b: Subject 1 + **hé** + subject 2 + action.

Pattern 3: Subject + action + object 1 + **hé** + object 2.

Examples:

1a Mike Lǎoshī hěn gāo, **yě** hěn shuài.

1b Tā yào tán jítā, **yě** yào chànggē.

2a Dàwèi **hé** Pèishān hěn qínláo.

2b Dàwèi **hé** Pèishān shì tóngshì.

3 Nàgè nánrén yào chī hànbǎo **hé** shǔtiáo.

Get to work

A Use "yě" to combine the following pairs of English sentences.

Ex: My mom is intelligent. She is beautiful, too. → Wǒ māma hěn piàoliàng, yě hěn cōngmíng.

1 I like hamburgers. I like french fries, too. ______

2 My older brother likes baseball. He also likes basketball. ______

3 His dog is hungry and thirsty. ______

4 She has to go to the bank. She has to go to the post office as well. ______

B Fill in the blanks with the appropriate translations, and use "hé" to create compound (more than one) subjects for the following sentences.

Ex: (Alan and Jack) shì (dentists). → Alan hé Jack shì yáyī.

1 (Elephants and hippopotamuses) shì hěn dàde (animals). ______

2 (My older sister and younger sister) ài qù (golf course) dǎ gāo'ěrfūqiú. ______

3 (Sam and Bob) xǐhuān zài (Chinatown) mǎi dōngxī. ______

4 (Her English teacher and her math teacher) hěn (good). ______

C Use "hé" to join the objects provided to answer the following questions.

Ex: Tā jīntiān zǎocān xiǎng chī shénme? (bacon and eggs) →
Tā jīntiān zǎocān xiǎng chī péigēn hé dàn.

1 Nǐ lǎopó xiànzài yào qù nǎ lǐ? (supermarket and gas station) ______

2 Tāmen xǐhuān zài cāntīng chī shénme? (pizza and hot dogs) ______

3 Jīntiān nǐ xiǎng chuān shénme yīfú? (a T-shirt and pants) ______

4 Lǎoshī jīnnián xiàtiān yào qù nǎ lǐ lǚxíng? (China and Japan) ______

D Read the sentence and decide if you need to add "yě" or "hé".

1 Tā ______ xǐhuān hē lǜchá.

2 Nǐmen yào bú yào chī dàngāo ______ bīnqílín?

3 Lǐ Tàitai ______ tā nǚ'ér xiǎng qù kàn yǎnzòuhuì.

4 Zhāng Jiàoshòu ______ tāde tóngshì hěn xiǎng fàng hánjià.

5 Wǒ hěn è, ______ hěn kě.

6 Tāmen bú huì shuō Zhōngwén, ______ bú huì shuō Hánwén.

Lesson 97

"I sing karaoke with my mom."

Hé and Gēn

On the rare occasion that you catch me outside of the garage in the winter, I'm usually carving ice sculptures or helping the neighborhood kids build snowmen. Today all I had time for was a few snow angels because I've got a lot going on. In fact, right now I have to:

- review the word **hé**
- introduce the important preposition / conjunction **gēn**

We're almost done with Season 4, so I think we'd better kick it into high gear. Let's learn some more tiny-yet-mighty new words!

Recap

Last time we focused on two words (**yě** and **hé**) that can translate as *and* in English. Remember, in everyday conversation, these words are less commonly used than the English word *and*.

A Let's make sure what I taught you last time is still fresh in your brain. Join the following sentences by combining their subjects with "hé" and then say them out loud.

1 (My older brother and younger brother) xīngqīliù yào qù gāo'ěrfūqiúchǎng.

2 (My teacher and your teacher) xiǎng yào zài cānguǎn chīfàn.

3 (Sarah and Rosie) zài chī pīsà.

B Now use "hé" to join the following objects. Then say them out loud.

1 Wǒ xiǎng qù chǒngwùdiàn mǎi (a dog and a cat.)

2 Tā xiǎng diǎn (a hamburger and french fries.)

3 Tāmen huì jiǎng (French and German.)

Words, phrases and stuff

97.01 Listen to the words and phrases then listen again and repeat.

Things to Do

hé	和	*and*
gēn	跟	*and; with*
pǎobù	跑步	*to run*
sànbù	散步	*to go for a walk; to take a walk*
diàoyú	钓鱼	*to go fishing; to fish*
wán pūkèpái	玩扑克牌	*to play poker; to play cards*
pūkèpái	扑克牌	*poker; playing cards*
dǎ bǎolíngqiú	打保龄球	*to go bowling*
kǎlāOK	卡拉	*karaoke*
tángguǒ	糖果	*candy*

Patterns

Gēn can mean *and*, *with* or *follow*. It's important to understand the context to determine the meaning.

Pattern 1a: Subject 1 + **gēn** + subject 2 + hěn + adjective.

Pattern 1b: Subject 1 + **gēn** + subject 2 + action.

Pattern 2: Subject + verb + object 1 + **gēn** + object 2.

Examples:

1a Mikě Lǎoshī **gēn** tāde péngyǒu hěn lǎnduò.

1b Wǒ **gēn** wǒde lǎopó bù xǐhuān kàn diànshì.

2 Zhègè nánhái xiǎng yào chī hànbǎo **gēn** shǔtiáo.

When they are used to join two subjects or objects, as in the patterns here, the words **hé** and **gēn** can be used interchangeably.

Get to work

A Use "hé" or "gēn" to translate the following sentences into Chinese.

Ex: (hé) This chair and and that table are extremely expensive. →
Zhèzhāng yǐzi hé nàzhāng zhuōzi fēicháng guì.

1 (hé) Susan and I like to go bowling. ______

2 (gēn) He and his mom don't like running. ______

3 (gēn) My mom and dad love walking. ______

4 (hé) Tomorrow my students and I are going to go to see a concert. ______

B Answer the questions by replacing the question words with the words in parentheses.

Ex: Nǐ gēn shéi xuéxí Zhōngwén? → Wǒ gēn tóngxué xuéxí Zhōngwén.

1 Nǐ gēn shéi dǎ gāo'ěrfūqiú? (my good friend) ______

2 Tā gēn shéi qù diàoyú? (my paternal grandfather) ______

3 Nǐmen érzi gēn shéi wán pūkèpái? (his brothers and sisters) ______

4 Nǐ nǚ'ér hé shéi chàng kǎlāOK? (her boyfriend) ______

C Given the answers, write questions about what these people want / like to do. For general questions, just use the verb "zuò" (*to do*).

Ex: Tāmen xǐhuān hē lǜchá gēn kāfēi. → Tāmen xǐhuān hē shénme?

1 Wǒ bàba xǐhuān dǎ wǎngqiú gēn bǎolíngqiú. ______

2 Tāde lǎobǎn yào kàn Zhōngwén bàozhǐ gēn zázhì. ______

3 Wǒde xuéshēng xiǎng qù lìshǐ bówùguǎn gēn měishùguǎn. ______

4 Tāde jiěmèi xiǎng yào qù Ōuzhōu hé Yàzhōu lǚxíng. ______

D 97.02 Listen and complete the sentences with the words you hear.

1 Wǒ ______ yào xué qí mótuōchē.

2 Tā ______ zuò huǒchē huíjiā.

3 Nàzhāng chuáng ______ piányí.

4 Nǐ ______ dǎ yǔmáoqiú?

5 Nàxiē xuéshēng yào mǎi Zhōngwén kèběn ______.

6 Zhègè lǎoshī yǒu fěnbǐ ______.

"This is sooooo not big enough for my fan mail!"

Dōu and Yīqǐ

Nǐ xǐhuān wǒde Shèngdànshù ma? I hope so; it took Justin three tries to get it right. So please, enjoy my decorative garage, as I teach you:

- how to say *both* or *all* using **dōu**
- how to say *together* using **yīqǐ**
- how to politely refuse a gift

Recap

In the past few lessons, we've been using **yě**, **hé** and **gēn** to express addition in Chinese. We've used **yě** to join longer sentences: **Wǒ xǐhuān chī pīsa, yě xǐhuān chī hànbǎo.** (*I like to eat pizza and (also like to eat) hamburgers.*) More recently, you've learned how to use **hé** and **gēn** to join subjects **Wǒ hé nǐ** (lit. *I and you*) as well as objects **Wǒ yào chī sānkē dàn hé sìwǎn fàn** (*I want to eat three eggs and four bowls of rice*).

A Use "yě", "hé" and "gēn" to combine the following sentences: *Joe has to go to the convenience store. He has to go the bank, too.*

1 (yě) ________________________________

2 (hé) ________________________________

3 (gēn) ________________________________

Words, phrases and stuff

98.01 Listen to the words and phrases then listen again and repeat.

Holiday Fun

dōu	都	*both; all*
yīqǐ	一起	*together*
Shèngdànjié	圣诞节	*Christmas*
Shèngdànshù	圣诞树	*Christmas tree*
Shèngdànjié Kuàilè!	圣诞节快乐！	*Merry Christmas!*
jiànkāng	健康	*healthy*
huàxué	化学	*chemistry*

Patterns

Let's go over a couple more useful words to spice up some of the Chinese that you already know! You know how to say **Wǒmen hěn è** (*We are hungry*). Now, we'll include a new word **dōu**, meaning *both* or *all*, which further emphasizes that *we are BOTH* or *we are ALL hungry* (**Wǒmen dōu hěn è**). Similarly, you know how to say **Wǒmen qù chīfàn** (*Let's go eat*) but by adding our new word **yīqǐ**, (**Wǒmen yīqǐ qù chīfàn**) you are emphasizing that we are going together – and you'll sound more like a native speaker. Let's cruise through this.

Pattern 1: Subject + **dōu** + hěn + adjective.

Pattern 2: Subject + **dōu** + verb.

Pattern 3: Subject + zài + **yīqǐ**.

Pattern 4: Subject + **yīqǐ** + verb.

When you use **dōu**, it translates as *both* when you are talking about two people / objects, and it translates as *all* when you are talking about three or more.

Examples:

1 Wǒmen **dōu** hěn máng. (*We are both busy. / We are all busy.*)

2 Tāmen **dōu** shì yīshēng. (*They are both doctors. / They are all doctors.*)

3 Wǒ gēn wǒ bàbamāma zài **yīqǐ**. (*I am with my mom and dad. / My mom and dad and I are together.*)

4 Wǒmen **yīqǐ** kàn diànshì. (*We watch TV together.*)

Get to work

 **A** 98.02 **Choose "dōu" or "yīqǐ" to complete the following sentences. Then say them out loud and compare your answers to the native speakers.**

Ex: Wǒ hé wǒde péngyǒu (dōu / yīqǐ) hěn kě.

1 Nǐ yào bú yào (dōu / yīqǐ) qù kàn diànyǐng?

2 Wǒmen (dōu / yīqǐ) hěn jiànkāng.

3 Nǐ xiǎng bù xiǎng (dōu / yīqǐ) zuò huàxué zuòyè?

4 Wǒ hé wǒde tóngxué (dōu / yīqǐ) xǐhuān wán diàndòng yóuxì.

5 Mike Lǎoshīde xuéshēng (dōu / yīqǐ) ài tā.

6 Zhōngguórén (dōu / yīqǐ) huì shuō Zhōngwén.

B Unscramble the sentences.

Ex: měitiān / shàngbān / yào / dōu / wǒ → Wǒ měitiān dōu yào shàngbān.

1 hé / tā / tā /dìdi / dōu / mán / ǎi. ______________________________

2 Xiànzài / yīqǐ / wǒ / wǒde / mèimei / zài / gēn. ______________________________

3 Nǐ / Yìdàlì / dōu / měinián / qù / ma? ______________________________

4 ma / zài / yīqǐ / zhù / nǐmen? ______________________________

C Use "hé" / "gēn" and "yīqǐ" to write an email about activities you routinely do (together) with other people.

Ex: Wǒ gēn wǒ jiārén yīqǐ chī wǎncān. (I eat dinner with my family.)

REPLY | REPLY ALL

From: ____________
Date: ____________
To: ____________
Subject: Activities

D 98.03 **Practice your pronunciation. Listen to the sentences with and without "dōu" and "yīqǐ". Repeat each sentence. Notice how you emphasize with dōu and "yīqǐ".**

1 Wǒ hé wǒ nǚ'ér yào yīqǐ qù yóulèchǎng.

2 Tā gēn tāde nánpéngyǒu dōu hěn jiànkāng

3 Wǒmen fēicháng xǐhuān qù dòngwùyuán kàn dòngwù.

4 Tāmen dōu shì dàxuéshēng.

Lesson 99

"Let's party like it's Lesson 99."

Háiyǒu

5 . . . 4 . . . 3 . . . 2 . . . 1 . . . Happy New Year! What's that in Chinese? You should be able to do that at the end of this lesson, but in the meantime, don't forget to:

- review the words **hái** (*still*) and **háishì** (*or*)
- learn the word **háiyǒu** to list multiple items

Let's take our conjunctions one step further by adding another important word: **háiyǒu** (lit. *still have*). While the literal meaning may be confusing, **háiyǒu** means *furthermore*, and is usually used to add on a third or fourth item in a series. Stick around to find out more . . .

Recap

Last time we covered **dōu** (*both; all*) and **yīqǐ** (*together*) to add subtle emphasis to some sentence patterns we had previously covered.

Translate the following sentences into English.

1 Tāmen zhù zài yīqǐ. ______________________________

2 Wǒmen dōu fēicháng lǎnduò. ______________________________

3 Nǐ xiǎng yīqǐ qù hǎitān ma? ______________________________

4 Wǒde xiōngdì dōu mán gāo. ______________________________

Words, phrases and stuff

99.01 Listen to the words and phrases then listen again and repeat.

Still and *Furthermore . . .*

hái	还	*still; yet*
hái méi	还没	*not yet*
háishì	还是	*or; still*
háiyǒu	还有	*in addition; furthermore; also*
gōngchǎng	工厂	*a factory*
chūzūchē / jìchéngchē	出租车/计程车	*taxi*
hūnlǐ	婚礼	*wedding*
Yuènán	越南	*Vietnam*

Patterns

Háiyǒu translates literally as *still have* and can be used in various ways. First, it can simply mean *still have* literally, in sentences such as **Nǐ hái yǒu duōshǎo qián?** It can function the same way as **hé** or **gēn** when joining two subjects or objects (**Zhègèyuè wǒmen yào qìngzhù Shèngdànjié háiyǒu wǒ bàbade shēngrì**). It's also commonly used to join more than two subjects or objects in a sentence (**Wǒ xiāng chī pīsà, règǒu, háiyǒu hànbǎo**). Furthermore, it can mean *in addition*, *also* or *furthermore* and be used to join two sentences (**Wǒ yào qù shūdiàn mǎi shū. Háiyǒu, wǒ yào qù jiāyóuzhàn jiāyóu**). No matter what the context, though, it is used to express addition.

Pattern 1: Subject 1 + subject 2 + **háiyǒu** + subject 3 + action.

Pattern 2: Subject + action + object 1 + object 2 + **háiyǒu** + object 3.

Pattern 3: Sentence 1. **Háiyǒu** + sentence 2.

Examples:

1 Pèishān, Dàwèi, **háiyǒu** wǒ zài gōngchǎng shàngbān.

2 Jīntiān wǎnshàng wǒde jiārén yào chī chūnjuǎn, niúròu chǎofàn, **háiyǒu** dàn.

3 Wǒ jīntiān zǎoshàng yào shàngbān. **Háiyǒu**, wǒ wǎnshàng yào shàngkè.

Get to work

A Use "hái", "háishì" or "háiyǒu" to complete the sentences.

Ex: Nǐmen xiǎng chī règǒu háishì hànbǎo?

1 Wǒ hé wǒde nánpéngyǒu xiǎng qù Fēizhōu. ________, wǒmen xiǎng qù Àozhōu.

2 Hěn duō rén yào lái wǒde shēngrì pàiduì: wǒde jiāren, wǒde péngyǒu, ________ wǒde tóngxué dōu yào lái.

3 Wǒ xiànzài bù néng qù nǐ jiā. Wǒ ________ zài zhǔfàn.

4 Nǐde xiǎohái yào wán diàndòng yóuxì ________ kàn diànshì?

5 Tā xiǎng yào mǎi shǔtiáo ________ kěle?

6 Nǐ jīntiān hǎo ma? Wǒ jīntiān ________ hǎo.

B Use "háiyǒu" to create compound subjects / objects for the following sentences.

Ex: Wǒ xiǎng xué ________________ →
Wǒ xiǎng xué Zhōngwén, Yīngwén, háiyǒu Xībānyáwén.

1 ________________ xǐhuān tī zúqiú.

2 Míngnián ________________ dōu yào qù wǒ mèimeide hūnlǐ.

3 Tā jīntiān fēicháng máng. Tā yào qù ________________.

4 Běijīng Dòngwùyuán yǒu hěn duō dòngwù. Yǒu ________________.

5 Wǒde shūbāo lǐ yǒu hěn duō dōngxī. Yǒu ________________.

C Use "háiyǒu" to express addition by joining and rewriting the following sentences in Chinese.

Ex: This evening I have to take the train. Also, I am going to take an airplane. →
Wǒ jīntiān wǎnshàng yào zuò huǒchē. Háiyǒu, (wǒ yào) zuò fēijī.)

1 Tomorrow she is going to English class. In addition, she must go grocery shopping.

2 Bob likes to drink red wine. Also, he likes to drink beer.

3 My dad works in a factory in the morning. In addition, he drives a taxi in the evening.

4 She and I both can speak Chinese. We can also write Chinese characters.

D Choose the correct words to complete each sentence.

1 Wǒmen (hé / yīqǐ / dōu) fēicháng xǐhuān kàn yǎnzòuhuì (gēn / yě / dōu) gējù.

2 Wáng Lǎoshī (gēn / yě / hái) tāde xuéshēng yào (dōu / yīqǐ / hé) fùxí zhètáng kè.

3 Xiànzài wǒ bù néng (gēn / yě / yīqǐ) nǐmen yīqǐ qù yèdiàn. Wǒ (hái / háiyǒu / hé) zài shàngbān.

4 Wǒ jiějie, dìdi, (hái / háiyǒu / yīqǐ) wǒ (yīqǐ / dōu / gēn) yào qù mǎi dōngxī.

5 Pèishān (hé / yīqǐ / dōu) Dàwèi xiǎng qù biànlì shāngdiàn. Tāmen (yīqǐ / yě / hé) xiǎng qù jiāyóuzhàn.

6 Tā měitiān zǎoshàng (hé / gēn / dōu) zuò gōnggòng qìchē qù shàngbān. (Háiyǒu / Hé / Yīqǐ), tā měitiān xiàwǔ dōu zuò jìchéngchē huíjiā.

Fireworks, Holidays and the Hero Li Tian

"When Mike Lǎoshī parties, he likes to set things ablaze. When I want to buy fireworks, I go to the fireworks capital of the world. The little-known (to the West) capital of fireworks is a city called Liuyang in south-central China, north of old Canton or modern-day Guangzhou. Li Tian was a monk who lived there long ago. According to one version of his story, Liuyang was being bullied by evil spirits, and Li wanted to do something about it. He knew the legend of the cook who had accidentally mixed up charcoal, sulfur, and potassium nitrate and caused a big bang with lots of colors. Later that mix was put into the hollow of a bamboo shoot and exploded loudly when ignited, convincing everyone that it was just the thing to drive evil spirits away. Li decided to give it a try. He put explosives into bamboo shoots and lit them, and made a great success, frightening the dragon so badly that he drove it away forever and making the people so happy that the citizens of Liuyang have said thanks to him every April 18 for more than a thousand years. (Hint: go online and check out Liuyang International Fireworks Festival to see some amazing displays.)"

"Don't cry (for me)."

Word Order with Prepositional Phrases

Forgive me if I break down and cry at any point during this episode; I have called a press conference to make an important announcement, and I'm feeling very emotional about it. Try and bear with me as we:

- review subject + time + place + action
- add prepositional phrases to our word order
- say goodbye for the last time ☹

We've reached the conclusion of Season 4 and – you guessed it – my retirement from my post as the World's Greatest Chinese Teacher. Well, I guess I will always own that title, but I will no longer be sharing my talents with the world. Anyway, enough about me. In Lesson 100, I'm leaving you with one final component to our Chinese sentence word order (prepositional phrases), so I think it's a good place for me to fade into the distance. I've given you your wings; now it's time for you to fly. And if you miss me too much, just watch re-runs.

Recap

The prepositional phrase that translates as *with . . .* in Chinese often begins with "gēn" or "hé". Translate the following expressions, so you're ready when we add this element to our word order.

1 gēn wǒmen ______________________

2 hé nǐmen ______________________

3 hé wǒ mèimei ______________________

4 gēn tāde nánpéngyǒu ______________________

5 gēn nǐde tóngshì ______________________

6 hé wǒde jiārén ______________________

Words, phrases and stuff

100.01 Listen to the words and phrases then listen again and repeat.

People, Places, Things, Actions

qìngzhù	庆祝	*to celebrate*	**Jiāzhōu**	加州	*California*
xīnnián	新年	*new year*	**línjū**	邻居	*a neighbor*
liáotiān	聊天	*to chat*	**bāshì**	巴士	*a bus*
jiànmiàn	见面	*to meet*	**jiàoliàn**	教练	*coach (sports)*
xiūchē	修车	*to repair a car*	**jiǔbā**	酒吧	*a bar*
shàngxué	上学	*to attend school*	**lánqiúchǎng**	篮球场	*basketball court*
Tàiguó	泰国	*Thailand*	**wàiguórén**	外国人	*foreigner*

Patterns

So far, we have used **hé** and **gēn** to form compound subjects, such as **Māma hé / gēn wǒ dōu xǐhuān zuòfàn** (*Mom and I both enjoy cooking*) and compound objects, such as **Wǒ yào chī tǔdòu hé / gēn yùmǐ**, (*I want to eat potatoes and corn*). This time, however, we are using **hé** and **gēn** to form prepositional phrases so that you can indicate you're doing something with someone. Notice that the overall meaning of your sentence using **hé / gēn** as a prepositional phrase is very similar to sentences where you use **hé** and **gēn** to form compound subjects (like **Māma hé / gēn wǒ . . .**). Only the placement of the prepositional phrase is different.

Pattern 1: Subject + time + place + **prepositional phrase** + action.

Pattern 2: Subject + time + verb 1 + place + **prepositional phrase** + verb 2

Examples:

1 Wǒ měitiān dōu zài dàxué **gēn wǒde tóngxué** shàngkè.

1 Pèishān tōngcháng zài gāozhōngde yóuyǒngchí **gēn tāde jiěmèi** yóuyǒng.

2 Wǒmen měinián qiūtiān xǐhuān zài gōngyuán **hé wǒde xiōngdì** dǎ gǎnlǎnqiú.

2 Tāmen jīntiān wǎnshàng xiǎng zài diànyǐngyuàn **gēn péngyǒu** kàn diànyǐng.

Get to work

A Let's first review subject + time + place + action by completing the sentences with the correct answers. Then translate the answers.

Ex: Nǐ xīngqījǐ zài jiànshēnfáng jiànshēn? (Monday and Wednesday) → Wǒ xīngqīsān hé xīngqíwǔ zài jiànshēnfáng jiànshēn. (I work out at the gym on Mondays and Wednesdays.)

1 Nǐmen měinián xiàtiān dōu qù nǎ lǐ lǚxíng? (Thailand and Vietnam)

2 Tāmen shénme shíhòu zài jiàoshì shàng Zhōngwén kè? (every Friday morning)

3 Nǐ gēn nǐde hǎo péngyǒu měitiān dōu xǐhuān zuò shénme? (play video games)

4 Nǐde nǚpéngyǒu hé nǐde jiějie jīntiān wǎnshàng yào zài nǎ lǐ jiànmiàn? (at the casino)

B Identify the different sentence pattern for each sentence. Match the pattern with the sentence. Then try to identify each part of the sentence.

Pattern 1: Subject + action.

Pattern 2: Subject + time + action.

Pattern 3: Subject + time + place + action.

Pattern 4: Subject + time + verb 1 + place + verb 2.

Pattern 5: Subject + time + place + prepositional phrase + action.

Pattern 6: Subject + time + verb 1 + place + prepositional phrase + verb 2.

Ex: Wǒ míngtiān wǎnshàng yào zài túshūguǎn kànshū. Pattern 4

1 Wǒ měitiān zǎoshàng xǐhuān zài kāfēitīng hē kafēi. ______

2 Wǒ měitiān zǎoshàng zài kāfēitīng hē kafēi. ______

3 Wǒ měitiān zǎoshàng xǐhuān zài kāfēitīng gēn tóngxué hē kāfēi. ______

4 Wǒ měitiān zǎoshàng zài kāfēitīng gēn tóngxué hē kāfēi. ______

5 Wǒ měitiān zǎoshàng hē kāfēi. ______

6 Wǒ hē kāfēi. ______

C Put the sentence parts in order to create logical sentences.

Ex: tī zúqiú / zhègèxīngqī / Tā / zài zúqiúchǎng / yào / gēn tóngxué yīqǐ. → Tā zhègèxīngqī yào zài zúqiúchǎng gēn tóngxué yīqǐ tī zúqiú.

1 gēn wǒde jiàoliàn / míngtiān xiàwǔ / xiǎng yào / Wǒ / zài lánqiúchǎng / jiànmiàn.

______

2 qùnián / Tā / gēn péngyǒu / qìngzhù tāde shēngrì / zài Niǔyuēshì.

______

3 zài Běijīng Dàxué / míngnián / yào / Wǒde línjūde érzi / kāishǐ shàngxué.

______

4 Nǐ / xiǎng bù xiǎng / gēn wǒ yīqǐ / xiàgèyuè / zuò bāshī qù Jiāzhōu?

______

D 100.02 Listen to the questions on the audio. Then match each question with the correct answer.

1	____ Tā míngtiān yào qù mǎi cài ma?	**a**	tāde péngyǒu
2	____ Tā jīntiān wǎnshàng xiǎng bù xiǎng zài zúqiúchǎng liànxí zúqiú?	**b**	Yào
3	____ Tā huì shuō Zhōngwén ma?	**c**	zài cāntīng
4	____ Tā zài nǎ lǐ shàngbān?	**d**	Bú huì
5	____ Tā měitiān zǎoshàng zài huǒchēzhàn gēn shéi děng huǒchē?	**e**	měitiān zǎoshàng
6	____ Tā shénme shíhòu xǐhuān zài jiànshēnfáng gēn tāde tóngshì jiànshēn?	**f**	Xiǎng

"This was supposed to be the end of the book and the beginning of my retirement. And well, my life away from the garage was going just fine until my secretaries told me about all of the heartbreaking letters they'd been receiving from my fans. If that isn't bad enough, apparently some French teenager climbed the Eiffel Tower and has refused to come down until there's a Season 5; an American has sued me for being the cause of his depression; and worst of all, a 90-year-old woman has been camped outside of my garage for two months! Anyway, I was taught to put others before myself, so I'm coming back for Season 5 to further feed people's addiction to *Chinese with Mike.*"

Lesson 101

"My fans missed me."

Comparisons with Bǐ

How did I let you talk me into this? I've given you 100 earth-shattering episodes, and you still want more? Aren't you sick of me yet? Anyway, as you could see from the intro of the video lesson, life as a retiree was pretty rough, but I'll tell you more about that later. For now, let's kick off Season 5 with:

- making comparisons with **bǐ**
- learning some new measure words

Season 5 was never meant to be, my friends, but I suppose miracles do happen. I figured that by now I had given you your wings and it was time for you to leave the nest, but well, I guess I was wrong. I might as well get back to what I do best – teaching the world Chinese.

Recap

Congratulations! If you're still with me, you've gotten pretty advanced as far as sentence constructions go. In Season 1, we started building sentences with just a subject plus an action. By the end of Season 4 (Lesson 100), we had been including time, place, prepositional phrases, more verbs, etc. all in the same sentence! Season 5 is designed to fill in the gaps with a nice mix of useful words and grammar points that we'll smoothly integrate into what you already know. Let's do it.

We're going to be using a lot of adjectives this time around to compare two people / objects. Let's make sure you remember some.

A Given the adjective, write its opposite.

1 gāo ____________________

2 pàng ____________________

3 cōngmíng ____________________

4 qínláo ____________________

5 piàoliàng; shuài ____________________

B Do you remember the meaning of the following compound adjectives? Match them with their English meaning.

1 ____ hǎochī	a tasty (beverages)
2 ____ hǎohē	b "good sounding" (for songs, etc.)
3 ____ hǎotīng	c tasty (food)
4 ____ hǎokàn	d useful
5 ____ hǎowán	e "good read / see / watch"
6 ____ hǎoyòng	f fun

Words, phrases and stuff

101.01 Listen to the words and phrases then listen again and repeat.

Measure Words and Taste Words

bǐ	比	a comparative particle like "than"	**kǔ**	苦	*bitter*
bù	部	MW for movies	**là**	辣	*spicy*
shǒu	首	MW for songs	**tián**	甜	*sweet*
bēi	杯	MW for cups; glasses	**suān**	酸	*sour*

Patterns

Think of the word **bǐ** the same way you think of the word *than* in English. By itself, it doesn't have a meaning, but it's used to compare two people / objects.

Pattern: Subject 1 + **bǐ** + Subject 2 + adjective.

Examples:

1 Bàba **bǐ** māma gāo. (*Dad is taller than Mom.*)

2 Zhèbù diànyǐng **bǐ** nàbù diànyǐng hǎokàn. (*This movie is better than that movie.*)

101.02 Put together the following words to create a comparison. Say the sentences out loud then compare yourself to the native speakers.

Ex: (lánqiú / yǔmáoqiú) → Lánqiú bǐ yǔmáoqiú hǎowán. (Basketball is more fun than badminton.)

1 (dàxiàng / lǎohǔ) ____________________

2 (Yīngguó / Měiguó) ____________________

3 (cǎoméi / píngguǒ) ____________________

4 (tǔdòu / yángcōng) ____________________

Get to work

A Use the words in parentheses to create comparative sentences about food. Then translate.

Ex: (Zhèbēi shuǐ / nàbēi shuǐ; bīng) → Zhèbēi shuǐ bǐ nàbēi shuǐ bīng.
(This glass of water is colder than that glass of water.)

1 (Zhègè píngguǒ / zhègè cǎoméi; tián) ______
2 (Nàxiē níngméng / nàxiē chéngzi; suān) ______
3 (Zhèbēi kāfēi / nàbēi kāfēi; kǔ) ______
4 (Zhèwǎn tāng / nàwǎn tāng; là) ______

B 101.03 Listen and write down the two objects being compared in each sentence.

1 Zhèshuāng ______ bǐ nàshuāng ______ shūfú.
2 ______ bǐ ______ piányí.
3 Nǐde ______ bǐ wǒde ______ kuài.
4 Nàshuāng ______ bǐ zhèshuāng ______ hǎoyòng.

C Use the compound adjectives "hǎochī", "hǎohē", "hǎotīng" and "hǎokàn" to compare the following pairs of items.

Ex: Steak / chicken → Niúpái bǐ jīròu hǎochī.

1 (Red wine / white wine) ______
2 (My book / your book) ______
3 (This song / that song) ______
4 (French fries / vegetables) ______

D Write a message to someone about your friends and / or family. Use your wealth of adjectives to create comparative sentences about them.

Ex: Wǒ gēge bǐ wǒ dìdi shòu. (My older brother is thinner than my younger brother.)

Lesson 102

"Introducing my *CWM* blanket."

Comparatives and Superlatives

Before you go online and try to order your very own customized *Chinese with Mike* blanket, I'm afraid I have to be the one to break the bad news: it's not for sale. Like my wardrobe, the *CWM* blanket was designed especially for me, and if a million other people had one too, it wouldn't be cool anymore. Get a T-shirt or bandana instead. Anyway, let's work on:

- reviewing comparatives using **bǐ**
- forming superlatives using **zuì**

I'm sure you've already caught on just fine with **bǐ**, and I'm sure you'll do the same in this lesson when we take it one step further.

Recap

I didn't want to overwhelm you since we're just starting a new season of *Chinese with Mike*, so I kept the last lesson pretty simple. Do you remember comparatives? Have a look at these two sentences:

Wǒ bǐ nǐ lèi.	(lit. *I compared with you tired.*)	*I am more tired than you.*
Zhōngguó bǐ Rìběn dà.	(lit. *China compared with Japan big.*)	*China is bigger than Japan.*

You list the first subject + **bǐ** + the second subject + the adjective. Are you ready to rock the superlative? Me too.

But first put these sentences in the correct order to make logical comparisons. Then translate.

1 chángjǐnglù / hóuzi / gāo / bǐ ______________________

2 bǐ / māma / wàipó / niánqīng ______________________

3 yéye / bǐ / lǎo / bàba ______________________

Words, phrases and stuff

102.01 Listen to the words and phrases then listen again and repeat.

Comparatives, Superlatives, etc.

bǐ	比	a comparative particle (used to form *-er / more . . .* comparatives)
zuì	最	*the most;* (used to form *-est / most . . .* superlatives)
huāshēng	花生	*peanuts*
bāo	包	MW for packs / packages
shēngwùxué	生物学	*biology*

1 What is the catch-all measure word?

2 What measure word do they use in Taiwan for small objects?

Patterns

Last time we compared two people / objects using **bǐ**. For example, we can say **Bob bǐ Dan pàng** (*Bob is fatter than Dan*). If we then add a third person / object (See Pattern 1) to the original comparison, we can use **zuì** to form the superlative, which is used when you are comparing three or more things. **Bob bǐ Dan pàng. Steve zuì pàng** (*Bob is fatter than Dan. Steve is the fattest).* However, you may also use **zuì** by itself (See Patterns 2 and 3) as long as what you're comparing is clear.

Pattern 1: Person / Object 1 + **bǐ** + Person / Object 2 + adjective. **Person / Object 3** + **zuì** + adjective.

Pattern 2: Subject + **zuì** + adjective (If context of your comparison is clear).

Pattern 3: Subject + verb + **zuì** + adjective(de) + noun.

Examples:

1 Wǒde nánpéngyǒu **bǐ** wǒ **cōngmíng**. Mike Lǎoshī **zuì cōngmíng**. (*My boyfriend is smarter than I am. Mike Lǎoshī is the smartest.*)

2 Zhèwǎn tāng **zuì** hǎohē. (*This bowl of soup is the best / tastiest.*)

3 Éguó shì **zuì** dàde guójiā. (*Russia is the largest country.*)

Get to work

A Use the words provided to create first a comparative and then a superlative sentence.

Ex: (The cat / the dog / the rabbit; cute) → Māo bǐ gǒu kě'ài. Tùzi zuì kě'ài.

1 (The bear / the lion / the elephant; big) ______

2 (The chicken / the pig / the mouse; small) ______

3 (The goat / the turtle / the horse; fast) ______

4 (The tiger / the zebra / the panda; slow) ______

B Fill in the blanks with words to create logical comparisons.

Ex: Tāde ______ bǐ tāde ______ lǎo. ______ zuì lǎo. →
Tāde gūgu bǐ tāde jiějie lǎo. Tāde wàipó zuì lǎo.

1 Wǒde ______ bǐ wǒde ______ ǎi. ______ zuì ǎi.

2 Wǒmende ______ bǐ wǒmende ______ piányí. Wǒmende ______ zuì piányí.

3 ______ bǐ ______ hǎohē. ______ zuì hǎohē.

4 ______ bǐ ______ hǎochī. ______ zuì hǎochī.

C Take it a step further and use "dànshì" / "kěshì" to create comparative and superlative sentences about three objects in your house. Then translate the sentences.

Ex: Wǒde diànshì bǐ wǒde píngbǎn diànnǎo guì, dànshì wǒde bǐjìběn diànnǎo zuì guì.

1 ______

2 ______

3 ______

4 ______

D What's your family like? Use comparatives and superlatives to describe your family.

Ex: My dad is busier than my mom. I am the busiest. →
Wǒ bàba bǐ wǒ māma máng. Wǒ zuì máng.

______

☑ What do you know about China? First, do some research. Then use Pattern 3 (adjective-noun combos) to create sentences about a few of China's most distinctive features. HINT: Think about its people, cities, famous locations, food, etc.)

Ex: Běijīng shì zuì yǒuqùde chéngshì. (Beijing is the most interesting city.)
Běijīng yǒu zuì yǒumíngde dòngwùyuán. (Beijing has the most famous zoo.)
Shànghǎi yǒu zuì piàoliàngde hǎitān. (Shanghai has the most beautiful beach.)

______

______

______

______

"Which Chinese teacher rocks?"

Which One?

In case you haven't noticed, I'm in the midst of training for a triathlon. As you'd expect, I am favored heavily in my next competition, but I'm not about to let my intense workouts get in the way of my teaching. So let's:

- learn the question word **nǎ(yī)** (*which*)
- practice using a new MW **shuāng**

Time for another question word: *which?* (**nǎ**) Interestingly, the question word for *which* is the same word as the question word for *where* (**nǎ**) that we learned back in Season 1. You'll know whether **nǎ** means *which* or *where* depending on the context.

Recap

Before I let you loose on this lesson, let's make sure you remember some of our basic measure words that you'll need in this lesson. Fill in the blanks with your best definition of what each of these measure words is used to quantify.

1 běn ______________________

2 tái ______________________

3 bēi ______________________

4 píng ______________________

5 zhāng ______________________

6 bù ______________________

Words, phrases and stuff

103.01 Listen to the words and phrases then listen again and repeat.

Which Country?

nǎ(yī)	哪(一)	*which?*	**Ruìdiǎn**	瑞典	*Sweden*
nǎguó	哪国	*which country?*	**Fēnlán**	芬兰	*Finland*
chūshēng	出生	*to be born*	**shuāng**	双	MW for a pair of something
Nuówēi	挪威	*Norway*	**bǐsài**	比赛	*a match; competition*

I reviewed a lot of expressions in the video lesson. Let's see what you remember.

A What are two ways to ask someone's nationality?

____

____

B How do you ask . . .

1 Which day? ______________

2 Which year? ______________

3 How many days / months / years? ______________

You've already learned two of the most common ways to ask about one's **guójí** (*nationality*). You may also ask **Nǐde guójí shì shénme?** (*What is your nationality?*). If someone asks you this question, your response should be **Wǒde guójí shì** (country name) (*My nationality is (country name)*).

Patterns

Nǎ means *which*, but it is also common to attach **yī** (*one*) to the word for emphasis (**nǎyī**), especially if you're offering a choice between two objects. For example, you might ask **Nǐ shì nǎguó rén?** (*Which country are you from?*) when there are several possibilities. On the other hand, if someone offers you the choice between two apples, he or she may ask **Nǐ yào chī nǎyīgè píngguǒ?**

Pattern 1: **nǎ(yī)** + noun

Pattern 2: **nǎ(yī)** + MW + noun

Pattern 3: Object 1 + gēn / hé + object 2: Subject + verb + **nǎ(yī)** + MW + ?

Examples:

1 **Nǎ(yī)** tiān? (*Which day?*)

2 **Nǎ(yī)** gè rén? (*Which person?*)

3 Chǎofàn gēn / hé chǎomiàn. Nǐ yào chī **nǎyīgè**? (*Fried rice and fried noodles: Which one do you want to eat?*)

You might be wondering why we say **nǎ(yī)tiān** (*which day?*) and **nǎ(yī)nián** (*which year?*) instead of using **jǐtiān** and **jǐnián**, respectively, the same way we did with **jǐyuè** (*which month?*). The reason is that **jǐtiān** and **jǐnián** are used to ask about duration (*How many days?* One, two, three days, etc.) and (*How many years?* One, two, three years, etc.).

Get to work

A Match the following phrases with their translations.

1 ____ nǎgèyuè	**a** which cup of tea
2 ____ nǎgèxīngqī	**b** which book
3 ____ nǎběn shū	**c** which month
4 ____ nǎbēi chá	**d** which computer
5 ____ nǎzhāng chuáng	**e** which bed
6 ____ nǎtái diànnǎo	**f** which week
7 ____ nǎnián	**g** which year?

B Translate the following sentences into Chinese.

Ex: Which book is yours? → Nǎběn shū shì nǐde?

1 Which chair is hers? ______________________

2 Which man is your teacher? ______________________

3 Which woman is a doctor? ______________________

4 Which dog is your friend's? ______________________

C Given the answer, write the question using "nǎ(yī)".

Ex: Wǒ 1980 nián chūshēng. → Nǐ nǎ(yī) nián chūshēng?

1 Tā xīngqīwǔ yào qù pàiduì. ______

2 Zhèbù chēzi shì wǒde. ______

3 Nàshuāng hóngsède xiézi shì tāde. ______

4 Zhèzhāng zhǐ shì wǒ dìdide. ______

D Look at the pictures and form questions using "nǎyī", then translate.

Ex: Nǐ xiǎng kàn nǎyīběn shū?

1 (drink) ______

4 (buy) ______

2 (wear) ______

5 (drive) ______

3 (use) ______

6 (sell) ______

E 103.02 Listen to the conversation. Then answer the questions. Then listen again and repeat using the pause button.

1 Where was Pèishān born? ______

2 What is Pèishān's nationality? ______

3 When does Pèishān have class? ______

4 When does Dàwèi have class? ______

Lesson 104

"Which Chinese teacher has the best fashion sense?"

Comparisons with Bǐjiào

Yep, I'm still training for my **sānxiàngquánnéng**. If you can't translate that, go back to the previous lesson where I mentioned it in English. But here's a hint: **sān** means *three*, as you know . . . Anyway, let me change my clothes and let's:

- review the question word **nǎ**
- use **bǐjiào** to make comparisons

Now that you know comparatives, superlatives and the question word for *which*, it's time to bring this full circle. When we worked with comparatives and superlatives in the first two episodes of this season, we explicitly stated the people / objects we were comparing. This time I'll roll out a new word (**bǐjiào**) so we can make implicit comparisons.

Recap

The question word *which* is useful on its own, and you'll see how useful it is when making comparisons in this lesson. My best advice is to separate the times you need a measure word after **nǎ** and the times you don't. For example, you'll ask **nǎ(yī)tiān** (*which day*) **nǎ(yī)nián** (*which year*) without a measure word, but you'll need one for **nǎgèxīngqī** (*which week*) and **nǎgèyuè** (*which month*).

Let's recall how to use "bǐ", "zuì" and "nǎyī" correctly. Make your own sentences with each.

Ex: Nǐ bǐ wǒ yǒuqián. (You are richer than I.) Wǒde lǎobǎn zuì yǒuqián. (My boss is the richest of all.)
Nǐmen nǎyītiān yào chūfā? (Which day are you guys leaving / setting off?)

1 (bǐ) Nàzhī gǒu bǐ wǒde gǒu dà. ______________________

2 (zuì) Zhèjiàn chènshān zuì piányí. ______________________

3 (nǎ(yī)) Nǎ(yī)běn Zhōngwén kèběn shì nǐde? ______________________

Words, phrases and stuff

104.01 Listen to the words and phrases then listen again and repeat.

Clothes

bǐjiào	比较	*to compare / contrast; relatively*
jiàn	件	MW for items of clothing
máoyī	毛衣	*sweater*
xīzhuāng	西装	*suit*
yángzhuāng	洋装	*dress*

Patterns

In this lesson, we are using **bǐjiào** to compare two objects when it's clear which two objects we're referring to. For example, if I know which two cars we are comparing, I can say **Zhèbù chēzi bǐjiào kuài** (*This car is faster*). Similarly, if I know which two watermelons I'm comparing, I can say **Nàgè xīguā bǐjiào tián** (*That watermelon is sweeter*).

Pattern 1:	Nǎ + (MW) + noun + **bǐjiào** + adjective?
Pattern 2:	Noun + **bǐjiào** + adjective.
Pattern 3:	Subject 1+ **bǐ** + subject 2 + adjective (used to make comparisons when two people / objects are explicitly stated).
Pattern 4:	Subject 1 / 2 + **bǐjiào** + adjective (used to make an implicit comparison when things you're comparing is clear).

Examples:

1 Nǎzhī bǐ **bǐjiào** hǎoyòng?

2 Zhèzhī bǐ **bǐjiào** hǎoyòng.

3 Wǒde nǚpéngyǒu **bǐ** nǐde nǚpéngyǒu piàoliàng.

4 Wǒde nǚpéngyǒu **bǐjiào** piàoliàng.

Get to work

A Complete the sentences with "bǐ" or "bǐjiào".

Ex: Nǎzhī qiānbǐ bǐjiào hǎoyòng?

1 Zhèshuāng kuàizi ____________ nǐde kuàizi hǎoyòng.

2 Nàzhāng zhuōzi ____________ cháng.

3 Nǎtái bǐjìběn diànnǎo ____________ piányí?

4 Nǎyījiàn T-xù ____________ shūfú?

5 Dàwèide fángzi ____________ Pèishānde fángzi dà.

6 Qù dòngwùyuán ____________ kàn qiúsài hǎowán.

B Complete the sentences with words that make sense. Then translate the sentences.

Ex: Wǒ gēge bǐ wǒ dìdi qínláo, dànshì wǒ bàba zuì qínláo.

1 Wǒ ____________ zhèjiàn chènshān, yě xǐhuān zhèjiàn máoyī. Nǎyījiàn ____________ shūfú?

2 Tāmende lǜchá hé tāmende kāfēi dōu hěn yǒumíng. ____________ gè bǐjiào hǎohē?

3 Wǒ jiějie, mèimei, háiyǒu gēge dōu kāi xīnde chēzi. Wǒ gēgede chēzi ____________ hǎokàn.

4 Yīnwèi tā hěn yǒuqián, suǒyǐ tāde xīzhuāng ____________ wǒde xīzhuāng guì.

C Find the mistake in the sentences below and change it to the correct word. If there are no mistakes, leave as is.

bǐ
Ex: Wǒ mèimei ~~bǐjiào~~ tāde péngyǒu lǎnduò.

1 Wǒ nǚ'ér bǐ wǒ érzi shòu. Wǒ nǚ'ér zuì shòu.

2 Diànyǐngyuàn yǒu hěn duō xīnde diànyǐng. Nǎbù zuì hǎokàn?

3 Wǒ xiǎng yào mǎi shǒujī. Nǎtái bǐ hǎoyòng?

4 Wǒ xǐhuān dǎ lánqiú kěshì wǒ bǐ xǐhuān kàn lánqiúsài.

D Read the paragraph about Lily and Cathy and list seven differences between them.

Lily bǐ Cathy gāoxìng. Lily bǐ Cathy gāo. Lily bǐ Cathy shòu. Lilyde ěrhuán bǐ Cathyde ěrhuán dà. Lilyde tóufǎ bǐ Cathyde tóufǎ cháng. Lilyde xiézi bǐjiào xīn. Lilyde yángzhuāng yě bǐjiào piàoliàng.

1 ____

2 ____

3 ____

4 ____

5 ____

6 ____

7 ____

Individualism vs. Collectivism

"Even though Mike Lǎoshī likes to boast about being the best Chinese teacher in the world, he really has to tone it down when he visits China. Why? Most Western countries (like the United States and much of Europe) are individualist cultures in which personal achievements / success take priority over the goals of the culture as a whole. On the other hand, China is a collectivist culture in which individual pursuits are sacrificed in favor of the collective society's well-being. Societal harmony can only be achieved if everyone performs his or her individual role and places more focus on the greater good. Due to Western influence, however, China is gradually becoming a more individualist society."

Lesson 105

"Which teacher do you like the most?"

Preferences and Favorites

We've been cruising right along here with forming comparatives and superlatives in Chinese, so let's keep the momentum going. Oh, in case you were interested, I won the triathlon I'd been training for and set a new world record. Who cares? I'm ready to teach you to:

- use **bǐjiào** and **zuì** with verbs

This time we'll use some of our new vocabulary (**bǐjiào** and **zuì**) to talk about preferences and the things you like the most in your life. Here's one I hear pretty often: **Wǒ zuì xǐhuān Mike Lǎoshī!** Can you guess what that means?

Recap

We've used other adverbs, such as "hěn", "fēicháng" and "mán" to modify verbs in previous lessons. Let's make sure you get the general concept before we dive into these new ones, so translate the following expressions for me.

1 Wǒ hěn huì shuō Zhōngwén. ______

2 Tā mán xǐhuān zhǔfàn. ______

3 Tāmen fēicháng xǐhuān dǎ lánqiú. ______

4 Wǒ mèimei hěn xiǎng qù kàn yǎnchànghuì. ______

Words, phrases and stuff

105.01 Listen to the words and phrases then listen again and repeat.

Like and Prefer

bǐjiào xǐhuān	比较喜欢	*to prefer; to like more*
zuì xǐhuān	最喜欢	*to like the most*
yǐnliào	饮料	*a beverage; a drink*
Āijí	埃及	*Egypt*
Yìndù	印度	*India*

The word **bǐjiào** has a variety of uses, and I will get to others later in this season. For now, you should know one important function of this word: to make implicit comparisons between two people / objects. For example, you learned in Lesson 101 how to say **Wǒ bǐ nǐ máng** (*I am busier than you*). With **bǐjiào**, you can indicate that you are busier than someone without explicitly mentioning him or her in the same sentence. For instance, your friend tells you **Wǒ hěn máng** and you reply **Wǒ bǐjiào máng**, indicating that you are busier (than your friend). With **bǐjiào**, the context of the comparison is clear.

Patterns

As I mentioned, we generally use **bǐjiào** – and in this case **bǐjiào xǐhuān** – (see Pattern 1) to talk about a preference of one object over another when the two objects you're comparing are clear. We use **zuì xǐhuān** (see Pattern 2) to indicate which you like the most / best of all.

Pattern 1: Subject + **bǐjiào xǐhuān** + (verb) + object.

Pattern 2: Subject + **zuì xǐhuān** + (verb) + object.

Examples:

1 Wǒ **bǐjiào xǐhuān** dǎ lánqiú. (*I prefer to play basketball.*)

2 Wǒ **zuì xǐhuān** dǎ bàngqiú. (*I like to play baseball the best.*)

Get to work

A Unscramble the sentences with "bǐjiào xǐhuān" and "zuì xǐhuān".

Ex: chī / zhūròu / bǐjiào / tā / xǐhuān. Tā bǐjiào xǐhuān chī zhūròu.

1 Wǒ xǐhuān / wǒ / kàn Měiguó diànyǐng / kàn diànyǐng / dànshì / zuì xǐhuān ____________.

2 zuì / Tā /xǐhuān / kǎlāOK / chàng ____________.

3 Nǐmen / bǐjiào / shàngwǎng / háishì / xǐhuān / kàn diànshì ____________?

4 hē hóngpútáojiǔ / Wǒ bàba / hē píjiǔ / xǐhuān / dànshì / wǒ / bǐjiào xǐhuān ____________.

B Complete and translate the conversation.

A: Nǐ ____________ qù yóulèchǎng háishì bówùguǎn? Wǒ xiǎng qù yóulèchǎng. Wǒ bǐjiào xǐhuān qù nà lǐ.

B: ____________________?

A: Yīnwèi yóulèchǎng ____________ bówùguǎn hǎowán.

B: ____________ ma? Zhēnde. Bówùguǎn tài wúliáo.

C Use the words in parentheses to answer the following questions.

Ex: Chén Xiānshēng bǐjiào xǐhuān kāichē háishì qí mótuōchē? (ride a motorcycle) →
Chén Xiānshēng bǐjiào xǐhuān qí mótuōchē.

1 Nǐ zuì xǐhuān zuò shénme? (play the piano)

2 Nǐmen bǐjiào xǐhuān lìshǐ kè háishì shùxué kè? (math class)

3 Jīnnián xiàtiān nǐ bǐjiào xiǎng qù Àozhōu hé Niǔ Xīlán háishì Āijí hé Yìndù? (Australia and New Zealand)

4 Tāmen zuì xǐhuān zài nǎ lǐ chī zǎocān? (at home)

D **What are some of your favorite things to do? Write a short blog entry about yourself and some of your preferences.**

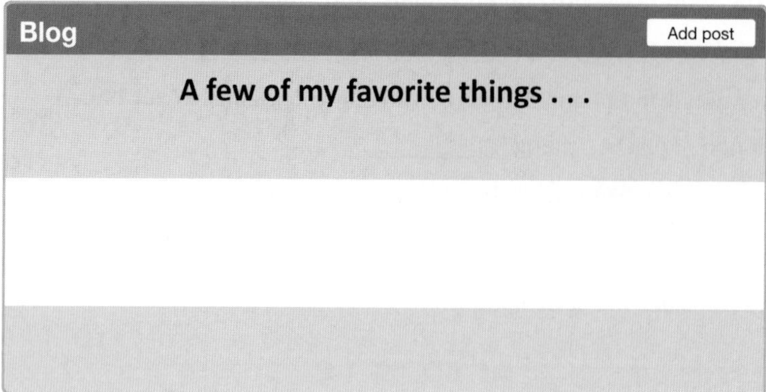

Lesson 106

"Mike Lǎoshī gèng lèi."

Gèng

Lately, we've been taping the show in the evening so I can practice for the croquet tournament. However, today we are doing a matinee performance, and, as you can see, these kids just can't wait to:

- learn the adverb **gèng**

Time for another important adverb: **gèng**. You'll see it's similar to **bǐjiào** when it's used to form implicit comparisons. The main thing to note is we use the word **gèng** to mean *even more . . .* when we have already established the fact that two people / objects are similar. For example, if we already know that you and I are both hungry, I can use **gèng** to emphasize that I am even hungrier. Similarly, if we know that we are both intelligent, I can use **gèng** to emphasize that I am even more intelligent.

Recap

Last time you learned another important use of **bǐjiào** and **zuì** when we combined them with verbs instead of adjectives to indicate preferences and favorites. Now you not only can say **Wǒ bǐjiào shuài** (*I am more handsome*) and **Wǒ zuì shuài** (*I am the most handsome*), but also **Wǒ bǐjiào xǐhuān chī Zhōngguó cài** (*I prefer eating Chinese food*).

For this lesson, however, you'll need to know the basics about **bǐ** comparisons. Let's make sure you do.

Complete the sentences with the correct definitions. Then translate the sentences.

1 Zhèzhāng yǐzi bǐ nàzhāng yǐzi ______ (comfortable) ______________________________

2 Zhèxiē yīngtáo bǐ nàxiē yīngtáo ______ (sweet) ______________________________

3 Zhètái píngbǎn diànnǎo bǐ nàtai píngbǎn diànnǎo ______ (expensive) ______________________________

4 Zhèpíng niúnǎi bǐ nàpíng niúnǎi ______ (cold) ______________________________

Words, phrases and stuff

106.01 Listen to the words and phrases then listen again and repeat.

Contrasting Things

gèng	更	*even more*
(qiáng)zhuàng	(强)壮	*strong; powerful*
(shòu)ruò	(瘦)弱	*thin and weak*
yìng	硬	*hard* (physically)
ruǎn	软	*soft*
xiǎomāo	小猫	*kitten*
xiǎogǒu	小狗	*puppy*
zhuōqiú	桌球	*table tennis; ping-pong; billiards* (in mainland China)

Patterns

Gèng is useful for making a comparison between two people / objects that have already been established as being similar in some way. For example, if we already know that two cars are both fast, we can use **gèng** to show one is even faster: **Zhèbù chēzi bǐ nàbù chēzi gèng kuài!** Similarly, we can say **Wǒde nǚ'érde jiǎo bǐ wǒde érzide jiǎo gèng xiǎo**. If you remember your body parts, you should be able to translate that one on your own!

Pattern 1: Subject + **gèng** + adjective.

Pattern 2: Subject 1 + **bǐ** + Subject 2 + **gèng** + adjective.

Examples:

1 Tā nǎinai **gèng** lǎo. (His / Her grandma is even older.)

2 Tā nǎinai **bǐ** wǒ nǎinai **gèng** lǎo. (His / Her grandma is even older than my grandma.)

106.02 Listen to what Dàwèi and Pèishān like to do and complete the sentences.

1 Dàwèi xǐhuān ____________ dànshì tā gèng xǐhuān ____________.

2 Pèishān xǐhuān ____________ kěshì tā gèng xǐhuān ____________.

3 Dàwèi xǐhuān ____________ dànshì tā gèng xǐhuān ____________.

4 Pèishān xǐhuān ____________ kěshì tā gèng xǐhuān ____________.

Get to work

A Translate the following sentences.

Ex: I love playing tennis, but I love playing table tennis even more. →
Wǒ ài dǎ wǎngqiú dànshì wǒ gèng ài dǎ zhuōqiú.

1 My brothers and I are all hungry, but my friend is even hungrier.

____

2 We are both strong, but our classmate is even stronger.

____

3 Your (pl.) girlfriends are all beautiful, but Mike Lǎoshī's girlfriend is even more beautiful.

____

4 Both of my cars are old, but my boyfriend's car is even older.

____

B Use the two subjects and adjectives in parentheses to write complete sentences.

Ex: (today's weather; yesterday's weather; even hotter) →
Jīntiān tiānqì bǐ zuótiān tiānqì gèng rè.

1 (your puppy; your kitten; even smaller)

____

2 (table tennis; bowling; even more fun)

____

3 (Chinese class; English class; even more difficult)

____

4 (my laptop computer; my tablet computer; even more expensive)

____

C Unscramble the following sentences.

Ex: chuáng / nàzhāng / wǒde / bǐ / chuáng / ruǎn / gèng →
Nàzhāng chuáng bǐ wǒde chuáng gèng ruǎn. OR Wǒde chuáng bǐ nàzhāng chuáng gèng ruǎn.

1 gèng / kāfēi / zhèbēi / bǐ / kāfēi / nàbēi / tàng

____

2 yìng / yǐzi / zhèzhāng / nàzhāng / gèng / yǐzi / bǐ

____

3 nàběn / gèng / hǎokàn / shū

____

4 érzide / bǐ / fángjiān / wǒ / gānjìng / wǒ / fángjiān / nǚ'érde / gèng

____

D Complete the sentences.

1 Wǒ xǐhuān kàn __________ dànshì wǒ gèng xǐhuān kàn __________

2 Wǒ hěn xǐhuān chī __________ dànshì wǒ gèng xǐhuān __________

3 Wǒ mán xǐhuān hē __________ dànshì wǒ gèng xǐhuān __________

4 Wǒ chāo xǐhuān dǎ __________ dànshì wǒ gèng xǐhuān __________

> We learned in Lesson 104 that the Chinese adhere to collectivist values, which emphasize the achievement of the society as a whole more than individual goals and accomplishments. As a result, the Chinese are very modest. For instance, you'll rarely hear Chinese people say **xièxie!** when others give them compliments. Instead, the Chinese often say **nǎ lǐ?!** (lit. *Where?!*) and politely deflect the compliment. On the other hand, you'll quickly find that the Chinese are quick to compliment **wàiguórén** (*foreigners*) on their Chinese-speaking abilities, even if they only know two or three sentences in Chinese. So, there is no excuse for you not to start practicing your amazing Mandarin!

Lesson 107

"No one can be the same as me."

Yīyàng

Yes, we did suffer a casualty about seven minutes into the video lesson when I almost took my producer's head off with a marker, but fortunately, I was the only one left in stitches. The good news is we were able to finish the video so you could learn:

- to use the word **yīyàng** to express "sameness"
- learn the MW **tiáo** to describe long, thin objects

You know how to form all kinds of comparatives and superlatives. Sweet! You should know how to tell me that the weather today is better than it was yesterday, that your mom is the most beautiful woman in the world, and that you are even cooler than Mike Lǎoshī (which would be a lie, of course). Today we'll talk about how to say two people / things are the same using our new word: **yīyàng**.

Recap

If you were conscious during Lesson 97, you should remember that both **gēn** and **hé** can mean *and* in Chinese. You'll need to make sure you're on the same page before we dive into our new sentence constructions with **yīyàng**.

Are the following "gēn" / "hé" phrases translated correctly?

1 Lín Xiānshēng hé tāde tàitai ____________ (*Mr Lin and his wife*)
2 Wáng Tàitai gēn tāde xiānshēng ____________ (*Mrs Wang and her student*)
3 Chén Yīshēng hé tāde lǎopó ____________ (*Doctor Chen and his teacher*)
4 Lǐ Jiàoshòu gēn tāde lǎogōng ____________ (*Professor Li and her husband*)

Words, phrases and stuff

107.01 Listen to the words and phrases then listen again and repeat.

Big, Small and Thin

yīyàng	一样	*the same*	**xiǎo**	小	*small; little; young*
Zhījiāgē	芝加哥	*Chicago*	**tiáo**	条	MW for long, thin objects; (e.g. fish, road)
dà	大	*big; large; old*	**lù**	路	*road*

Patterns

We use Pattern 1 to talk about how two people / objects are the same (when we already know the context or the reason for *why* they are the same). In Patterns 2 and 3, however, we include a specific adjective so that we can specify exactly how two or more people / objects are the same.

Pattern 1: Subject 1 + **gēn** / **hé** + subject 2 + (bù) **yīyàng**

Pattern 2: Subject 1 + **gēn** / **hé** + subject 2 + **yīyàng** + **adjective**

Pattern 3: **Zhè** / **Nà** + number + **MW** + subject + **yīyàng** + **adjective**

Examples:

1a Nǐ **gēn / hé** wǒ **yīyàng**.
(*You and I are the same.*)

1b Nǐ **gēn / hé** wǒ bù **yīyàng**.
(*You and I are NOT the same.*)

2 Nǐ **gēn / hé** wǒ **yīyàng** gāo.
(*You are just as tall as I am.*)

3 **Zhè** sì**zhāng** chuáng **yīyàng piányí**.
(*These four beds are equally inexpensive.*)

When we state in Chinese that two people / objects are the same, we use the word **gēn** (*and; with*) to join them, but it is also acceptable to use **hé** (*and*) in place of **gēn**.

107.2 Listen to a few people making comparisons. Write down in Chinese what you hear. Then translate into English. Good luck.

1 ______

______

2 ______

______

3 ______

______

4 ______

______

5 ______

______

Get to work

A Translate the following sentences using the various meanings of "dà" and "xiǎo".

Ex: Nǐde bǐjìběn diànnǎo gēn wǒde bǐjìběn diànnǎo yīyàng xiǎo. →
Your laptop computer is just as small as mine.

1 Tāde nánpéngyǒu gēn tā yīyàng dà.

2 Nàzhāng yǐzi hé zhèzhāng yǐzi yīyàng xiǎo.

3 Zhèliǎnggè chéngshì yīyàng dà.

4 Zhèxiē chuáng yīyàng xiǎo.

B Form your own sentences with "yīyàng" using the words in parentheses.

Ex: (My older brother; my younger brother; handsome) →
Wǒ gēge gēn (hé) wǒ dìdi yīyàng shuài.

1 (Your class; his class; easy)

2 (My cell phone; my girlfriend's cell phone; small)

3 (This chicken; that beef; tasty)

4 (This green fish; that blue fish; long)

5 (This road; that road; good)

C Use the phrases given to form your own sentences.

Ex: (These three books . . .) → Zhè sānběn shū dōu hěn hǎokàn.

1 (Those two cars . . .) ______

2 (These five dogs . . .) ______

3 (These ten people . . .) ______

4 (Those eight students . . .) ______

D 107.03 Listen to the comparisons and write down what you hear.

1 ______

2 ______

3 ______

4 ______

Lesson 108

"My advanced class"

Review of Comparisons

Just after I finished complaining about those kids interrupting my croquet game, somehow I agree to attend a daycare's end-of-the-year picnic and deliver a quick lesson on body parts. I'm such a nice guy. In fact, I'm so nice that I am going to let you:

- review all patterns on comparatives

Let's see what you remember. Don't let me down.

Recap

Pop Quiz on Yīyàng!

If I I'm 21 years old, and I say to you, "Wǒ gēn nǐ yīyàng dà", how old are you? If I'm 185 cm (6'1") tall, and I say to you, "Wǒ gēn nǐ yīyàng gāo", how tall are you? If you answered incorrectly, go back and review the last lesson and join the big boys (and girls) when you're ready.

Words, phrases and stuff

108.01 Listen to the words and phrases then listen again and repeat.

Soccer

zúqiúsài 足球赛 *soccer game; soccer match / (football Br)*

Patterns

I recommend at this point you go back and review of all patterns in Season 5 thus far (Lessons 101–7).

Match the words for comparatives we have covered to their definitions.

1 ____ bǐ	a which?
2 ____ zuì	b the most
3 ____ gèng	c the same
4 ____ yīyàng	d even more
5 ____ nǎ(yī)	e comparative particle

Get to work

A Complete the sentences with words from the box.

bǐ	bǐjiào	zuì	gèng	yīyàng	nǎ(yī)

1 Nǐ bǐjiào xǐhuān ______ bù chēzi?
2 Zhègè chéngzi ______ nàgè chéngzi ______ suān.
3 Dàwèi hěn cōngmíng. Tāde gēge bǐ tā ______ cōngmíng. Tāde jiějie ______ cōngmíng.
4 Diànyǐngyuàn yǒu liǎngbù diànyǐng. Nǐ ______ xiǎng kàn nǎbù?

B Locate and fix the errors. Then rewrite the sentences correctly.

Ex: Tā bǐjiào tā jiějie shòu. (Error: bǐjiào; Correction: bǐ)

1 Kàn zúqiúsài bǐ kàn lánqiúsài zuì hǎowán. ______
2 Bàba hé māma dà yīyàng. ______
3 Wǒde péngyǒu xǐhuān bǐjiào chuān hēisède xīzhuāng. ______
4 Pèishān bǐjiào tāde tóngxué cōngmíng. ______

C Given the words in parentheses, form your own sentences to compare people you know.

Ex: (bǐ; gèng) Wǒde péngyǒu bǐ wǒ gèng máng.

1 (bǐ) ______
2 (bǐ; gèng) ______
3 (bǐ; zuì) ______
4 (yīyàng) ______

Lesson 109

"Meet my newest pupil."

The Particles A, Wa, and Ba

Due to the recent economic downturn, a lot of people have had to slow down on luxury purchases (like private Chinese lessons with me) so I've had to take on some non-traditional students. I don't mind – I need money to refinish my whiteboard. Anyway, hope you're ready to:

- use the particles **a**, **wa**, and **ba** to express exclamation and surprise

We've learned some particles in Chinese before, most importantly **ma** and **ne**. Here I'm going to introduce three more (**a**, **wa**, and **ba**) which will allow you to spice up your everyday conversations in Chinese and sound more like a native speaker. Our new particles are helpful in adding emphasis to statements and slightly altering your tone.

Recap

Define the particles you already know. What are they used for?

1 ma ______________________________

2 bǐ ______________________________

3 ne ______________________________

4 de ______________________________

Words, phrases and stuff

109.01 **Listen to the words and phrases then listen again and repeat.**

Particles

a / ā	啊	particle expressing exclamation / surprise
ba	吧	particle expressing a suggestion / command
wā	哇	particle meaning "Wow"
shàng	上	*to go to; to use (the bathroom)*
zǒu ba	走吧	*Let's go!*
dài	带	*to bring; to carry*

Patterns

Pattern 1 is used to add exclamation / enthusiasm to a statement whereas Pattern 2 is used to indicate surprise. Last, Pattern 3 is used to either make a suggestion or reluctantly agree to a suggestion.

Pattern 1: Sentence + **a**!

Pattern 2: **Ā / Wā** + sentence!

Pattern 3: Sentence + **ba**.

Examples:

1 Hǎo **a**! (OK!)

2 **Ā / Wā**, nǐde fángzi hǎo dà!

3 Wǒmen qù kàn diànyǐng **ba**.

Wā is another important particle that is similar to the particle **ā** when **ā** is used to express surprise at the beginning of a sentence. As you can see, **wā** is very similar in pronunciation to the English interjection *wow* and is used the same way.

Get to work

A Fill in the blanks with "a" or "ba".

Ex: Xiǎohái hěn kě. Wǒmen qù mǎi yínliào ba.

1 Tiānqì hǎo rè! Wǒmen qù chī bīngqílín ______!

2 Nǐ xiǎng bù xiǎng gēn wǒ yīqǐ qù dòngwùyuán? Xiǎng ______!

3 Wǒ kě bù kěyǐ hē shuǐ? Kěyǐ ______!

4 Nǐde Zhōngwén bú tài hǎo. Qù fùxí nǐde Zhōngwén zuòyè ______.

B Match the possible answers with the statements.

1 Wǒmen yīqǐ kàn *Chinese with Mike*!

2 Wǒ xiàgèxīngqīliù yào qù wǒde péngyǒude hūnlǐ.

3 Wǒde nǚpéngyǒu hěn è.

4 Wǒmen jiā bù xǐhuān zuò fēijī.

5 Wǒde chēzi tài jiù.

a Qù mǎi xīnde yángzhuāng ba.

b Hǎo a!

c Zuò huǒchē ba.

d Qù mǎi xīnde ba.

e Dài tā qù chīfàn ba.

C Use "ba" to provide solutions to the following sentences.

Ex: Jīntiān shì wǒde tàitaide shēngrì. → Qù mǎi lǐwù ba.

1 Wǒ hěn lèi. ____________________

2 Tāde yáchǐ hěn tòng. ____________________

3 Nǐde māma hěn máng. ____________________

4 Wǒ méi yǒu qián. ____________________

D 109.02 First, listen to the conversation. Then answer the questions. Then listen again and repeat.

1 What time of day is it? ____________________

2 Who is hungry? ____________________

3 What does Pèishān suggest they do? ____________________

4 What does Dàwèi like to eat most? ____________________

5 Why doesn't Dàwèi like pancakes? ____________________

E How would you respond if someone were to suggest the following? Use "hǎo a!" or "hǎo ba" to answer.

1 Let's study Chinese! ____________________

2 Let's go to the beach! ____________________

3 Let's throw a huge party when my parents are out of town! ____________________

4 Let's clean the house! ____________________

"I will rock you!"

The Future Tense

Unfortunately, these days it's hard for me to leave my garage without being recognized and mobbed by fans, so I do what I can to entertain myself in the garage. Anyway, let me finish this football game (I'm beating myself 9–8) and I promise we'll soon:

- learn another way to express future tense

I'm bringing back a word you learned in Season 1: **huì**. If you don't remember what it means, allow me to **mà** (*scold*) you for an hour for not remembering. After that's taken care of, I'll remind you that it means *can* or *to know how to (do something)*. You then should be able to translate the following with no problem: 1 **Wǒ huì jiǎng Zhōngwén** and 2 **Wǒ bú huì kāichē**. In this lesson, we are getting into a totally different definition of **huì**. It means *will* and is used to express future tense. **Huì** is used pretty much the same way that *will* is in English, so you shouldn't have any problems.

Recap

Last time we learned a few important particles: **a**, **wa**, and **ba**, which are used to express exclamation, surprise, suggestion, etc. Try incorporating them into your conversations and impress your Chinese-speaking friends! If you're really good, you might even impress me.

Words, phrases and stuff

110.01 Listen to the words and phrases then listen again and repeat.

Future Weather

huì 会 *will (future tense)*

xiàyǔ 下雨 *to rain*

xiàxuě 下雪 *to snow*

Patterns

We learned in Season 2 that we can express the future tense by using **yào** (*to be going to; to be about to*). **Huì** is basically interchangeable with **yào**, but using **huì** is a little stronger. By using **huì**, you are indicating that you are very committed to your plan and won't let anything stop you from accomplishing it.

Pattern 1: Subject + **huì** + (action) + ma?

Pattern 2: Huì / Bú huì. Subject + **(bú) huì** + (action).

Pattern 3: Subject + **huì bú huì** + (action)?

Pattern 4: **Huì / Bú huì**. Subject + **(bú) huì** + (action).

Examples:

1 Wáng Xiānshēng míngtiān **huì** qù shàngbān ma?

2 Huì / Bú huì. Wáng Xiānshēng míngtiān **(bú) huì** qù shàngbān.

3 Nǐ xīngqīsān **huì bú huì** qù chāojí shìchǎng mǎi cài?

4 **Huì / Bú huì**. Wǒ xīngqīsān **(bú) huì** qù chāojí shìchǎng mǎi cài.

Remember from last season that if a sentence contains two verbs AND a location, we must split the verbs. For example, the sentence **Wǒ yào chīfàn** has two verbs (**yào** and **chīfàn**). If we also include a place in the sentence, we must split **yào** and **chīfàn** by inserting the place. Therefore, we would say **Wǒ yào zài cāntīng chīfàn** (*I want to eat at a / the restaurant*). Two-verb sentences with **huì** follow the same pattern. **Wǒ huì zài wǒ jiā shuìjiào** (*I will sleep at my house*).

Get to work

A Use the words in parentheses to make sentences about your future plans.

Ex: (This evening) → Wǒ jīntiān wǎnshàng huì xǐwǎn. (This evening I will do the dishes.)

1 (Tomorrow) ______

2 (Next week) ______

3 (Next month) ______

4 (Next year) ______

B Give long answers to the following questions using the words in parentheses.

Ex: Tā jīnnián wǔyuè huì bú huì bìyè? (No) → Bú huì. Tā jīnnián wǔyuè bú huì bìyè.

1 Tā xiàgèyuè huì kāishǐ gōngzuò ma? (Yes) ______

2 Míngtiān huì bú huì xiàyǔ? (Yes) ______

3 Tāmen jīntiān wǎnshàng huì zài diànyǐngyuàn kàn diànyǐng ma? (Yes) ______

4 Xiàgèxīngqīyī huì xiàxuě ma? (No) ______

C Decide whether the meaning of "huì" means *will* or *can* based on the context.

Ex: Yīnwèi tiānqì hěn wēnnuǎn, suoyi míngtiān bú huì xiàxuě. **A:** Will

1 Nǐde nánpéngyǒu huì bú huì shuō Rìwén?

2 Yīnwèi wǒ nǎinai bú huì kāichē, suǒyǐ tā méiyǒu jiàzhào.

3 Wǒ xiàgèyuè bú huì qù Jiānádà.

4 Wǒ bù zhīdào wǒ érzi jīnnián huì bú huì jiéhūn.

jiàzhào = driver's license

E 110.02 Listen. Then list three things that Dàwèi will and will not do in the future.

Dàwèi will . . .

1 ______

2 ______

3 ______

Dàwèi will not . . .

1 ______

2 ______

3 ______

"A thing of the past"

Yǐqián (General Past)

So, I try to beautify an ugly brick wall and get busted for vandalizing public property. What's this world coming to?! Anyway, I've got to do community service, so I've agreed to donate a few autographed photos to the silent auction at the local police department's annual charity event. Could have been worse. For now, though, let's:

- learn the word **yǐqián** to talk about the general past

We've talked a little bit about verb tense in Chinese, but so far we've stuck mainly to the present tense, which is used to state general facts (**Mike Lǎoshī shì zuì hǎode Zhōngwén lǎoshī**) or habitual actions (**Wǒ měitiān wǎnshàng chī wǎncān**). We have used time words (e.g. **zuótiān**, **míngtiān**, **xiàgèyuè**, **qùnián**, etc.) to indicate events that occurred in the past or will occur in the future, but we have never learned how to talk about the general past without giving a specific time. That's about to change, as you can now use **yǐqián** to make statements about the general past.

Recap

We learned another meaning of the word **huì** last time, and I'm sure you found it laughably easy. That's why I only devoted one lesson to it – I didn't want to insult your intelligence. Remember that **huì** has multiple meanings, including *can; know how to* (See Season 2) and *will*, when it's used to express future tense. Can you translate this? **Yīnwèi wǒ bú huì shuō Zhōngwén, suǒyǐ míngtiān wǒ huì kāishǐ shàng Zhōngwén kè.**

A Use time words you're already familiar with to translate the following sentences in two different ways – one with the time + subject + action pattern and one with the subject + time + action pattern.

Ex: We would like to watch a movie this evening. → Jīntiān wǎnshàng wǒmen xiǎng kàn diànyǐng.
OR Wǒmen jīntiān wǎnshàng xiǎng kàn diànyǐng.

1 I am going to drive (a car) to work today.

2 On Monday evenings I play soccer.

3 She will go abroad next year.

4 He has to go to the bank tomorrow.

5 They wait for the bus every morning.

6 We are going to a wedding next month.

Words, phrases and stuff

111.01 Listen to the words and phrases then listen again and repeat.

The Past

yǐqián 以前 *before; in the past*

juéde 觉得 *to think; to feel*

zhù 住 *to live*

Patterns

Yǐqián's placement in your sentence is the same as other time words (e.g. **jīnnián**, **shànggèyuè**, **xīngqīrì**, etc.) that you already know. You may place it before or after the subject. If you place it before the subject, you are emphasizing the time; if you place it after the subject, you are emphasizing the subject.

Pattern 1: **Yǐqián** + subject + action.

Pattern 2: Subject + **yǐqián** + action.

Examples:

1 **Yǐqián** wǒ hěn ǎi. (*I used to be short.*)

2 Tā **yǐqián** shì wǒ zuì hǎode péngyǒu. (*He / She used to be my best friend.*)

Get to work

A Choose "yǐqián" or the specific time word given to complete the sentences. Then translate them into English.

Ex: Wǒ māma (yǐqián / zuótiān) zhù zài Zhōngguó. → yǐqián

1 (Yǐqián/Míngtiān) wǒ mán xǐhuān dǎ zhuōqiú. ____________________

2 (Yǐqián/Shànggèxīngqī) wǒ hěn qiángzhuàng. ____________________

3 (Yǐqián/Hòutiān) huì xiàyǔ. ____________________

4 Wǒ mèimei (hòunián/yǐqián) xǐhuān wán yángwáwa. ____________________

B Tell Mike Lǎoshī about your past. Use "yǐqián" to make five sentences.

Ex: Wǒ yǐqián hěn yǒuqián. OR Wǒ yǐqián hěn xiǎng xué Xībānyáwén.

1 ____________________

2 ____________________

3 ____________________

4 ____________________

5 ____________________

C Given the answer, write the question.

Ex: Huì. Wǒ yǐqián hěn huì tán jítā. → Nǐ yǐqián huì tán jítā ma? Nǐ yǐqián huì bú huì tán jítā?

1 Xǐhuān. Tā yǐqián hěn xǐhuān kàn diànshì. ____________________

2 Shì. Nàgè nǚrén yǐqián hěn piàoliàng. ____________________

3 Xiǎng a! Wǒ bàba yǐqián xiǎng yào qù Bālí. ____________________

4 Bú huì. Wǒmen yǐqián bú huì tiàowǔ. ____________________

D 111.02 Listen to the statements about Pèishān and Dàwèi and answer the following questions.

1 Who didn't like to do homework in the past?

2 What instruments did Pèishān and Dàwèi play before?

3 With whom did Pèishān and Dàwèi live in the past?

Lesson 112

"Relax. I'm going to put my shirt on."

Yǐhòu (General Future)

Most people I know store their fishing poles in their garages. Me too! And you can see I have a good reason for that. Where else can you catch a 25-inch Hawaiian shirt? But more importantly, where can you:

- learn the word **yǐhòu** to talk about the future?

Last time we learned how to say *before* or *in the past*. Wouldn't it make sense if we now learned how to say *after* or *in the future*? Yes, I am a genius!

We use the word **yǐhòu** (*after; in the future*) the same way we use **yǐqián**, but of course, their meanings are opposite. Anyway, I'm dying to hear about all of your hopes and dreams for the future, so we'd better get cranking on this one.

Recap

Last time we learned the important word **yǐqián** to talk about the general past. Like other time words that we know (e.g. **zuótiān**, **shànggèyuè**, **míngnián**, **xiàgèxīngqī**, etc.) we can place the word **yǐqián** before or after the subject of our sentence. Have a look at these two sentences, and notice you have flexibility with your placement of the time word: **Yǐqián wǒ hěn xǐhuān tán gāngqín** and **Wǒ yǐqián hěn xǐhuān tán gāngqín** (*I used to really like playing the piano*).

Translate the following sentences with "yǐqián".

1 Yǐqián wǒ bù chī ròu. ____________________

2 Tā yǐqián yǒu lǎopó. ____________________

3 Yǐqián tāmen zhù zài Zhījiāgē. ____________________

4 Wǒmen yǐqián bù xiǎng bānjiā. ____________________

Words, phrases and stuff

112.01 Listen to the words and phrases then listen again and repeat.

The Future

yǐhòu	以后	*after; in the future*
zuò	做	*to make; to do; to become*
dāng	当	*to become*
líhūn	离婚	*to get divorced*
xīnlǐ yīshēng	心理医生	*psychologist*
duì	对	*yes; right; correct*

Patterns

As was the case with **yǐqián**, **yǐhòu** can be placed before or after the subject of the sentence. The only slight difference is that when **yǐhòu** is placed before the subject, you are emphasizing the time; when it is placed after the subject, you are emphasizing the subject.

Pattern 1: **Yǐhòu** + subject + action.

Pattern 2: Subject + **yǐhòu** + action.

Examples:

1 **Yǐhòu** wǒ huì jiéhūn. (*In the future, I will get married.*)

2 Wǒ **yǐhòu** xiǎng xué Xībānyáwén. (*In the future, I would like to learn Spanish.*)

Get to work

A Fill in the blank with yǐqián or yǐhòu to create sensible sentences.

Ex: Nàzhāng shāfā (yǐqián / yǐhòu) hěn gānjìng. **A:** yǐqián

1 Wǒ xiānshēng (yǐqián / yǐhòu) hěn shuài. ______

2 Wǒmen (yǐqián / yǐhòu) yào mài wǒmende fángzi. ______

3 Nǐmen (yǐqián / yǐhòu) zhù zài Měiguó. ______

4 Nàxiē dà gǒu (yǐqián / yǐhòu) hǎo kě'ài. ______

B Tell Mike Lǎoshī about what you would like to do in the future. Make five sentences with "yǐhòu".

Ex: Wǒ yǐhòu xiǎng dāng xīnlǐ yīshēng. (In the future, I'd like to be a psychologist.)

1 ______

2 ______

3 ______

4 ______

5 ______

C Given the answer, write the question using "yǐhòu".

Ex: Duì. Yǐhòu wǒ xiǎng dāng yáyī. → Yǐhòu nǐ xiǎng dāng yáyī ma?

1 Duì. Yǐhòu tāmen xiǎng shàng dàxué. ______

2 Yào. Wǒ érzi yǐhòu yào zhǎo xīnde gōngzuò. ______

3 Bù xiǎng. Yǐhòu wǒ yéye bù xiǎng zhù zài Zhōngguó. ______

4 Huì. Dàwèi hé Pèishān yǐhòu huì líhūn. ______

D 112.02 Listen. Provide the English translation for what the following individuals would like to do for work in the future.

1 Ross ______

2 Ella ______

3 Melissa ______

4 Sarah ______

5 David ______

6 Robert ______

7 Rosie ______

8 Yassine ______

"Believe it or not, I do my own grocery shopping."

. . . De Shíhòu (When; At the Time)

I enjoy grocery shopping quite a bit! The only problem is that one of my personal assistants has to call the store in advance and arrange a private shopping session after normal business hours. Otherwise, I get mobbed by fans asking for autographs and pictures, and I don't get back to the garage for several hours. Anyway, are you ready to:

- learn how to use **. . . de shíhòu** to talk about events that happened at / during a particular time

In Season 4, we learned the question word *when* (**shénme shíhòu**), and we used it only to ask questions. For example, **Nǐ shénme shíhòu shàng Zhōngwén kè?** (*When do you attend Chinese class?*) or **Nǐ bàba shénme shíhòu qù shàngbān?** This time we will drop **shénme** because we're not asking questions – we're making statements.

Recap

In the past two lessons, we've learned two important words: **yǐqián** and **yǐhòu**, which mean *in the past* and *in the future*, respectively. Like other time words we know, they can be placed before or after the subject of the sentence and more importantly, we can use these time markers to indicate past or future actions / events.

Look at the following sentences with "yǐqián" and "yǐhòu". Are the following translations correct? If they are incorrect, provide the correct translation.

1 Lǎoshī yǐqián zhù zài Táiběi. (*The teacher used to live in Taipei.*)

____

2 Nǐmen yǐhòu xiǎng zhù zài Shànghǎi ma? (*Did you live in Shanghai in the past?*)

____

3 Wǒ yǐqián bù xǐhuān zhù zài zhè lǐ. (*I would not like to live there in the future.*)

____

4 Lili yǐhòu bú huì zhù zài tā bàbamāma jiā. (*In the future, Lili won't live at her parents' house.*)

____

Words, phrases and stuff

113.01 Listen to the words and phrases then listen again and repeat.

During The Time When . . .

de shíhòu	的时候	*when; at / during the time when . . .*
dào	到	*to arrive*
huílái	回来	*to come back; to return*
mà(rén)	骂人	*to scold; yell at; curse (someone)*
xiǎo(de) shíhòu	小的时候	*childhood*
hǎibiān	海边	*the seaside*
tàiyáng yǎnjìng	太阳眼镜	*sunglasses*
lǎobǎn	老板	*boss*
yángé	严格	*strict*
zuò mèng	做梦	*to dream; to have a dream*
bàomǐhuā	爆米花	*popcorn*
tángguǒ	糖果	*candy*
Táiběi	台北	*Taipei*
Shànghǎi	上海	*Shanghai*

Patterns

We attach the phrase **. . . de shíhòu** to statements so that we can indicate that two actions / events have happened or will happen concurrently (or at the same time). We already know that **Wǒ shàng Zhōngwén kè** means *I attend Chinese class*. However, by adding **de shíhòu**, it now translates as *When I attend Chinese class*. Since this clause cannot stand by itself, we need another statement along with it: **Wǒ shàng Zhōngwén kède shíhòu zuì xǐhuān liànxí xiě Zhōngwén zì** (*When I attend Chinese class, I like to practice writing Chinese characters the most*). In English we call these complex sentences, but believe me, they're not that bad. I'll hold your hand through it if you need me.

Pattern 1: Word / Phrase / Action + **. . . de shíhòu**

Pattern 2: Subject + **. . . de shíhòu** + action.

Pattern 3: **. . . de shíhòu** + subject + action.

Examples:

1 (Wǒ) zài xuéxiào**de shíhòu** (*When (I am) at school*)

2 Tāmen zài jiā**de shíhòu** xǐhuān yīqǐ wán diàndòng yóuxì. (*When they are at home, they like to play video games together.*)

3 Gōngzuò**de shíhòu** wǒ xǐhuān hē chá. (*I like to drink tea when I am at work.*)

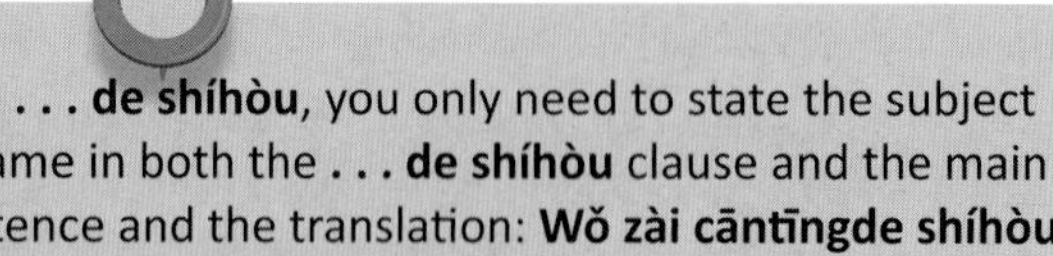

Note that when forming sentences with **. . . de shíhòu**, you only need to state the subject once, provided that the subject is the same in both the **. . . de shíhòu** clause and the main action of the sentence. Look at this sentence and the translation: **Wǒ zài cāntīngde shíhòu xǐhuān diǎn niúròu miàn** (*When I am at the restaurant, I like to order beef noodles*). In the Chinese sentence, *I* (**Wǒ**) is stated only once; in the English translation, *I* is used twice.

Get to work

A Translate the following clauses with "de shíhòu".

Ex: Wǒ zài yínhángde shíhòu . . . → When I am / was at the bank . . .

1 Tā shuìjiàode shíhòu . . . ____________________

2 Bàba dào bàngōngshìde shíhòu . . . ____________________

3 Wǒ lǎogōng gōngzuòde shíhòu . . . ____________________

4 Tā māma zuòfànde shíhòu . . . ____________________

B Given the *when* clauses with "de shíhòu", complete the sentence with a statement that makes sense.

Ex: Wǒ zài jiāde shíhòu . . . → Wǒ zài jiāde shíhòu xǐhuān xiūxi.

1 Wǒde lǎopó zài gōngzuòde shíhòu . . . ____________________

2 Wǒde jiārén chī wǎncānde shíhòu . . . ____________________

3 Wǒde gǒu zài wàimiànde shíhòu . . . ____________________

4 Wǒde lǎoshī xiàkède shíhòu . . . ____________________

C Convert the following sentences from ". . . de shíhòu", Subject + action (Pattern 3) to Subject + ". . . de shíhòu" + action (Pattern 2) or vice versa.

Ex: Xiǎode shíhòu wǒ bú tài xǐhuān hē niúnǎi. → Wǒ xiǎode shíhòu bú tài xǐhuān hē niúnǎi. (When I was a child, I didn't really like to drink milk.) OR Wǒ xǐ zǎode shíhòu ài chànggē. Xǐ zǎode shíhòu wǒ ài chànggē.

1 Kàn diànyǐngde shíhòu xiǎopéngyǒu xǐhuān chī tángguǒ. ____________________

____

2 Kāichēde shíhòu Dàwèi xǐhuān tīng yīnyuè. ____________________

____

3 Gēge jiéhūnde shíhòu huì chuān xīzhuāng. ____________________

____

4 Jiějie bìyède shíhòu huì hěn gāoxìng. ____________________

____

D Match the following sentence parts to create a complete sentence.

1 ____ Zài túshūguǎnde shíhòu

2 ____ Wǒde nǚpéngyǒu zài shìchǎngde shíhòu

3 ____ Chī zǎocānde shíhòu

4 ____ Mike Lǎoshī jiāo wǒmende shíhòu

5 ____ Māma mà wǒde shíhòu

a xǐhuān mǎi shūcài gēn shuǐguǒ.

b wǒ hěn nánguò.

c wǒmen fēicháng gāoxìng.

d tāmen xǐhuān kàn xīnde shū.

e tāmen bàba xǐhuān kàn bàozhǐ.

Lesson 114

"No funny business in my garage."

Yǐqián (Before a Specific Time)

As you can see, I am an experienced wedding officiant, but it's not every day that I get to witness one of my good friends (**Xiǎo Màikè**) marry his true love. In fact, the ceremony was so beautiful, I almost cried. (Well, I did, actually, but don't tell anybody. I have a reputation to protect.) Anyway, enough of this sappy %$#%. I need to teach you:

- another definition of **yǐqián**

I'm bringing back the word **yǐqián**, but this time we're going to plug it into the sentence pattern from the last lesson when we used (**. . . de shíhòu**) to talk about two simultaneous events. The difference is that this time we're using **yǐqián** not to mean *in the general past*, but rather *before* (a specific action / event) so that we can put two events in sequential order. You got that?

Recap

We learned how to attach **. . . de shíhòu** to statements, which allowed us to indicate that when action / event 1 occurs, action / event 2 occurs as well. For example, **Wǒ zài jiā** means *I am at home*. By attaching **de shíhòu** to the aforementioned statement, we are left with **Wǒ zài jiāde shíhòu**, meaning *WHEN I am at home*. If we then add another complete sentence to it, we will have a full sentence. So, if I say **Wǒ zài jiāde shíhòu (wǒ) zuì xǐhuān kàn *Chinese with Mike***, what does that mean?

Complete the sentences.

1 Wǒ ____________ wǒ péngyǒu jiāde shíhòu (When I am at my friend's house)
2 Tā ____________ de shíhòu (When he / she boards the airplane)
3 Tāmen ____________ de shíhòu (When they eat lunch)
4 Wǒmen ____________ Jiānádàde shíhòu (When we arrive in Canada)

Words, phrases and stuff

114.01 Listen to the words and phrases then listen again and repeat.

Yǐqián; *To Meet*

yǐqián	以前	*in the past; before (a specific event); ago*
huíguó	回国	*to return to one's home country*
rènshì	认识	*to meet; to know*
xiǎoshí	小时	*an hour*
kāfēiyīn	咖啡因	*caffeine*

Patterns

When **yǐqián** is used to mean before a specific time / ago, as it is in this lesson, you may abbreviate it by omitting **yǐ**. Therefore, instead of saying **Bāgè xiǎoshí yǐqián**, you may simply say **Bāgè xiǎoshí qián**.

Pattern 1: Sentence + **yǐqián**

Pattern 2: Sentence + **yǐqián** + action.

Pattern 3: Time / Event + **yǐqián**

Examples:

1 Wǒde lǎobān shàngbān **yǐqián** (*Before my boss goes to work*)

2 Wǒde lǎobān shàngbān **yǐqián** xǐhuān chī zǎocān. (*Before my boss goes to work, he likes to eat breakfast.*)

3a 5 tiān **yǐqián** (*Five days ago*)

3b Shèngdànjié **yǐqián** (*Before Christmas*)

Get to work

A Translate the following Chinese clauses to English.

Ex: Wǒ shàng dàxué yǐqián → Before I attend university

1 Wǒde xiǎohái shuìjiào yǐqián ______________________

2 Tā rènshì tā lǎopó yǐqián ______________________

3 Wǒmen bānjiā yǐqián ______________________

4 Nǐ bàba chūmén yǐqián ______________________

5 Tāmen huíguó yǐqián ______________________

B Match the time expressions with "yǐqián" to their meanings.

1	____ Liùtiān yǐqián	a	Six years ago
2	____ Liùgè xiǎoshí yǐqián	b	Six hours ago
3	____ Liùnián yǐqián	c	Six months ago
4	____ Liùgè xīngqī yǐqián	d	Six minutes ago
5	____ Liùgèyuè yǐqián	e	Six days ago
6	____ Liù fēnzhōng yǐqián	f	Six weeks ago

C Given the clause with "yǐqián", complete the sentence with an action that makes sense.

Ex: Wǒ xǐliǎn yǐqián → shuā yá

1 Wǒmen chīfàn yǐqián ____________

2 Tā shàngbān yǐqián ____________

3 Bob jiéhūn yǐqián ____________

4 Tāmen qù jīchǎng yǐqián ____________

D Given the main action, make up a "yǐqián" clause.

Ex: . . . yào zuò zuòyè. → Tā shuìjiào yǐqián yào zuò zuòyè.

1 . . . xǐhuān hē kāfēi. ______________________

2 . . . xiǎng bìyè. ______________________

3 . . . huì mǎi cài. ______________________

4 . . . yào xǐzǎo. ______________________

"I love winning."

Yǐhòu (After a Specific Time)

I must confess that I do enjoy a friendly game of blackjack in the garage before I get into teaching mode. I figure that by playing for **qiānyǔbǐng** (instead of real money) I'm sure to earn a fortune! (Cue laughter.) Anyway, you'd better pay attention so you can:

- learn another definition of **yǐhòu**

Note: Mike Lǎoshī does not promote gambling.

Recap

Last time we learned that **yǐqián** can also mean *before* (a specific event) that is used to indicate that one action / event occurred before another. All we had to do was tack on **yǐqián** to the end of a statement. So watch and be amazed: **Wǒ dǎ lánqiú** (*I play basketball*) → **Wǒ dǎ lánqiú yǐqián** (*Before I play basketball*). I've seen two-year-olds master this stuff!

A Translate the main action (in parentheses) to create full sentences. Remember, you only state the subject once.

Ex: Chūmén yǐqián (she would like to make coffee) → Chūmén yǐqián tā xiǎng zhǔ kāfēi.

1 Tā shuìjiào yǐqián (he likes to drink milk) ______________________

2 Chīfàn yǐqián (you must wash your hands) ______________________

3 Shàngkè yǐqián (I must do my homework) ______________________

4 Tāmen shàngbān yǐqián (they must wait for the bus) ______________________

Words, phrases and stuff

115.01 Listen to the words and phrases then listen again and repeat.

In the Future

yǐhòu	以后	*in the future; after (a specific event)*
dàojiā	到家	*to arrive home*
shēng	生	*to give birth; to have a baby*
huàn yīfú	换衣服	*to change (clothes)*
kāixué	开学	*to begin school*

Patterns

Once again, we have a companion lesson to the previous one. Last time we learned another meaning of **yǐqián**, and this time we'll learn another meaning of **yǐhòu**. We already know **yǐhòu** means *in the future*, but it can also mean *after* (a specific event). If I say **Wǒ chī wǎncān**, it means *I eat dinner*. However, if I attach **yǐhòu** to that statement (**Wǒ chī wǎncān yǐhòu**), the translation becomes *After I eat dinner*.

Pattern 1: Sentence + **yǐhòu**

Pattern 2: Sentence + **yǐhòu** + action.

Pattern 3: Time phrase / event + **yǐhòu**

Examples:

1 Wǒ huàn yīfú **yǐhòu** (*After I change my clothes*)

2 Wǒ huàn yīfú **yǐhòu** yào chūqù. (*After I change my clothes, I am going to go out.*)

3a 5 diǎn **yǐhòu** (*After 5 o'clock*)

3b Chūnjié **yǐhòu** (*After Chinese New Year*)

Get to work

A Translate the following clauses with yǐhòu.

Ex: Wǒ qǐchuáng yǐhòu. → After I wake up

1 Tā chī wǎnfàn yǐhòu. ____________________

2 Wǒmen xiàkè yǐhòu. ____________________

3 Sarah bìyè yǐhòu. ____________________

4 Wǒ jiějie dàojiā yǐhòu. ____________________

B Match the following time expressions with "yǐhòu".

1 ____ Shítiān yǐhòu

2 ____ Shínián yǐhòu

3 ____ Shígè xiǎoshí yǐhòu

4 ____ Shífēnzhōng yǐhòu

5 ____ Shígèyuè yǐhòu

6 ____ Shígèxīngqī yǐhòu

a After / In ten minutes

b After / In ten weeks

c After / In ten days

d After / In ten months

e After / In ten years

f After / In ten hours

C Given the "yǐhòu" clause, finish the sentence.

Ex: Wǒ yùndòng yǐhòu yào xǐ zǎo.

1 Wǒ gēge xiàbān yǐhòu ____________________

2 Tā chī wǔfàn yǐhòu ____________________

3 Tāmen jiéhūn yǐhòu ____________________

4 Dàwèi gēn Pèishān pǎobù yǐhòu ____________________

D Given the main action, make up a "yǐhòu" clause to create a full sentence.

Ex: . . . tā huì qù shàngkè. → Tā chī zǎofàn yǐhòu huì qù shàngkè.

1 . . . tāde nánpéngyǒu yào xiūxi. ____________________

2 . . . wǒmende jiàoshòu xǐhuān hē pútáojiǔ. ____________________

3 . . . wǒ érzi yào shuìjiào. ____________________

4 . . . nǐ wàipó xiǎng dǎ tàijíquán. ____________________

E Unscramble the following sentences. Begin each sentence with the subject.

1 huíjiā / wǒ / yǐhòu / huàn / yào / yīfú. ____________________

2 zhuōqiú / tāmen / yǐhòu / ài / dàojiā / dǎ. ____________________

3 yǐhòu / báipútáojiǔ / Mike Lǎoshī / xiàkè / hē / yībēi / xǐhuān. ____________________

4 Lili / yǐhòu / qǐchuáng / shuā yá / yào. ____________________

5 Nǐ nǚ'ér / kāixué / máng / yǐhòu / huì / bǐjiào. ____________________

Lesson 116

"Get ready for some fireworks."

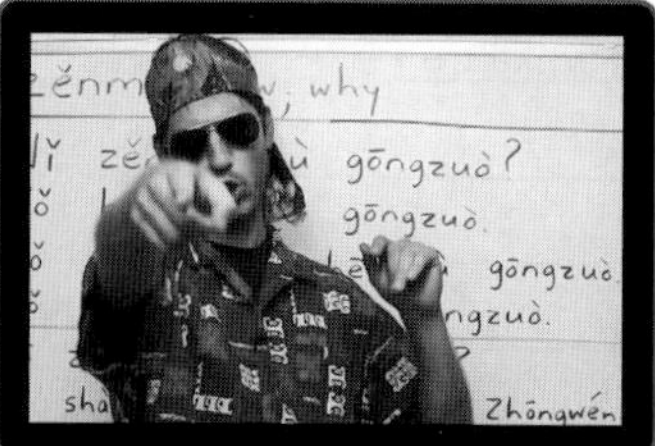

Zěnme (How?)

So my neighbor probably won't be too pleased that he can't recognize his own lawn when he comes home later this summer. Oh well, he'll get over it. Besides, I'd rather blow off some fireworks and spend my time teaching you:

- the important question word **zěnme**

Shéi, **shénme**, **nǎ lǐ**, **wèishénme**, **jǐ**, **duōshǎo**, **shénme shíhòu**, **nǎ(yī)** . . . What do these words all have in common? Correct. They're all question words that we've studied before, and today I'm finishing off the list by introducing your final question word: **zěnme**, which among other things, means *how*. I'll roll out some of **zěnme**'s other meanings in the next few lessons, but for now we'll use it to form questions about how we do certain things.

Recap

Last time we learned the second meaning of **yǐhòu**, meaning *after* (a specific event). Like its counterpart, **yǐqián**, the word **yǐhòu** allows us to put actions / events in sequential order. For example, I can say **Wǒ shàng fēijī yǐhòu xǐhuān shuìjiào**. Even though we're not working with **yǐqián** and **yǐhòu** in this lesson, let's make sure you're still on your toes.

Fill in the blanks with "yǐqián" or "yǐhòu" to create logical sentences, then translate.

Ex: Tā chī wǎncān ________ huì xǐ shǒu. (yǐqián) → He will wash his hands before he eats.

1 Tā qǐchuáng ________ chī zǎocān. ________________

2 Tā shuìjiào ________ xǐhuān kànshū. ________________

3 Tā xiàbān ________ yào qù jiǔbā hē píjiǔ. ________________

4 Tā kǎoshì ________ yào fùxí tāde zuòyè. ________________

Words, phrases and stuff

116.01 Listen to the words and phrases then listen again and repeat.

How and Crustaceans

zěnme	怎么	*how*
shàngwǎng	上网	*to go online; to use the Internet*
yáokòngqì	遥控器	*a remote control*
liánluò	联络	*to get in touch with; to contact*
wǎnglù	网路	*the Internet; a network*
lóngxiā	龙虾	*lobster*
pángxiè	螃蟹	*crab*

Patterns

Think about the question words we've learned before: **nǎ lǐ**, **shénme**, **shéi**, etc. Usually we just had to substitute the answer for the question word. For example, **Tā shì shéi? Tā shì Tom. Tā zài nǎ lǐ? Tā zài jiā (lǐ).** It was pretty straightforward. With **zěnme**, however, you often have to describe how to do something, how to eat something, how to use something, etc. Therefore, sometimes your answer will require more than a single sentence.

Pattern 1: Subject + **zěnme** + action?

Example:

1 Nǐ **zěnme** qù cāntīng? (*How do you get to the restaurant?*)

Get to work

A Given the answer, write the question with "zěnme".

Ex: Wǒ dā huǒchē qù shàngbān. → Nǐ zěnme qù shàngbān?

1 Tā zuò fēijī qù Zhījiāgē. ______

2 Wǒmen yòng kuàizi chī chǎofàn. ______

3 Tā jiějie yòng wǎnglù gēn tāde péngyǒu liánluò. ______

4 Wǒ māma yòng xǐyījī xǐ yīfú. ______

B Unscramble the questions. Then translate.

Ex: Nǐ xiūlǐ zěnme chēzi? → Nǐ zěnme xiūlǐ chēzi?

1 zěnme qù tā túshūguǎn? ______

2 hē nàgè zěnme rén tāng? ______

3 hànbǎo chī zěnme tāmen? ______

4 nǐmen zěnme yīfú mǎi? ______

C Translate the following sentences into Chinese.

Ex: How do you eat beef fried rice? → Nǐ zěnme chī niúròu chǎofàn?

1 How do you ride a motorcycle? ______

2 How do you guys play mahjong? ______

3 How do they use their dryer? ______

4 How does your mom cook lobster? ______

D Look at the pictures and answer the questions.

1 Tā zěnme chī niúpái?

3 Tā zěnme qù xuéxiào?

2 Tā zěnme xǐ wǎn?

4 Tā zěnme hē tāng?

"This guy needs my Chinese lessons."

Zěnme (How? or Why?)

As always, I agree to play the humanitarian role and rent out my garage ($2000 / hr.) for weddings, birthday parties, and corporate events, and now I'm supposed to pay taxes on it? Sorry, that's just not going to happen. And this dude certainly isn't going to get in my way of teaching you:

- another definition of **zěnme**

You've probably picked up on the ongoing pattern in this season of *Chinese with Mike*. We're learning a lot of important new words, and we're learning how several of them have multiple definitions. The same is true for **zěnme**, which not only means *how*, but can also mean *why*. Most of the time, it can be used interchangeably with the question word (**wèishénme**), which we learned back in Season 1.

Recap

Last time we learned the primary definition of **zěnme**, (*how*) and used it to ask how to do things, such as: get to work, use a remote control, cook a steak, etc.

Let's see if you remember how to use "zěnme" to mean *how*. Provide translations for the following questions.

1 Nǐ zěnme qù bǎolíngqiúchǎng? ______________________________

2 Nǐ zěnme yòng zhètái píngbǎn diànnǎo? ______________________________

3 Nǐ zěnme dǎ zhuōqiú? ______________________________

4 Nǐ zěnme kǎo hànbǎo? ______________________________

Words, phrases and stuff

117.01 **Listen to the words and phrases then listen again and repeat.**

Why and Hurt

zěnme 怎么 *how; why*

tòng 痛 *to hurt*

Patterns

Pattern 1: Subject + **zěnme** + action?

Pattern 2: **Yīnwèi** + subject + action.

Examples:

1 Nǐ **zěnme** bù hē zhèwǎn tāng? (*Why aren't you eating this bowl of soup? / How come you don't eat this bowl of soup?*)

2 **Yīnwèi** zhèwǎn tāng tài là. (*Because this bowl of soup is too spicy.*)

Get to work

A Given the question, write an answer that makes sense.

Ex: Nǐ zěnme bú qù shàngkè? → Yīnwèi wǒ bù xǐhuān wǒde jiàoshòu.

1 Nǐ nǚ'ér zěnme bú shuìjiào? ______________________

2 Nǐ érzi zěnme bù chīfàn? ______________________

3 Nǐmen zěnme bù chūqù? ______________________

4 Tā zěnme bù xiūxi? ______________________

B Match the questions and answers that make sense.

Ex: Tā xīngqīrì zěnme bù lái wǒde shēngrì pàiduì? → Yīnwèi tā xīngqīrì yào shàngbān.

1 _____ Nǐ zěnme bú yào lái wǒmen jiā?

2 _____ Nǐ zěnme bù shuō huà?

3 _____ Tā zěnme bù jiē diànhuà?

4 _____ Tā zěnme bù kāichē?

a Yīnwèi tāde shǒujī méi yǒu diàn.

b Yīnwèi tā bǐjiào xǐhuān qí zìxíngchē.

c Yīnwèi nǐmen jiā tài zāng.

d Yīnwèi wǒde hóulóng tòng.

C Why don't your family members want to eat / drink the following items?

Ex: Nǐ āyí zěnme bù chī Tàiguó cài? (too spicy) → Yīnwèi Tàiguó cài tài là.

1 Nǐ bàba zěnme bù hē kāfēi? (too bitter) ______________________

2 Nǐ māma zěnme bù chī tángguǒ? (too sweet) ______________________

3 Nǐ gēge zěnme bù hē zhèbēi níngméngzhī? (too sour) ______________________

4 Nǐ dìdi zěnme bù hē nàbēi chá?(too hot (temperature)) ______________________

D Translate the following questions and answers.

1 **Q:** Tāmen zěnme bù xǐhuān shàng shùxué kè?

A: Yīnwèi shùxué tài nán.

____

____

2 **Q:** Nǐ lǎogōng zěnme bú qù shàngbān?

A: Yīnwèi tā tóu tòng.

____

____

3 **Q:** Nǐ zěnme bú yào tīng wǒde CD?

A: Yīnwèi wǒ bù xǐhuān tīng Yīngwén gē.

____

____

4 **Q:** Nǐde péngyǒu zěnme méi yǒu qián?

A: Yīnwèi tā méi yǒu gōngzuò.

____

____

Lesson 118

"Listen up!"

Zhème & Nàme

Shadowboxing is part of my daily workout routine, but as you can see, it's not that much of a challenge. You want to know what is? Trying to balance a panda on your head while delivering an awesome Chinese lesson. Watch me do that while you:

- learn the adverbs **zhème** and **nàme**

We're done with **zěnme** – for now. Don't worry, though, I'll be bringing it back next lesson for some fun and games. At the moment, I'd like to kick off Lesson 118 with a couple of important adverbs (**zhème** and **nàme**) that we use to modify (and emphasize) adjectives.

Recap

By now you should know that **zěnme** can mean *how* or *why*.

Look at the following sentences and write whether "zěnme" means *how* or *why*.

Ex: Tā zěnme qù shàngxué? → How

1 Tā zěnme bú zuò zuòyè? ________________

2 Nǐmen zěnme wán zhègè yóuxì? ________________

3 Wǒ zěnme qù jīchǎng? ________________

4 Nǐ zěnme bù mǎi nàjiàn yángzhuāng? ________________

Words, phrases and stuff

118.01 Listen to the words and phrases then listen again and repeat.

So So

zhème	这么	*this much; so much*
nàme	那么	*so*
chénggōng	成功	*to succeed*

Patterns

Zhème means *this (much)* or *so (much)* and **nàme** means *that (much)* or *so (much)*. The major difference in their usage is that you usually use **zhème** to describe objects that are closer to you and **nàme** for objects that are farther away.

Pattern 1: **Q:** Subject + **zěnme** + **zhème / nàme** + adjective?

Pattern 1b: **A: Yīnwèi** + subject + action.

Pattern 2: **Q:** Subject + **zěnme** + **zhème / nàme** + action?

Pattern 2b: **A: Yīnwèi** + subject + action.

Examples:

1 Nǐde xiǎohái **zěnme zhème** shòu? (*Why is your child this thin?*)

1b **Yīnwèi** tā bù xǐhuān chīfàn. (*Because he / she doesn't like to eat.*)

2 Nǐ **zěnme nàme** xǐhuān chī dàngāo? (*Why do you like to eat cake so much?*)

2b **Yīnwèi** wǒ xǐhuān chī hěn tiánde dōngxī! (*Because I like to eat sweet things!*)

Get to work

A Provide answers to the following questions.

Ex: Tāmen zěnme zhème chòu? → Yīnwèi tāmen bù xǐhuān xǐzǎo.

1 Nǐmen zěnme nàme lèi? ______
2 Nǐde lǎoshī zěnme nàme shēngqì? ______
3 Nǐmende wàigōng zěnme nàme qiángzhuàng? ______
4 Tāmende dìdi zěnme zhème máng? ______

B Translate the following into English.

Ex: Nǐ zěnme nàme fán? → Why are you so annoying?

1 Nǐde gǒu zěnme nàme chǎo (loud)? ______
2 Xiǎohái zěnme nàme kě'ài? ______
3 Tā zěnme nàme ài jiǎng diànhuà? ______
4 Tāmen zěnme zhème xǐhuān wán diàndòng yóuxì? ______

C Talk about the weather. Match the descriptions with the pictures.

Ex: → Tàiyáng zěnme zhème dà?

a

b

c

d

1 Tiānqì zěnme nàme rè? ______
2 Tiānqì zěnme zhème lěng? ______
3 Fēng zěnme zhème dà? ______
4 Cǎihóng zěnme zhème piàoliàng? ______

D 118.02 Listen to the dialogues and fill in the blanks with "zhème / nàme" and an adjective. Listen again and repeat after the native speakers.

1 Nǐ nǚ'ér zěnme ______?
2 Tā zěnme ______?
3 Nǐ zěnme chī ______?
4 Nǐ zěnme chuān______ yīfú?

Lesson 119

"Some people say I look like a movie star."

Zěnmeyàng

Have you ever played washers? I know I make it look easy, but for the amateur, it can be a challenge. The same goes for understanding our new question word **zěnmeyàng**, but I promise I'll make that easy too. Sit back, take a deep breath, and let's:

- learn the question word **zěnmeyàng** to ask *How is it?* or *What's it like?*

Recap

Last time we learned two important adverbs: **zhème** (*this; so*) and **nàme** (*that; so*) that we can use to modify adjectives.

A Match the "zhème / nàme" statements to a final word that makes sense.

1 Tā zěnme nàme ài chī ____?	**a** piàoliàng
2 Nǐ māma zěnme nàme ____?	**b** pīsà
3 Nǐ bàba zěnme zhème ____?	**c** diànshì
4 Nǐmen zěnme zhème xǐhuān kàn ____?	**d** qiángzhuàng

Words, phrases and stuff

119.01 Listen to the words and phrases then listen again and repeat.

Words That Describe, Measure Words and Some Food

zěnmeyàng	怎么样	*how; how is it?; how about it?*
zuìjìn	最近	*recently; in the near future*
bú cuò	不错	*not bad; pretty good*
làngmàn	浪漫	*romantic*
hǎoxiào	好笑	*funny*
hǎokāi	好开	*"good drive" (a car that drives well)*
hǎoqí	好骑	*"good ride" (a bike / motorcycle that rides well)*
jiémù	节目	*a program; (e.g., a television program / show)*
jiā	家	MW for stores; shops
jiān	间	MW for rooms; spaces
hǎixiān	海鲜	*seafood*
shuǐ jiǎo	水饺	*Chinese dumplings* (food)

Patterns

The question word **zěnmeyàng** has a variety of functions and translations depending on the context. As you probably guessed, it is related to the question word **zěnme** (*how; why*). However, when you attach the word **yàng** (*shape; way; appearance*), you have a lot more flexibility in using it. For one, you can use **zěnmeyàng** to ask how somebody is doing. For instance, **Nǐ jīntiān zěnmeyàng?** is more casual way to ask **Nǐ jīntiān hǎo ma?** even though both have basically the same meaning.

Pattern 1: Subject + **zěnmeyàng**?

Examples:

1 Nǐde xīnde píngbǎn diànnǎo **zěnmeyàng**? (*How's your new tablet computer?*)

Zuìjìn can mean both *recently* or *in the near future*. Therefore, don't be alarmed if you hear Chinese people use **zuìjìn** to ask about your upcoming plans.

Get to work

A Translate the following questions.

Ex: Nàbù gējù zěnmeyàng? → How is / was that opera?

1 Nàjiā diànyǐngyuànde bàomǐhuā zěnmeyàng? ______

2 Zhèjiān kāfēitīngde kāfēi zěnmeyàng? ______

3 Nǐ juéde Yīngguó(de) hóngchá zěnmeyàng? ______

4 Měiguó(de) shíwù zěnmeyang? ______

B Using the words in the box, answer the following questions.

hǎochī	hǎohē	hǎokàn	hǎoyòng	hǎoqí

Ex: Nàgè diànshì jiémù zěnmeyang? → Nàgè diànshì jiémù hěn hǎokàn.

1 Zhètái xǐwǎnjī zěnmeyàng? ______

2 Nǐde mótuōchē zěnmeyàng? ______

3 Tā bàbade pútáojiǔ zěnmeyàng? ______

4 Zhèjiā cāntīngde shuǐ jiǎo zěnmeyàng? ______

C Given the answer, write the question with "zěnmeyàng".

Ex: Wǒ juéde Niǔyuē hěn hǎowán. → Nǐ juéde Niǔyuē zěnmeyàng?

1 Wǒmen juéde Wáng Lǎoshīde Zhōngwén kè hěn wúliáo. ______

2 Tāmen juéde nàgè diànshì jiémù hěn hǎoxiào. ______

3 Wǒ érzi juéde zhèshǒu gē bù hǎotīng. ______

4 Pèishān juéde *Chinese with Mike* fēicháng yǒuqù. ______

D Match the question to the picture.

1 

3 

2 

4 

a Zhèjiàn yīfú zěnmeyàng? ______

b Zhèwǎn tāng zěnmeyàng? ______

c Zhètái zìxíngchē zěnmeyàng? ______

d Nàběn zázhì zěnmeyàng? ______

Lesson 120

"It's time to leave the garage."

Xiān . . . Zài . . . Ránhòu

Most adults think it's a nice gesture to let kids win when it comes to games and sports. Not me. In fact, humiliating children in dodgeball games is one of my favorite pastimes. If you think that sounds mean, think about this: My title as *World's Greatest Chinese Teacher* wasn't just handed to me, nor were my Olympic medals. I worked hard for them. And if these kids don't get a taste of reality, they may never accomplish anything and might wind up living in a garage. Anyway, let's:

- learn some important transitions to put events in sequence
- watch Mike Lǎoshī make his triumphant exit from Season 5

I can't believe this is our final lesson and the conclusion of my second book. I guess it's time to rest up a bit, then make a few public appearances, and finally embark on my next world tour. Maybe I'll see you along the way . . .

Recap

In this final lesson, let's learn a few important transitions, which are words that allow us to connect sentences smoothly. Today we'll learn time-order transitions so you can put events in sequence and give people step-by-step instructions.

A Match the "zěnmeyàng" questions with their short answers.

1 Nǐde mótuōche zěnmeyàng? ____	a hěn hǎoyòng
2 Tāde chēzi zěnmeyàng? ____	b mán hǎoqí
3 Nàbù diànyǐng zěnmeyàng? ____	c fēicháng hǎokāi
4 Nàbēi níngméngzhī zěnmeyàng? ____	d bù hǎochī
5 Zhèxiē chūnjuǎn zěnmeyàng? ____	e bú tài hǎohē
6 Nàgè diànzuān zěnmeyàng? ____	f hǎo hǎoxiào

Words, phrases and stuff

120.01 **Listen to the words and phrases then listen again and repeat.**

Sequence Words, Meals and Verbs

xiān	先	*first*
zài	再	*then; again*
ránhòu	然后	*then; after that*
zǎofàn	早饭	*breakfast*
wǔfàn	午饭	*lunch*
wǎnfàn	晚饭	*dinner*
zhé (yīfú)	折（衣服）	*to fold* (clothes)
zǒu	走	*to walk; to go*
zhízǒu	直走	*to walk (go) straight*
zhuǎn	转	*to turn*
zuǒzhuǎn	左转	*to turn left*
yòuzhuǎn	右转	*to turn right*

Patterns

Last time we tackled the important question word **zěnmeyàng**, which is an extension of the question word **zěnme**, meaning *how* or *why*, primarily. We use **zěnmeyàng** in a variety of situations, mainly to ask questions like *How is it? What's it like?*

Pattern 1: (Subject) + **xiān** + action 1 + **zài** + action 2.

Pattern 2: (Subject) + **xiān** + action 1 + **zài** + action 2 + **ránhòu** + action 3.

Examples:

1 Wǒde nánpéngyǒu xiān zhé yīfú zài chī wǔfàn. (*First, my boyfriend folds clothes. Then, he eats lunch.*)

2 Wǒde nánpéngyǒu xiān zhé yīfú, zài chī wǔfàn, ránhòu chūmén. (*First, my boyfriend folds clothes. Then, he eats lunch. After that, he leaves the house.*)

Get to work

A Take a look at Dàwèi's routines in his life. Fill in the missing words, and then put the entire sentence into Chinese.

Ex: (Every morning) Dàwèi xiān (brushes his teeth) zài chī zǎofàn. →
Měitiān zǎoshàng Dàwèi xiān shuā yá zài chī zǎofàn.

1 (Every day) tā xiān pǎobù zài (goes to work).

____

2 (Every Wednesday) tā xiān (brings his children to school) zài gēn péngyǒu qù (the coffee shop).

____

3 (Every afternoon) Dàwèi xiān (does the laundry) zài (folds his clothes).

____

4 (Every evening) tā xiān (takes a shower) zài (watches TV).

____

B Let's take it a step further. What are the following people going to do today? Use the "xiān . . . zài . . . ránhòu" pattern to sequence the following actions in Chinese.

Ex: My mom: goes grocery shopping, meets her friends, goes home →
Wǒ māma xiān qù mǎi cài zài gēn tāde péngyǒu jiànmiàn ránhòu huí jiā.

1 My dad: goes to the bank, plays tennis, goes home and cooks

____

2 My older brother: wakes up, drinks coffee, reads the newspaper

____

3 My older sister: takes a shower, gets dressed, combs her hair

____

4 My younger brother: plays soccer, drinks water, rides his bicycle home

____

C Provide two ways to ask the following questions.

Ex: How do I get to the restaurant? → Wǒ zěnme qù cāntīng? Cāntīng zěnme qù?
Cāntīng zěnme zǒu?

1 How do we get to the movie theater?

____

2 How do I get to your house?

____

3 How do I get to the post office?

____

4 How do we get to the golf course?

____

D Translate the following directions into Chinese.

Ex: First, turn right. Then go straight. After that, turn right. →
<u>(Nǐ) xiān yòuzhuǎn zài zhízǒu ránhòu yòuzhuǎn.</u>

1 First, go straight. Then, turn left. After that, turn right.

____

2 First, turn right. Then, turn left. After that, go straight.

____

3 First, turn left. Then, go straight. After that, turn left.

____

4 First, go straight. Then, turn right. After that, turn left.

____

Pīnyīn Review Table

		Initials (Consonants)																				
Finals (Vowels)		b	p	m	f	d	t	n	l	g	k	h	j	q	x	zh	ch	sh	r	z	c	s
a	a	ba	pa	ma	fa	da	ta	na	la	ga	ka	ha				zha	cha	sha		za	ca	sa
ai	ai	bai	pai	mai		dai	tai	nai	lai	gai	kai	hai				zhai	chai	shai		zai	cai	sai
an	an	ban	pan	man	fan	dan	tan	nan	lan	gan	kan	han				zhan	chan	shan	ran	zan	can	san
ang	ang	bang	pang	mang	fang	dang	tang	nang	lang	gang	kang	hang				zhang	chang	shang	rang	zang	cang	sang
ao	ao	bao	pao	mao		dao	tao	nao	lao	gao	kao	hao				zhao	chao	shao	rao	zao	cao	sao
e	e			me		de	te	ne	le	ge	ke	he				zhe	che	she	re	ze	ce	se
ei	ei	bei	pei	mei	fei	dei		nei	lei	gei		hei						shei		zei		
en	en	ben	pen	men	fen	den		nen		gen	ken	hen				zhen	chen	shen	ren	zen	cen	sen
eng		beng	peng	meng	feng	deng	teng	neng	leng	geng	keng	heng				zheng	cheng	sheng	reng	zeng	ceng	seng
er	er																					
i	yi	bi	pi	mi		di	ti	ni	li				ji	qi	xi	zhi	chi	shi	ri	zi	ci	si
ia	ya					dia			lia				jia	qia	xia							
ian	yan	bian	pian	mian		dian	tian	nian	lian				jian	qian	xian							
iang	yang							niang	liang				jiang	qiang	xiang							
iao	yao	biao	piao	miao		diao	tiao	niao	liao				jiao	qiao	xiao							
ie	ye	bie	pie	mie		die	tie	nie	lie				jie	qie	xie							
in	yin	bin	pin	min				nin	lin				jin	qin	xin							
ing	ying	bing	ping	ming		ding	ting	ning	ling				jing	qing	xing							
io	yo																					
iong	yong												jiong	qiong	xiong							
iu	you			miu		diu		niu	liu				jiu	qiu	xiu							
o	o	bo	po	mo	fo				lo													
ong	weng					dong	tong	nong	long	gong	kong	hong				zhong	chong		rong	zong	cong	song
ou	ou		pou	mou	fou	dou	tou	nou	lou	gou	kou	hou				zhou	chou	shou	rou	zou	cou	sou
u	wu	bu	pu	mu	fu	du	tu	nu	lu	gu	ku	hu				zhu	chu	shu	ru	zu	cu	su
ua	wa									gua	kua	hua				zhua		shua				
uai	wai									guai	kuai	huai					chuai	shuai				
uan	wan					duan	tuan	nuan	luan	guan	kuan	huan				zhuan	chuan	shuan	ruan	zuan	cuan	suan
uang	wang									guang	kuang	huang				zhuang	chuang	shuang				
ue	yue							nüe	lüe				jue	que	xue							
ui	wei					dui	tui			gui	kui	hui				zhui	chui	shui	rui	zui	cui	sui
un	wen					dun	tun		lun	gun	kun	hun				zhun	chun	shun	run	zun	cun	sun
uo	wo					duo	tuo	nuo	luo	guo	kuo	huo				zhuo	chuo	shuo	ruo	zuo	cuo	suo
ü	yu							nü	lü				ju	qu	xu							
üan	yuan												juan	quan	xuan							
ün	yun												jun	qun	xun							

The Writing System

General Rules for Writing Characters

Size, Shape and Spacing

All characters occupy imaginary rectangular (or square) areas to standardize size, shape, and spacing. Notice these features in the sentence **Wǒ shì lǎoshī** (*I am a teacher*):

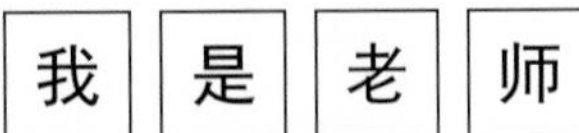

Horizontal and Vertical

Historically, Chinese was written vertically right to left. Today, it is usually written horizontally left to right, primarily due to the influence of Western languages and of computer software programs.

Stroke Count

A stroke is a single written mark contributing to the formation of a character. Horizontal, vertical, and curved lines are common (一, 八). One method of locating characters in Chinese dictionaries is by stroke count.

Radicals

Radicals are components of characters and can usually provide a clue to a word's meaning. For example, words related to water usually contain the radical **sāndiǎnshuǐ** (氵) on the left side of the character: 湖 (*lake*), 河 (*river*) and 海 (*sea*).

There are about 214 total radicals. Here are some common ones:

CHARACTER	MEANING	RADICAL	EXAMPLE
人	**rén** *(person)*	亻	你 *(you)*
手	**shǒu** *(hand)*	扌	打 *(to hit)*
水	**shuǐ** *(water)*	氵	海 *(sea)*
木	**mù** *(tree)*	木	森 *(forest)*
心	**xīn** *(heart)*	忄	情 *(feeling)*
口	**kǒu** *(mouth)*	口	吃 *(to eat)*

The Six Classifications

Characters are classified into these six categories.

1 Pictograms (form imitation): words represented by pictures (a small percentage of characters). Ancient pictograms have often evolved into modern characters: → 山 **shān** (*mountain*)

2 Ideograms or "Indication" characters: characters representing ideas, such as numbers or directions: 三 **sān** (*three*), 上 **shàng** (*up*)

3 Ideogrammatic compounds (joined meaning characters): two or more pictograms or ideograms combined to form new words: 木 **shù** (*tree*) → 林 **lín** (*grove*) → 森 **sēn** (*forest*)

4 Phono-semantic compounds (form & sound): the most common type of character (over 90 per cent), consisting of two parts: the general category (semantic) and the approximate pronunciation (phono):

ice (**bīng**)	*river* (**hé**)	*lake* (**hú**)	*sea* (**hǎi**)	*wave* (**làng**)
冰	河	湖	海	浪

5 Transformed cognate (reciprocal meaning): now basically disappeared from the modern classification system but essentially consisting of pairs of words historically related but whose meanings and pronunciation have since drifted apart: 老 **lǎo** (*old*) and 考 **kǎo** (*to test*)

6 Rebus: "borrowed characters": modern characters carrying the default meaning associated with an original character of different meaning which is now changed to indicate its original meaning. For example, the modern 要 **yào** (*to want*) originally meant *waist* and the character 腰 **yāo** was later created to mean *waist*.

Traditional Versus Simplified

In an effort to increase literacy, the Chinese government began in the 1950s to "simplify" the traditional more complicated characters used for about 1,500 years: 書 → 书 **shū** (*book*).

Transcripts

65 **Dàwèi:** Good morning, Peishan.
Pèishān: Hello!
Dàwèi: (pointing) Is that your older sister?
Pèishān: Yes. That's my older sister. Her name is Yan Xin. Do you have brothers and sisters?
Dàwèi: Yes. I have two older brothers, and I also have a younger sister.
Pèishān: Is your younger sister a student?
Dàwèi: Yes. She is a very smart girl.

81 Peishan is busy. Today she has to go / is going to go to the post office. She also must go / is going to the pharmacy. Tomorrow Peishan is going to go to the bakery. The day after tomorrow she is going to go to the nightclub. On Sunday, Peishan is going abroad.

91 David practices Chinese at the library.
Peishan practices Chinese at home.
David eats in the kitchen.
Peishan eats at the restaurant.
David watches TV in the living room.
Peishan watches TV in the bedroom.

103 **Dàwèi:** Hello, I am Dàwèi.
Pèishān: I am Pèishān.
Dàwèi: Where are you from?
Pèishān: I am Singaporean but I was born in Beijing.
Dàwèi: What is your nationality?
Pèishān: My nationality is Chinese.
Dàwèi: Which days do you have class?
Pèishān: I have class on Monday, Wednesday and Thursday. What about you? What day(s) do you have class?
Dàwèi: I attend class on Wednesday and Friday.

109 **Dàwèi:** Zǎoshàng hǎo!
Pèishān: Zǎo a!
Dàwèi: Wǒ hěn è.
Pèishān: Wǒmen yīqǐ qù chī zǎocān ba.
Dàwèi: Hǎo a! Zǒu ba!
Pèishān: Nǐ zuì xǐhuān chī shénme?
Dàwèi: Wǒ zuì xǐhuān chī pèigēn hé dàn. Nǐ ne? Nǐ yě xǐhuān chī pèigēn hé dàn ma?
Pèishān: Hái hǎo. Wǒ bǐjiào xǐhuān chī tǔsī gēn sōngbǐng.
Dàwèi: Wǒ yě xǐhuān chī tǔsī dànshì wǒ juéde sōngbǐng tài tián.

Answer Key

Pīnyīn **Patterns:** **1** 1, **2** 2, **3** 2, **4** 4, **5** 1, **6** 3, **7** 2, **8** 4, **9** 3, **10** 4

61 **Recap: A 1** shì, **2** yào, **3** xǐhuān
Words, phrases and stuff: běn
Get to work: A 1 f, **2** h, **3** g, **4** k, **5** d, **6** a, **7** j, **8** b, **9** c, **10** i, **11** l, **12** e; **B 1** yǒu, **2** xǐhuān, **3** yǒu, **4** yào; **C 1** Tā yǒu zìdiǎn. **2** Lǎoshī yǒu xīnde kèběn ma? **3** Nǐde Zhōngwén liànxíběn nán bù nán? **4** Zhèxiē huā shì shéide? OR Zhèxiē shì shéide huā? **D 1** Tā yǒu hěn guìde bǐjìběn diànnǎo. **2** Yōupán shì shénme? **3** Wǒmen yǒu píngbǎn diànnǎo. **4** Bill yǒu shénme? **E 1** Tā yǒu shénme? **2** Tā(de) māma yǒu shénme? **3** Nǐ yǒu shénme? **4** Tāmen yǒu shénme? **F 1** Lín Xiānshēng yǒu xīnde píngbǎn diànnǎo. **2** Tā bàbade péngyǒu xǐhuān kàn tāde Zhōngwén kèběn. **3** Wǒmende jiàoshòu yào mǎi diànzishū yuèdúqì. **4** Wáng Tàitai yǒu hěn piàoliàngde huā. **5** Zhè shì wǒ érzide yōupán.

62 **Recap: 1** Wǒ bú yào, **2** Wǒ bú huì, **3** Wǒ bù xǐhuān, **4** Wǒ bù néng
Words, phrases and stuff: A bǐ; **B 1** Because I am a teacher, I have markers. **2** Because they are children, they love using crayons. **3** Because my little sister has to do homework, she is going to use my laptop. **4** Because he / she has to practice writing Chinese characters, he / she is going to buy a brush pen. **5** Because Lili likes reading, she has an eBook reader.
Patterns: A 1 Yes: Yǒu. (Wǒ yǒu bǐ.) **2** No: Méi yǒu. (Wǒ méi yǒu bǐ.); **B** Wǒ gēge yǒu (zhào)xiàngjī.
Get to work: A 1 Wǒ **méi** yǒu làbǐ. **2** Tāmen **méi** yǒu (zhào)xiàngjī. **3** Xuéshēng **méi** yǒu qiānbǐ. **4** Wǒmende yéye **méi** yǒu máobǐ. **B 1** bú, **2** méi, **3** méi, **4** bù; **C 1** Méi yǒu, **2** Yǒu, **3** Tāde nǚ'ér yǒu mǎkèbǐ ma? **4** Wǒde lǎogōng méi yǒu píngbǎn diànnǎo.

63 **Recap: 1** Chg méi to bù, **2** Chg méi to bú, **3** chg bú to méi, **4** Correct
Words, phrases and stuff: A 1 gōngyuán **2** gōngkè **3** wánjù **4** yáshuā; **B 1** telephone, **2** cell phone case, **3** chōngdiànqì; **C** shǒu (hand) diàn (electric) jī (machine)
Patterns: Question: Nǐmen yǒu méi yǒu shǒujī?
Review: A 1 N, **2** Y, **3** Y, **4** Y; **B 1** Nǐ yǒu méi yǒu chōngdiànqì? **2** Tāmen yǒu méi yǒu Zhōngwén zìdiǎn? **3** Tāde mèimei yǒu méi yǒu hēisède shǒujīké? **4** Nǐmen yǒu méi yǒu máobǐ? **C 1** Nǐ yǒu xīnde píngbǎn diànnǎo ma? **2** Chúshī yǒu hěn chángde dāozi ma? **3** Tā yǒu hěn guìde bǐjìběn diànnǎo ma? **4** Nǐde nǚ'ér yǒu gōngzuò ma? **D 1** d, **2** a, **3** e, **4** c, **5** b; **E 1** bù, **2** méi, **3** bú, **4** méi; **F 1** Nǐmen yào zhìnéng shǒujī ma? Nǐmen yào bú yào zhìnéng shǒujī? **2** Nǐmen yǒu shǒujī ma? Nǐmen yǒu méi yǒu shǒujī? **3** Nǐ yǒu shǒujīké ma? Nǐ yǒu méi yǒu shǒujīké? **4** Zhè shì chōngdiànqì.

64 **Recap:** yǒu shuǐ; Yào
Words, phrases and stuff: A work; **B 1** much, **2** many, **3** a lot of, **4** a lot of
Get to work: A 1 Mùgōng yǒu hěn duō chuízi. **2** Jìgōng yǒu hěn duō bānshǒu. **3** Luósīdāo zài nǎ lǐ? **4** Nǐ yǒu diànzuān ma? **B 1** Wèishénme nǐ yǒu hěn duō Yīngwén zìdiǎn? **2** Tāmen bù néng chī

tài duō ròu. **3** Wǒde lǎogōng shì jìgōng. **4** Mùgōng yào mǎi xīnde chuízi. **C 1** Yǒu. Wǒde yéye yǒu hěn duō gōngjù. **2** Méi yǒu. Tāmende fùqīn méi yǒu diànzuān. **3** Shì. Wǒde gēge shì hěn bàngde mùgōng. **4** Bú huì. Wǒ bú huì yòng jùzi. **D** Answers will vary.

65 **Recap:** wǔ 五 5, bā 八 8, jiǔ 九 9, sì 四 4, èr 二 2, liù 六 6, yī 一 1, sān 三 3, qī 七 7, shí 十 10
Words, phrases and stuff: A èr is used for counting; liǎng is used for giving number of people / objects. **B** Wǒ yǒu mèimei indicates that you have one or more younger sisters, but it does not specify how many. Wǒ yǒu yīgè mèimei makes it clear that you have only one younger sister.
Patterns: 10 people shígè rén; 37 sānshíqīgè rén; 14 shísìgè rén; 100 yībǎigè rén
Get to work: A Answers will vary. **B 1** Tā yǒu liǎnggè yīshēng. **2** Tā méi yǒu péngyǒu. **3** Lǎoshī yǒu èrshísāngè xuéshēng. **4** Tāmen yǒu sìgè jiàoshòu. **5** Wǔgè jǐngchá yào kāfēi. **6** Shígè shāngrén yào qù dǎ gāo'ěrfūqiú. **7** Tā méi yǒu nánpéngyǒu. **8** Tā yǒu yīgè dìdi. **C 1** Pèishān's older sister. **2** Yes, he has 2. **3** No. **4** He has a younger sister. **5** She's a student.

66 **Review: A** ask date of the month; ask day of the week; ask time of day; use for small numbers; ask age; **B 1** b, **2** a, **3** d, **4** e, **5** c
Words phrases and stuff: b – answer with a number
Get to work: A 2 How many brothers do you have? **3** How many sisters do you have? **B 1** d six farmers, **2** f four carpenters, **3** e nine mechanics, **4** a one nurse, **5** b five chefs, **6** c two lawyers: **C 1** Nǐmen yǒu jǐgè jiàoshòu? **2** Tāmen yǒu jǐgè háizi? **3** Nǐde lǎoshī yǒu jǐgè xuéshēng? **4** Nǐ yǒu jǐgè xiōngdì jiěmèi? **D** Answers will vary. **F 1** jìmǔ Who is this? This is my stepmother. **2** érzi Is he your son? Yes. He is our son. **3** nǚ'ér Are they your daughters? Yes, they are our daughters. **4** jìfù Whose stepfather is that? That is my stepfather.

67 **Recap:** nǚrén, nǚháizi, xiōngdì, jiěmèi, xuéshēng, lǎoshī, yīshēng, chúshī, péngyǒu
Get to work: A 1 farm, **2** pet store, **3** house pet, **4** animals, **5** books; **B 1** sìzhī māo, **2** liùběn shū, **3** wǔzhī xióng, **4** yīgè jiàoshòu, **5** shíběn zázhì, **6** liǎnggè Jiānádàrén; **C 1** yīgè nánrén, **2** liǎngzhī gǒu, **3** sānběn shū; **D 1** háizi, **2** dàxiàng, **3** gēge, **4** shīzi, **5** māo; **E 1** Wǒde nǚpéngyǒu yǒu yīzhī lǎoshǔ. **2** Wǒ yǒu sānzhī gǒu. **3** Wǒde mèimei yǒu sìzhī niú. **4** Wǒde gēge yǒu liǎngběn bǐjìběn. **5** Wǒde dìdi yǒu yīběn zìdiǎn. **6** Wǒ(de) māma yǒu shíyīzhī niǎo. **7** Wǒ(de) bàba yǒu bāzhī qīngwā. **8** Wǒ(de) wàipó yǒu jiǔběn zázhì. **9** Wǒ(de) wàigōng yǒu wǔběn shū.

68 **Recap: 1** gè, **2** zhī, **3** běn, **4** jǐgè
Words, phrases and stuff: cháhú (pot): teapot, chábēi: teacup, chábāo (bag): teabag, lǜchá: green tea, nǎichá: milk tea; **Video: 1** bed, **2** paper, **3** table
Get to work: A 1 hóngpútáojiǔ, **2** píngzi, **3** qǐng, **4** hóngchá, **5** bēi, **6** lǜchá, **7** zhāng, **8** píjiǔ, **9** báipútáojiǔ, **10** píng; **B** Read the shopping list and put it in Chinese. Answers in order for B – **1** sānpíng shuǐ, **2** liǎngběn Déwén shū, **3** wǔshízhāng zhǐ, **4** sìzhī tùzi, **5** sìbēi kāfēi; **C** All begin with Qǐng gěi wǒ . . . along with the answers in B. **D 1** Xǐhuān. Wǒ xǐhuān Fǎguó pútáojiǔ. **2** Shì. Tāde xīnde gōngjùxiāng hěn dà. **3** Méi yǒu. Wǒde xiǎoháizi méi yǒu hěn duō wánjù. **4** Bú yào. Wǒ bú yào hē lǜchá. **5** Shì. Nàxiē mùgōng hěn qínláo.

69 **Recap: 1** Zhè shì shuǐ. Nà shì ròu. (No MW required); **2** Zhè shì hěn hǎode shū. Nà shì hěn kuàide chēzi. (No MW required); **3** Yīgè lǎoshī. Wǔgè xuéshēng. (MW required)

Patterns: Video: Answer (2) is correct. You must use a measure word after zhè / nà if a noun immediately follows.

Get to work: A 1 dàxué, **2** gāozhōngshēng, **3** dàxuéshēng, **4** nàgè, **5** gāozhōng, **6** zhègè; **B 1** zhègè hùshì, **2** nàgè mùgōng, **3** zhègè lǎoshī, **4** nàgè dàxuéshēng, **5** nàgè nánhái(zi), **6** zhègè gāozhōngshēng; **C 1** (Nàgè hěn shuàide nánrén) jiào Mike Lǎoshī; That handsome man is called Mike Lǎoshī. **2** (Nàgè hěn lǎnduòde gāozhōngshēng) bù xǐhuān zuò tāde zuòyè; That lazy high school student doesn't like to do his / her homework. **3** (Zhègè hěn lǎode jiàoshòu) yǒu shíwǔběn Zhōngwén kèběn; This old professor has 15 Chinese textbooks. **4** (Nàgè hěn kě'àide xiǎohái(zi)) yào qù mǎi xīnde làbǐ; That cute child is going to go buy new crayons. **D 1** Nàgè rén shì Joede bàba. **2** Shì. Zhègè nǚháizi shì wǒde nǚ'ér. **3** Bù xǐhuān. Nàgè xiāofángyuán bù xǐhuān zuò yùndòng. **4** Nàgè nǚrén jiào Lily. **E 1** zhègè, **2** wánpíde háizi, **3** nàgè, **4** niánqīngde jǐngchá.

70 **Recap: 1** Wǒ yǒu liǎnggè mèimei. Nǐ yǒu jǐgè gēge? **2** Tāmen yào mǎi èrshíběn shū. Tā yào yībēi kāfēi.

Words, phrases and stuff: Video: A 4 This pig is so big. **B 1** c, **2** a, **3** e, **4** g, **5** f, **6** d, **7** b

Get to work: A 1 zhòng, **2** bīng, **3** cháng, **4** zhè, **5** xiǎoxīn, **6** tàng, **7** wǎn, **8** ruǎn, **9** nà, **10** yìng; **B 1** Kěyǐ. Wǒ kěyǐ gěi nǐ nàzhāng zhǐ. **2** Bú yào. Wǒ bú yào mǎi nàpíng pútáojiǔ. **3** Shì. Nàbēi lǜchá tài tàng. **4** Méi yǒu. Nàzhī gǒu méi yǒu hěn duō wánjù. **5** Shì. Nàzhuāng chuáng hěn yìng. **C 1** c, **2** a, **3** e, **4** b, **5** f, **6** d; **D 1** Zhègè hěn ǎide nánrén. **2** Nàběn Yīngwén shū. **3** Nàzhī hěn chǒude gǒu. **4** Zhèbēi lǜchá. **5** Zhèpíng niúnǎi. **6** Nàzhāng hěn ruǎnde chuáng.

71 **Recap: Video: 1** Nǐ yě zài nǐde chēkù ma? **2** Nǐ zài nǐde wòshì ma? **3** Nǐ zài túshūguǎn ma? **4** Nǐ zài cèsuǒ ma?

Words, phrases and stuff: A biān; **B 1** Tā bú zài lóushàng. (He isn't upstairs.) **2** Tā bú zài tāde fángjiān. (He's not in his room.) **3** Tā bú zài wàimiàn. (He's not outside.) **4** Tā zài lóuxià. (He's downstairs.)

Patterns: 1 Nǐ zài nǎ lǐ? **2** Wǒ zài jiā. **3** Nǐ zài xuéxiào. **4** Māma zài yínháng. **5** Tāmen zài lóuxià.

Get to work: A 1 b, **2** d, **3** a, **4** c, **B 1** CORRECT, **2** INCORRECT: Does your dog like to go outside to play? **3** CORRECT, **4** INCORRECT: My mother really likes teaching foreigners English. **C** Gǒu zài lóushàng. Gǒu zài yùshì. Mèimei zài lóushàng. Mèimei zài tāde fángjiān. Māma zài lóuxià. Māma zài chúfáng. Bàba zài lóuxià. Bàba zài xǐyīfáng. Gēge zài wàimiàn. **D** Answers will vary.

72 **Recap: 1** Wǒ(de) bàba zài lóushàng. **2** Wǒ(de) māma zài lóuxià. **3** Wǒde māo zài lǐmiàn. **4** Wǒde gǒu zài wàimiàn.

Words, phrases and stuff: Discovery: 2 a board

Patterns: 1 Jīròu zài kǎoxiāng lǐ. **2** Nǐde Zhōngwén kèběn zài chuángde shàngmiàn.

Get to work: A 1 tiānhuābǎn, **2** dìbǎn; dìtǎn, **3** xióngmāo, **4** báibǎnbǐ, **5** hēibǎn; **B 1** Bǐjìběn diànnǎo zài shǒujīde xiàmiàn. **2** Wǒ māma zài wǒ jiějiede hòumiàn. **3** Píngbǎn diànnǎo zài Zhōngwén shūde xiàmiàn. **4** Wǒmen zài qiángbìde qiánmiàn. **C 1** Xiāngjiāo zài bīngxiāngde shàngmiàn. **2** Chéngzhī zài bīngxiāngde lǐmiàn. **3** Píngguǒ zài bīngxiāngde wàimiàn. **4** Kělè zài bīngxiāngde shàngmiàn. **5** Lǎoshǔ zài bīngxiāngde xiàmiàn. **6** Chǎofàn zài bīngxiāngde lǐmiàn.

73 **Recap: 1** Nǐde kèběn zài zhuōzide shàngmiàn. **2** Jǐngchá zài wǒde hòumiàn. **3** Wǒde shū zài wǒde shūbāode lǐmiàn.

Words, phrases and stuff: A 1 b, **2** c, **3** a; **B 1** My friend is next to me. **2** I am between the cars. **C 1** R, **2** L

Patterns: 1 a, **2** c, **3** a, **4** c, **5** a, **6** b

Get to work: A 1 d, **2** c, **3** b, **4** a; **B 1** Wǒde shǒujī bú zài wǒde shūbāode pángbiān. (My cell phone is not next to my bookbag.) **2** Tāde bǐjìběn diànnǎo bú zài nǐde bǐjìběn diànnǎode yòubiān. (His / Her laptop isn't to the right of your laptop.) **3** Yīshēng bú zài hùshìde zuǒbiān. (The doctor is not to the left of the nurse.) **4** Yínháng bú zài túshūguǎnde duìmiàn. (The bank is not across from the library.) **C 1** Nàzhī gǒu zài yǐzide zhōngjiān. **2** Chuānghu zài shízhōngde xiàmiàn. **3** Nàgè jǐngchá zài xiāofángyuánde yòubiān. OR Jǐngchá zài nàgè xiāofángyuánde yòubiān. **4** Nǐde / wǒde pánzi zài wǒde / nǐde pánzide zuǒbiān. **D 1** Dìtǎn zài zhuōzide xiàmiàn. **2** Xióngmāo zài shāfāde hòumiàn. **3** Yǐzi zài shāfāde duìmiàn. **4** Yībēi pútáojiǔ zài bǐjìběn diànnǎode shàngmiàn. **5** Bǐjìběn diànnǎo zài zìdiǎnde pángbiān. / Bǐjìběn diànnǎo zài zìdiǎnde yòubiān. **6** Bǐjìběn diànnǎo zài zhuōzide shàngmiàn. **7** Tiānhuābǎn zài xióngmāode shàngmiàn.

74 **Recap: A** 1, 2, and 3; **B 1** a, **2** b, **3** a, **4** c, **5** b

Words, phrases and stuff: A The major difference is that you use xiǎng to express that you're thinking about or would like to something; however, if you use yào, you are indicating that you already have a definite plan to do it. **B** 2; **C 1** F, **2** F

Get to work: A 1 zāng, **2** xǐ zǎo, **3** tóufǎ; cháng, **4** guā; **B 1** xǐ shǒu, **2** jiǎn tóufǎ, **3** shuā yá, **4** xǐ tóufǎ; **C 1** yào, **2** xiǎng, **3** yào, **4** xiǎng

75 **Recap: 1** want / would like (now); **2** would like to (at some point in the future); **3** to think about; **4** to miss something / someone

Words, phrases and stuff: A 1, 3, 4; **B** 1; **C** With yào qù: you have a definite plan; xiǎng qù: you are only thinking about going

Get to work: A 1 C sìwǎn báifàn; four bowls of white rice, **2** C liǎngbù diànyǐng; two movies, **3** X yīběn bǐjìběn diànnǎo; (tái); a laptop computer, **4** C yīpíng píjiǔ; a bottle of beer, **5** X yīgè xióng; (zhī); a bear, **6** C wǔběn Fǎwén liànxíběn; five French workbooks, **7** C sānfèn chūnjuǎn; three portions / orders of spring rolls; **B 1** a, **2** c, **3** d, **4** d, **5** a, **6** b; **C 1** d, **2** e, **3** a, **4** b, **5** c

76 **Recap: A 1** C, **2** X, **3** X; **B** Definition 3 is interchangeable

Words, phrases and stuff: 1 c, **2** a, **3** e, **4** d, **5** f, **6** b

Get to work: A 1 Míngtiān nǐ yào qù kàn yáyī. **2** Hòutiān tā xiǎng dǎ wǎngqiú. **3** Jīntiān wǒmen bú yào qù gōngyuán. **4** Wǒ (xiǎng) yào diǎn liǎngfèn chūnjuǎn. **5** Míngtiān nǐ xiǎng zuò shénme? **6** Jīntiān tā yào xǐ yīfú ma? **B 1** Jīntiān tā yào / xiǎng xǐ tóufǎ. **2** Míngnián tā yào / xiǎng qù Jiùjīnshān. **3** Hòutiān tā yào / xiǎng qù tāde péngyǒu jiā. **4** Xīngqīwǔ tā yào / xiǎng qù pàiduì. **5** Jīntiān tā yào / xiǎng dǎ bàngqiú. **6** Jīnnián tā yào / xiǎng qù Luóshānjī.

Review: Part 1: Basics: A 2 to want, **4** must, **6** be going to; **B 1** would like to, **2** to want, **3** to miss, **5** to think about; **Part 2: Patterns: A 1** a; b, **2** d, **3** a, **4** d, **5** b, **6** c, **7** a **B 1** a **2** b, **3** c, **4** f, **5** a, **6** c, **7** a, **8** d, **9** c, **10** e

77 **Recap: A** 2; **B** 2; **C 1** Nǐ yǒu shénme? **2** Nǐ yǒu shǒujī ma? OR Nǐ yǒu méi yǒu shǒujī? **3** Nǐ yǒu jǐgè jiěmèi?

Words, phrases and stuff: Video: b zhī

Get to work: A 1 zhōu, **2** kē, **3** zhī, **4** tái; **B 1** jīběn, **2** duōshǎo, **3** duōshǎo, **4** jīběn; **C 1** c, **2** d, **3** a, **4** b

78 **Recap:** Kàn: to see, read, watch; chī: eat; chàng(gē): to sing (a song); děng: to wait; xiàngjī: camera; mài: to sell; hē: to drink; chuān: to wear; chéngshì: city; pǎo(bù): to run

Words, phrases and stuff: A 1; **B** 2

Get to work: A 1 d, **2** f, **3** e, **4** a, **5** c, **6** b; **B 1** Tā zài xiě Rìwén zì. **2** Tāmen zài chī Zhōngguó cài. **3** Wǒmen zài hē lǜchá. **4** Tāde mèimei zài shuō Xībānyáwén. **C** Note that all of these could also be: subject + zài zuò shénme? **1** Q: Nàzhī māo zài hē shénme / zuò shénme? **2** Q: Zhègè nǚrén zài mài shénme / zuò shénme? **3** Q: Tā zài tīng shénme / zuò shénme? **4** Q: Nǐ nǎinai zài xǐ shénme / zuò shénme? **5** Q: Tāmen zài chī shénme / zuò shénme? **D 1** A: Tā zài xué Yīngwén. **2** A: Nàxiē yīshēng zài dǎ gāo'ěrfūqiú. **3** A: Zhèxiē xuéshēng zài chī wǔcān. **4** A: Tāmen zài pào chá. **E a** Tā zài tiàowǔ. (He is dancing.) **b** Tā zài zhǔ (zuò) wǎncān. (She is making dinner.) **c** Tāmen zài wán yóuxì. (They are playing a game.)

79 **Recap: A** 2 is correct; **B 1** g, **2** e, **3** a, **4** h, **5** f, **6** b, **7** d, **8** c, **9** j, **10** l, **11** k, **12** i; **C 1** zài tiàowǔ, **2** zài kàn diànyǐng, **3** zài tī zúqiú, **4** zài tīng yīnyuè, **5** zài pǎo(bù), **6** zài zǒu(lù), **7** zài kàn diànshì, **8** zài wán yóuxì, **9** zài shuā yá, **10** zài xǐ shǒu, **11** zài dǎ bàngqiú, **12** zài kàn bàozhǐ

Words, phrases and stuff: Video icon: Wǒmen zài děng wǒmende péngyǒu; **1** Tā gēge (zhèng) zài tī zúqiú. **2** Wǒ (zhèng) zài hē niúnǎi. **3** Wǒmen(zhèng) zài chī chǎofàn. **4** Nǐ mèimei (zhèng) zài shuìjiào. **5** Tāmen (zhèng) zài kàn xīnwén. **6** Tā (zhèng) zài xǐliǎn.

Patterns: Video: I am at work / I am working.

Get to work: A 1 a, **2** f, **3** e, **4** d, **5** b, **6** c; **B 1** pǎo(bù), **2** dǎ wǎngqiú, **3** tīng yīnyuè, **4** shuā yá

80 **Recap: 1** Shì / Bú shì, **2** Yào / Bú yào, **3** Yǒu / Méi yǒu, **4** Xǐhuān / Bù xǐhuān, **5** Huì / Bú huì

Words, phrases and stuff: 1 fángdōng, **2** gōngyù, **3** zū, **4** zhuànqián

Review: Part 1: méi; bú / bù. **Part 2:** Shì; Bù; adjective. **Part 3:** Shì; Bù

Get to work: A 1 Máng / Bù máng, **2** Yào / Bú yào, **3** Yào / Bú yào, **4** Xǐhuān / Bù xǐhuān, **5** Shì / Bù, **6** Yǒu / Méi yǒu, **7** Huì / Bú huì, **8** Yǒu / Méi yǒu, **9** Zài / Bú zài. **10** Kěyǐ / Bù kěyǐ, **11** Shì / Bù (Méi yǒu); **B 1** zhuàn hěn duō qián, **2** fù hěn duō qián, **3** Yīnwèi tāmende (apartment building) tài yuán, suǒyǐ tāmen xiǎng zhǎo xīnde. (gōngyù), **4** gōngzuò. **C** Here are some sample answers: **1** (Bú) Huì. Wǒ (bú) huì shuō Zhōngwén. **2** (Bù) Xiǎng. Wǒ (bù) xiǎng qù Zhōngguó. **3** (Bú) Yào. Míngtiān wǒ (bú) yào kàn wǒde Zhōngwén kèběn. **4** Shì / Bù. Wǒ hěn / bù cōngmíng. **5** (Bù) Xǐhuān. Wǒ (bù) xǐhuān xuéxí Zhōngwén. **6** (Bú) Zài. Xiànzài wǒ (bú) zài jiā.

81 **Recap: Video: 1** Today Jīntiān, **2** Tomorrow Míngtiān, **3** Next year Míngnián, **4** Yesterday Zuótiān

Word, phrases and stuff: 1 xīngqīrì, **2** jīntiān, **3** míngtiān, **4** hòutiān, **5** jīntiān

Get to work: A 1 Nǐ jīntiān máng ma? **2** Wǒmen xīngqīrì bù xiǎng qù nǐde pàiduì. **3** Wǒde fùmǔ wǔyuè yào chūguó. **4** Tāde yáchǐ zuótiān hěn tòng. **B 1** Xiànzài wǒ bàba bú zài zhè lǐ. **2** Zuótiān tāmen hē lǜchá. **3** Qiántiān māma qù yóujú. **4** Míngtiān nǐde yéye yào qù miànbāodiàn ma? **C 1** Wǒmende jiàoshòu qīyuè yào chūguó. Qīyuè wǒmende jiàoshòu yào chūguó. **2** Tā míngtiān bù xiǎng qù yèdiàn. Míngtiān tā bù xiǎng qù yèdiàn. **3** Wǒ xīngqī'èr yào gōngzuò. Xīngqī'èr wǒ yào gōngzuò. **4** Wǒ dìdi zuótiān chī chǎofàn. Zuótiān wǒ dìdi chī chǎofàn. **5** Wǒmen xīngqīrì yào qù jiàotáng. Xīngqīrì wǒmen yào qù jiàotáng. **6** Nǐ jīntiān yào qù yàofáng ma? Jīntiān nǐ yào qù yàofáng ma? **D 1** Hòutiān nǐ yào bú yào lái wǒ jiā? **2** Nǐ (jīntiān / míngtiān / hòutiān, etc.) yào qù kāfēitīng ma? **3** Wǒde nǚpéngyǒu míngtiān xiǎng xuéxí Zhōngwén. / Míngtiān wǒde nǚpéngyǒu xiǎng xuéxí Zhōngwén; **4** Correct

82 **Recap: A 1** b, **2** c, **3** a; **B 1** Jīntiān wǒ yào qù miànbāodiàn. **2** Míngtian wǒde péngyǒu xiǎng qù yèdiàn. **3** Yào. Hòutiān tāmen yào qù kàn qiúsài.

Get to work: A 1 b, **2** c, **3** e, **4** f, **5** a, **6** d; **B 1** tán, **2** lā, **3** chuī, **4** dǎ; **C 1** Tā jīntiān xiǎng lā xiǎotíqín ma? Jīntiān tā xiǎng lā xiǎotíqín ma? **2** Tāmen jīnnián xiǎng bānjiā ma? Jīnnián tāmen xiǎng bānjiā ma? **3** Nǐ lǎopó zuótiān hěn shēngqì ma? Zuótiān nǐ lǎopó hěn shēngqì ma? **4** Dàwèi míngtiān yào qù yínháng ma? Míngtiān Dàwèi yào qù yínháng ma?

83 **Recap: 1** What time is it? **2** What month is it? **3** What day of the week is it? **B 1** Wǒ zuótiān fēicháng máng. Zuótiān wǒ fēicháng máng. **2** Wǒ míngtiān yào qù yínháng. Míngtiān wǒ yào qù yínháng. **3** Nǐ jīntiān xiǎng qù nǎ lǐ? Jīntiān nǐ xiǎng qù nǎ lǐ?

Get to work: A 1 b, **2** c, **3** a; **B 1** Tāmen jǐdiǎn yào chūmén? **2** Tā jǐdiǎn (jǐfēn) chī zǎocān? **3** Nǐ bàbamāma jǐyuè yào bānjiā? **4** Nǐ zuótiān hěn lèi ma? / Zuótiān nǐ hěn lèi ma? OR Nǐ zuótiān lèi bú lèi? / Zuótiān nǐ lèi bú lèi? **C** Answers will vary. **D 1** Nàxiē dàxuéshēng jǐyuè fàng shǔjià? **2** Nǐde háizi jǐdiǎn yào chūmén? **3** Nǐ lǎogōng xīngqījǐ fàngjià? **4** Nǐ jīntiān xiǎng bù xiǎng gōngzuò? Jīntiān nǐ xiǎng bù xiǎng gōngzuò?

84 **Recap: 1** sìdiǎn bàn / sìdiǎn sānshí fēn, **2** shíyīyuè, **3** wǔdiǎn, **4** xīngqīyī (lǐbàiyī; zhōuyī), **5** liù diǎn sìshíwǔ fēn, **6** míngtiān; **B** Sample answers. Answers will vary. **1** Wǒ 7 diǎn 45 fēn chī zǎocān. **2** Wǒ 12 diǎn chī wǔcān. **3** Wǒ 6 diǎn bàn chī wǎncān. **4** Wǒ 10 diǎn qù shuìjiào.

Get to work: A 1 Míngtiān wǒ yào shàngbān / gōngzuò. Wǒ míngtiān yào shàngbān / gōngzuò. **2** Jīntiān nǐ yào shàngbān ma? / Nǐ jīntiān yào shàngbān ma? **3** Nǐde tàitai / lǎopó jǐdiǎn xiàbān? **4** Nǐ jiějie jǐdiǎn xiàkè? **B 1** shàngkè, **2** kāishǐ, **3** xiàkè, **4** táng; **C 1** Nàgè jiàoshòu xīngqīsān shàngkè. **2** Zhèxiē xuéshēng sāndiǎn bàn xiàkè. OR Zhèxiē xuéshēng sāndiǎn sānshí fēn xiàkè. **3** Dàxuéshēng shí'èryuè fàng hánjià. **4** Gāozhōngshēng liùyuè fàng shǔjià. **D** Sample answer: Wǒ bādiǎn kāishǐ shàngbān.

85 **Recap: A 1** chàng Yīngwén gē, **2** kàn Xībānyáwén shū, **3** xiě Zhōngwén zì; **B** Sample answer: Wǒ (bú) huì . . . , Wǒ (bù) xǐhuān . . .

Words, phrases and stuff: 1 lìshǐ kè (history), **2** Zhōngwén kè (Chinese), **3** diànnǎo kè (computer class), **4** shùxué kè (math), **5** wǔdiǎn (5:00)

Get to work: A 1 5th, **2** 3rd, **3** 7th, **4** 2nd, **5** 1st, **6** 16th, **7** 84th, **8** 9th, **9** 4th, **10** 100th; **B 1** Wǒ xǐhuān kāichē dànshì, **2** Tā xǐhuān kànshū dànshì, **3** Tāmen xǐhuān tīnggē dànshì, **4** Wǒmen xǐhuān chànggē dànshì; **C 1** Pèishān 8 diǎn shàng Rìwén kè. **2** Pèishān 9 diǎn shàng Zhōngwén kè. **3** Pèishān 12 diǎn chī wǔcān. **4** Pèishān 2 diǎn shàng diànnǎo kè; **D 1** Tāmen jiā lǐ yǒu sìzhī gǒu. **2** Wǒmende Zhōngwén bānjí yǒu shíjiǔgè xuéshēng. **3** Wǒde shūbāo lǐ yǒu wǔběn shū. **4** Wǒ yào gěi wǒde lǎoshī liǎnggè píngguǒ. (Also: liǎngkē píngguǒ is acceptable)

86 **Recap: A 1** b, **2** d, **3** a, **4** e, **5** f, **6** c; **B 1** Dàwèi qīyuè yào fàng shǔjià. **2** Tā xīngqīliù xǐhuān qù gōngyuán dǎ lánqiú. **3** Tā jiǔdiǎn yào shàng Zhōngwén kè.

Words, phrases and stuff: TIP: yǎnyuán (演员)

Get to work: A 1 Wǒmen liù diǎn xiǎng qù kàn yǎnchànghuì. **2** Tāmen xiàtiān yào jiéhūn. **3** Wǒde nánpéngyǒu hòutiān yào qù kàn gējù. **4** Wǒ xīngqīwǔ yào qù kàn yǎnzòuhuì. **B 1** Dàwèi shénme shíhòu yào qù kàn yǎnchànghuì? **2** Nǐmen shénme shíhòu xiǎng bānjiā? **3** Nǐmende nǚ'ér shénme shíhòu bìyè? **4** Nǐde péngyǒu shénme shíhòu yào qù kàn gējù? **C 1** Nǐde jiārén shénme shíhòu xiǎng mǎi xīnde fángzi? **2** Wǒ xīngqīrì bù néng qù kàn yǎnzòuhuì. **3** Tā wǔyuè yào bìyè ma? **4** Tāmen shénme shíhòu xiǎng mǎi nàbù hēisède chēzi?

87 **Recap: 1** b, **2** e, **3** g, **4** d, **5** c, **6** a, **7** h, **8** f

Get to work: A 1 míngnián dōngtiān, **2** qùnián qiūtiān, **3** míngtiān xiàwǔ, **4** jīntiān zǎoshàng, **5** wǎnshàng liùdiǎn, **6** zǎoshàng qīdiǎn, **7** jīnnián shíyuè, **8** qùnián liùyuè, **9** sānyuè shíwǔ hào, **10** míngtiān zǎoshàng; **B 1** Dàwèi jīntiān zǎoshàng yào dǎ lánqiú. **2** Dàwèi míngtiān wǎnshàng yào chuī lǎba. **3** Dàwèi jīntiān xiàwǔ yào fùxí Zhōngwén. **4** Dàwèi míngtiān zǎoshàng yào shàng shùxué kè. **5** Dàwèi jīntiān wǎnshàng yào kàn diànshì. **6** Dàwèi míngtiān xiàwǔ yào zuò lìshǐ zuòyè. **C** Answers will vary; **D 1** Tāde érzi xīngqī'èr zǎoshàng shàng tǐyù kè. **2** Nàxiē xuéshēng xiàwǔ sāndiǎn bàn xiàkè. **3** Nàgè xiǎoháizi wǎnshàng liùdiǎn yào huíjiā. **4** Wǒmen jīntiān wǎnshàng yào chūfā.

88 **Recap: A 1** bicycle, **2** car, **3** motorcycle

Words, phrases and stuff: Vocabulary: fēi = to fly; piào = a ticket; jiāyóuzhàn (gas station);
Discovery: jiāyóuzhàn

Get to work: A 1 Fēijīchǎng zài dǔchǎngde pángbiān. **2** Gōnggòng qìchē chē / gōngchē zài gōngyuánde duìmiàn. **3** Tāde chēpiào zài tāde shūde xiàmiàn. OR Tāde chēpiào zài tāde shū xià. **4** Wǒde jīpiào zài zhuōzide shàngmiàn. OR Wǒde jīpiào zài zhuōzi shàng. **B 1** e, **2** c, **3** d, **4** b, **5** a; **C 1** Are you guys getting on the plane this afternoon? **2** Is your bus / train ticket cheap? **3** When are they going to take the bus? / When do they have to take the bus? **4** What time does your mom get off the plane? **5** Tomorrow evening at 8:00 we are going to take the train. **6** These plane tickets are too expensive! **D** Sample answer: Wǒ míngnián xiàtiān yào zuò fēijī qù Zhōngguó. Wǒ xiǎng qù Běijīng Dòngwùyuán kàn xióngmāo. Wǒ yě xiǎng zuò huǒchē qù kàn Wànlǐ Chángchéng. Yīnwèi wǒ xǐhuān chī Zhōngguó cài, suǒyǐ wǒ xiǎng qù hěn duō hǎochīde cāntīng. Wǒ yě xiǎng yào zuò gōngchē qù kàn hěn duō bówùguǎn. (Next summer I am going to take a plane to China. I would like to go to Beijing Zoo to see the pandas. I would also like to take the train to go see the Great Wall of China. Because I like eating Chinese food, I would like to go to many good restaurants. I would also like to take the bus to go see many museums.)

89 **Recap: A 1** F xīngqī, **2** F yuè, **3** T, **4** T, **5** TTTTT; **B 1** shàng – on; to attend (class, school, work); to get on (a train, plane, etc.), **2** xià – under; to finish (class, school, work); to get off (a train, plane, etc.)

Words, phrases and stuff: East: dōng; West: xī

Get to work: A 1 Tā jiějie míngnián qiūtiān xiǎng qù Àozhōu. **2** Tā dìdi jīnnián yào qù Nán Měizhōu. **3** Wǒmende bàbamāma míngnián xiǎng qù Běi Měizhōu. **4** Wǒde jiěmèi xiàgèyuè yào qù Yàzhōu. **B 1** Shànggèyuè tiānqì hěn lěng. **2** Zhègèxīngqī wǒ chāo máng. **3** Xiàgèxīngqī wǒ yào qù Fēizhōu. **4** Xiàgèyuè wǒ kāishǐ shàng Zhōngwén kè. **5** Shànggèxīngqī wǒde nǚpéngyǒu /

nánpéngyǒu fēicháng lèi. **6** Zhègèyuè Lín Jiàoshòu zài Zhōngguó. **C 1** Nǐ shénme shíhòu kāishǐ nǐde xīnde gōngzuò? **2** Tāmen shénme shíhòu yào zuò fēijī? **3** Nǐmen shénme shíhòu xiǎng qù Yàzhōu? **4** Nǐ jiějie shénme shíhòu zài Běijīng? OR Nǐ jiějie shànggèxīngqī zài nǎ lǐ?

90 **Recap: 1** c, **2** a, **3** d, **4** b
Get to work: A 1 měitiān wǎnshàng (I practice writing Chinese characters every evening.) **2** měigèxīngqīsì (You play basketball every Thursday.) **3** měigèyuè (He / She must go abroad every month.) **4** měinián xiàtiān (We like to travel every summer.) **5** měigèxīngqī (You (pl.) go to the gas station every week.) **6** měinián liùyuè (They go on summer vacation (from school) every June.) **B** Answers will vary depending on the individual's habits. **1** Wǒ WOL chī wǎncān. (eat dinner) **2** Wǒ WOL shuā yá. (brush my teeth) **3** Wǒ . . . jiǎn tóufǎ. (get my hair cut) **4** Wǒ . . . qù kàn yīshēng. (go see the doctor) **5** Wǒ . . . qù chāojí shìchǎng. (go to the supermarket) **C 1** Tā tōngcháng wǎnshàng shídiǎn shuìjiào. **2** Wǒmen tōngcháng zǎoshàng bādiǎn qù shàngbān. **3** Wǒ tōngcháng xiàwǔ sāndiǎn zuò gōnggòng qìchē. **4** Wǒ jiā tōngcháng wǎnshàng liùdiǎn bàn chī wǎncān. OR Wǒ jiā tōngcháng wǎnshàng liùdiǎn sānshí fēn chī wǎncān. **D** Answers will vary. Sample answers. Wǒ měinián xiàtiān xǐhuān qù hǎitān yóuyǒng. Wǒ yě xǐhuān qí mótuōche. Wǒde jiārén měinián xiàtiān xǐhuān qù kàn bàngqiúsài. Wǒmen yě xǐhuān qù diànyǐngyuàn kàn xīnde diànyǐng. (Every summer I like to to swimming at the beach. I also like to ride my motorcycle. Every summer my family likes to go watch baseball games. We also like to go to the movie theater to watch new movies.)

91 **Recap: 1** Tā zài jiā. **2** Tā zài gōngzuò. **3** Tā zài cèsuǒ. **4** Tā zài xuéxiào. **5** Tā zài tāde péngyǒu jiā. **6** Tā zài gōngyuán.
Get to work: A Dàwèi zài túshūguǎn liànxí Zhōngwén. (David practices Chinese at the library.) Pèishān zài jiā liànxí Zhōngwén. (Peishan practices Chinese at home.) Dàwèi zài chúfáng chīfàn. (David eats in the kitchen.) Pèishān zài cāntīng chīfàn. (Peishan eats at the restaurant.) Dàwèi zài kètīng kàn diànshì. (David watches TV in the living room.) Pèishān zài wòshì kàn diànshì. (Peishan watches TV in the bedroom.) **B 1** Yóujú zài túshūguǎnde zuǒbiān. **2** Wǒ érzide dàxué zài Lúndūn. **3** Yínháng zài cāntīngde hòumiàn. **4** Tāde shǒujī zài tāde chuángde shàngmiàn. (zài tāde chuáng shàng.) **5** Lǎoshīde fěnbǐ zài hēibǎnde qiánmiàn. **6** Wǒde péngyǒu zài (fēi)jīchǎng. **C 1** a, **2** c, **3** d, **4** f, **5** b, **6** e; **D** Answers will vary. Example included in unit. **E 1** kètīng (the living room), **2** cèsuǒ (the bathroom), **3** wòshì (the bedroom), **4** shūdiàn (the bookstore)

92 **Recap:** Answers will vary. Example provided in lesson.
Words, phrases and stuff: 1 fàndiàn (hotel); cāntīng (restaurant), **2** a type of location (e.g. shop, building, etc.)
Get to work: A 1 bàngqiúchǎng; gōngyuán, **2** xuéxiào; dàxué; gāozhōng, **3** cháguǎn; cāntīng; kāfēitīng, **4** wòshì; chuáng shàng; **B 1** Nǐmende péngyǒu zài cháguǎn shàngbān ma? **2** Lǚguǎnde tíngchēchǎng zài nǎ lǐ? **3** Wǒ měigèxīngqī zài shìchǎng mǎi hěn duō dōngxī. **4** Nàxiē xuéshēng zài túshūguǎn liànxí Zhōngwén. **C 1** Tāmen xiǎng zài nǎ lǐ gōngzuò? **2** Nǐmen xǐhuān zài nǎ lǐ wán zhuō mí cáng? **3** Zhāng Yīshēng zài nǎ lǐ shàngbān? **4** Nǐ yào zài nǎ lǐ chī zǎocān? **D** Answers will vary.

93 **Recap: A 1** Wǒ xīngqīliù dǎ gāo'ěrfūqiú. **2** Tā měigèxīngqī'èr qù chāojí shìchǎng. **3** Wǒmen měigèxīngqīwǔ wǎnshàng qù yèdiàn. **B 1** Tāmen zài fàntīng chī wǔcān. **2** Wǒ bàba zài yínháng shàngbān. **3** Tā māma zài dàxué jiāoshū.

Get to work: A 1 měinián xiàtiān – Every summer we swim at the beach. **2** huǒchēzhàn – They wait for the train at the train station at seven o'clock in the morning. **3** rè qiǎokèlì – Mrs Gao drinks hot chocolate at the coffee shop every winter. **4** lǚguǎn – That businessman usually sleeps at a motel. **5** jiànshēnfáng; tǐyùguǎn – Pèishān exercises at the gym every afternoon. **B 1** měitiān zǎoshàng, **2** měitiān xiàwǔ, **3** chāojí shìchǎng, **4** hǎitān, **5** měigèyuè, **6** xuéxiào; **C** Answers will vary. **D 1** CORRECT, **2** Wáng Jiàoshòu wǎnshàng zài xuéxiào shàng Zhōngwén kè. **3** Wǒmen měinián xiàtiān zài gōngyuán chī bīngqílín. **4** Wǒde nánpéngyǒu xīngqīyī zài dǔchǎng dǎ májiàng.

94 **Recap: 1** Wǒmen měitiān wǎnshàng zài dìxiàshì dǎ pīngpāngqiú. **2** Nǐmen měitiān zǎoshàng zài chúfáng pàochá. **3** Lín Xiānshēng zǎoshàng zài jiànshēnfáng / tǐyùguǎn zuò yùndòng. **4** Bill xīngqīsān xiàwǔ zài tāde wòshì liànxí xiǎotíqín. **5** Mike Lǎoshī měitiān zài chēkù jiāo Zhōngwén.

Get to work: A 1 (Nàgè nǚrén) xǐ bù xǐhuān zài tǐyùguǎn dǎ tàijí? Does that woman like to do tai chi in the gym? (Pattern 2), **2** Nǐ měinián shí'èryuè zài nǎ lǐ (huáxuě)? Where do you ski every December? (Pattern 1), **3** Wǒmen xiànzài yào zài (yóuyǒngchí) yóuyǒng. We are going to the pool to swim now. (Pattern 2), **4** Wǒmen míngnián xiàtiān xiǎng zài Yìdàlì (lǚxíng). Next summer we would like to travel in Italy. (Pattern 2); **B** Answers will vary. **C 1** Wǒ míngtiān wǎnshàng xiǎng zài bàngqiúchǎng kàn qiúsài. **2** Tāmen míngnián chūntiān xiǎng zài Běi Měizhōu lǚxíng. **3** Wǒ māma měitiān zǎoshàng xǐhuān zài gōngyuán dǎ tàijí. **4** Nǐmen jīntiān xiàwǔ yào zài cāntīng chīfàn ma? **D** Answers will vary.

95 **Recap: A 1** b, **2** c, **3** a; **B 1** c, **2** a, **3** b

Words, phrases and stuff: Video: dōngxī

Get to work: A Sample Answers: **1** Wǒ fùqīn xiàwǔ yīdiǎn zài cāntīng chī wǔcān. **2** Wǒde mìshū zǎoshàng bādiǎn zài bàngōngshì hē kāfēi. **3** Tā xīngqīliù zài fàndiàn gōngzuò. **4** Tāmende nǚ'ér wǔyuè yào zài Yìdàlì kāishǐ gōngzuò. **B** Sample Answers: **1** Tāmen míngtiān wǎnshàng yào zài gōngyuán dǎ wǎngqiú. **2** Wǒmen xiàgèxīngqī yào zài chāojí shìchǎng mǎi cài. **3** Tā érzi měitiān zài fàntīng zuò zuòyè. **4** Lili tōngcháng xǐhuān zài biànlì shāngdiàn mǎi dōngxī. **C** Answers will vary. Example given in lesson.

96 **Recap: A 1** You are intelligent and hardworking. **2** He likes to play baseball and tennis. **3** We would like to go to Beijing and Toyko. **B 1** Wǒmen hěn ǎi yě hěn shòu. **2** Tā xǐhuān chī píngguǒ yě xǐhuān chī xiāngjiāo. **3** Wǒ huì tán gāngqín yě huì dǎ gǔ.

Get to work: A 1 Wǒ xǐhuān hànbǎo. Wǒ yě xǐhuān shǔtiáo. **2** Wǒ gēge xǐhuān bàngqiú, yě xǐhuān lánqiú. **3** Tāde gǒu hěn è, yě hěn kě. **4** Tā yào qù yínháng, yě yào qù yóujú. **B 1** Dàxiàng hé hémǎ shì hěn dàde dòngwù. **2** Wǒ jiějie hé mèimei ài qù gāo'ěrfūqiúchǎng dǎ gāo'ěrfūqiú. **3** Sam hé Bob xǐhuān zài Zhōngguóchéng mǎi dōngxī. **4** Tāde Yīngwén lǎoshī hé shùxué lǎoshī hěn hǎo. **C 1** Wǒ lǎopó xiànzài yào qù chāojí shìchǎng hé jiāyóuzhàn. **2** Tāmen xǐhuān zài cāntīng chī pīsà hé règǒu. **3** Jīntiān wǒ xiǎng chuān T-xù hé kùzi. **4** Lín Jiàoshòu jīnnián xiàtiān yào qù Zhōngguó hé Rìběn lǚxíng. **D 1** yě, **2** hé, **3** hé, **4** hé, **5** yě, **6** yě

97 **Recap: A 1** Wǒ gēge hé wǒ dìdi. **2** Wǒde lǎoshī hé nǐde lǎoshī. **3** Sarah hé Rosie. **B 1** yīzhī gǒu hé yīzhī māo. **2** hànbǎo hé shǔtiáo. **3** Fǎwén hé Déwén.

Get to work: A 1 Susan hé wǒ xǐhuān qù dǎ bǎolíngqiú. **2** Tā gēn tā māma bù xǐhuān pǎobù. **3** Wǒ bàbamāma ài sànbù. **4** Míngtiān wǒde xuéshēng hé wǒ yào qù kàn yǎnchànghuì. **B 1** Wǒ gēn wǒde hǎo péngyǒu dǎ gāo'ěrfūqiú. **2** Tā gēn tāde yéye qù diàoyú. **3** Wǒmen érzi gēn tāde xiōngdì jiěmèi wán pūkèpái. **4** Wǒ nǚ'ér hé tāde nánpéngyǒu chàng kǎlāOK. **C 1** Nǐ bàba xǐhuān zuò shénme (yùndòng)? **2** Tāde lǎobǎn yào zuò / kàn shénme? **3** Nǐde xuéshēng xiǎng qù nǎ lǐ? **4** Tāde jiěmèi xiǎng yào qù nǎ lǐ lǚxíng? **D 1** Wǒ **gēn wǒde nǚpéngyǒu** yào xué qí mótuōchē. **2** Tā hé **tāde tóngshì** zuò huǒchē huíjiā. **3** Nàzhāng chuáng **hé zhèzhāng shāfā** hǎo piányí. **4** Nǐ **gēn shéi** dǎ yǔmáoqiú? **5** Nàxiē xuéshēng yào mǎi Zhōngwén kèběn **hé liànxíběn**. **6** Zhègè lǎoshī yǒu fěnbǐ **hé mǎkèbǐ.**

98 **Recap: 1** Joe yào qù biànì shāngdiàn, yě yào qù yínháng. **2** Joe yào qù biànì shāngdiàn hé yínháng. **3** Joe yào qù biànì shāngdiàn gēn yínháng.

Get to work: A 1 yīqǐ, **2** dōu, **3** yīqǐ, **4** dōu, **5** dōu, **6** dōu; **B 1** Tā hé tā dìdi dōu mán ǎi. **2** Xiànzài wǒ gēn wǒde mèimei zài yīqǐ. **3** Nǐ měinián dōu qù Yìdàlì ma? **4** Nǐmen zhù zài yīqǐ ma? **C** Answers will vary. Example provided in exercise. **D** Listen to audio.

99 **Recap: 1** They live together. **2** We are all extremely lazy. **3** Would you like to go to the beach together? **4** My brothers are both quite tall.

Get to work: 1 háiyǒu, **2** háiyǒu, **3** hái, **4** háishì, **5** háishì, **6** hái; **B** Answers will vary. Example provided. **C 1** Míngtiān tā yào shàng Yīngwén kè. Háiyǒu, tā yào qù mǎi cài. **2** Bob xǐhuān hē hóngpútáojiǔ. Háiyǒu, tā xǐhuān hē píjiǔ. **3** Wǒ bàba zǎoshàng zài gōngchǎng gōngzuò / shàngbān. Háiyǒu, tā wǎnshàng kāi chūzūchē / jìchéngchē. **4** Tā hé wǒ dōu huì shuō Zhōngwén. Háiyǒu, wǒmen yě huì xiě Zhōngwén zì. **D 1** dōu; gēn, **2** gēn; yīqǐ, **3** gēn; hái, **4** háiyǒu; dōu, **5** hé; yě, **6** dōu; Háiyǒu

100 **Recap: 1** with us, **2** with you guys, **3** with my younger sister, **4** with her boyfriend, **5** with your co-workers / colleague(s), **6** with my family (members)

Get to work: A 1 Wǒmen měinián xiàtiān dōu qù Tàiguó hé/gēn Yuènán lǚxíng. (Every summer we go traveling in Thailand and Vietnam.) **2** Tāmen měigèxīngqīwǔ zǎoshàng zài jiàoshì shàng Zhōngwén kè. (Every Friday morning they attend Chinese class in the classroom.) **3** Wǒ gēn wǒde hǎo péngyǒu měitiān dōu xǐhuān wán diàndòng yóuxì. (My good friend and I like to play video games every day.) **4** Wǒde nǚpéngyǒu hé wǒde jiějie jīntiān wǎnshàng yào zài dǔchǎng jiànmiàn. (My girlfriend and my older sister are going to meet at the casino this evening.) **B 1** Pattern 4, **2** Pattern 3, **3** Pattern 6, **4** Pattern 5, **5** Pattern 2, **6** Pattern 1; **C 1** Wǒ gēn wǒde jiàoliàn míngtiān xiàwǔ xiǎng yào zài lánqiúchǎng jiànmiàn. OR Wǒ míngtiān xiàwǔ xiǎng yào zài lánqiúchǎng gēn wǒde jiàoliàn jiànmiàn. **2** Tā qùnián zài Niǔyuēshì gēn péngyǒu qìngzhù tāde shēngrì. OR Tā gēn péngyǒu qùnián zài Niǔyuēshì qìngzhù tāde shēngrì. **3** Wǒde línjūde érzi míngnián yào zài Běijīng Dàxué kāishǐ shàngxué. **4** Nǐ xiàgèyuè xiǎng bù xiǎng gēn wǒ yīqǐ zuò bāshì qù Jiāzhōu? **D 1** b, **2** f, **3** d, **4** c, **5** a, **6** e

101 **Recap:** **A 1** ǎi, **2** shòu, **3** bèn, **4** lǎnduò, **5** chǒu; **B 1** c, **2** a, **3** b, **4** e, **5** f, **6** d
Patterns: **1** Dàxiàng bǐ lǎohǔ dà. (The elephant is bigger than the tiger.) **2** Yīngguó bǐ Měiguó xiǎo. (England is smaller than America.) **3** Cǎoméi bǐ píngguǒ tián. (The strawberries are sweeter than the apples.) **4** Tǔdòu bǐ yángcōng hǎochī. (The potato tastes better than the onion.)
Get to work: **A 1** Zhègè píngguǒ bǐ zhègè cǎoméi tián. (This apple is sweeter than this strawberry.) **2** Nàxiē níngméng bǐ nàxiē chéngzi suān. (Those lemons are more sour than those oranges.) **3** Zhèbēi kāfēi bǐ nàbēi kāfēi kǔ. (This cup of coffee is more bitter than that cup of coffee.) **4** Zhèwǎn tāng bǐ nàwǎn tāng là. (This bowl of soup is spicier than that bowl of soup.) **B 1** This pair of shoes; that pair of shoes, **2** tablet computers; laptop computers, **3** Your motorcycle; my motorcycle, **4** That pair of chopsticks; this pair of chopsticks; **C 1** Hóngpútáojiǔ bǐ báipútáojiǔ hǎohē. **2** Wǒde shū bǐ nǐde shū hǎokàn. **3** Zhèshǒu gē bǐ nàshǒu gē hǎotīng. **4** Shǔtiáo bǐ shūcài hǎochī. **D** Example given. Answers will vary.

102 **Recap:** **A 1** Chángjǐnglù bǐ hóuzi gāo. (The giraffe is taller than the monkey.) **2** Māma bǐ wàipó niánqīng. (Mom is younger than grandma.) **3** Yéye bǐ bàba lǎo. (Grandpa is older than dad.)
Words, phrases and stuff: **1** gè, **2** kē
Get to work: **A 1** Xióng bǐ shīzi dà. Dàxiàng zuì dà. **2** Jī bǐ zhū xiǎo. Lǎoshǔ zuì xiǎo. **3** Shānyáng bǐ wūguī kuài. Mǎ zuì kuài. **4** Lǎohǔ bǐ bānmǎ màn. Xióngmāo zuì màn. **B** Answers will vary. Example given. **C** Answers will vary. Example given. **D** Answers will vary. Example given.

103 **Recap:** **1** běn – books; book-like objects, **2** tái – electronic devices, **3** bēi – cups; glasses, **4** píng – bottles, **5** zhāng – flat objects, **6** bù – movies; machines (e.g. cars)
Words, phrases and stuff: **A** Nǐ shì nǎlǐ rén? Nǐ shì nǎguó rén? **B 1** nǎ(yī)tiān, **2** nǎ(yī)nián, **3** jǐtiān, jǐgèyuè, jǐnián
Get to work: **A 1** c, **2** f, **3** b, **4** a, **5** e, **6** d, **7** g; **B 1** Nǎzhāng yǐzi shì tāde? **2** Nǎgè nánrén shì nǐde lǎoshī? **3** Nǎgè nǚrén shì yīshēng? **4** Nǎzhī gǒu shì nǐde péngyǒude? **C 1** Tā nǎ(yī)tiān yào qù pàiduì? **2** Nǎ(yī)bù chēzi shì nǐde? **3** Nǎ(yī)shuāng xiézi shì tāde? **4** Nǎ(yī)zhāng zhǐ shì nǐ dìdide? **D 1** Nǐ xiǎng hē nǎyībēi kāfēi? (Which cup of coffee would you like to drink?) **2** Nǐ xiǎng chuān nǎyījiàn kùzi? (Which pair of trousers would you like to wear?) **3** Nǐ xiǎng yòng nǎyīzhī bǐ? (Which pen would you like to use?) **4** Nǐ xiǎng mǎi nǎyīzhāng chuáng? (Which bed would you like to buy?) **5** Nǐ xiǎng kāi nǎyībù chēzi? (Which car would you like to drive?) **6** Nǐ xiǎng mài nǎyītái diànnǎo? (Which computer would you like to sell?) **E 1** Beijing, **2** Chinese, **3** Monday, Wednesday and Thursday, **4** Wednesday and Friday

104 **Recap:** Answers will vary. Sample answers provided. **1** Nàzhī gǒu bǐ wǒde gǒu dà. **2** Zhèjiàn chènshān zuì piányí. **3** Nǎ(yī)běn Zhōngwén kèběn shì nǐde?
Get to work: **A 1** bǐ, **2** bǐjiào, **3** bǐjiào, **4** bǐjiào, **5** bǐ, **6** bǐ; **B 1** xǐhuān; bǐjiào, **2** Nǎyī, **3** zuì, **4** bǐ; **C 1** Wǒ nǚ'ér bǐ wǒ érzi shòu. Wǒ nǚ'ér zuì shòu. (bǐjiào intead of zuì), **2** Diànyǐngyuàn yǒu hěn duō xīnde diànyǐng. Nǎbù zuì hǎokàn? (Correct), **3** Wǒ xiǎng yào mǎi shǒujī. Nǎtái bǐ hǎoyòng? (zuì), **4** Wǒ xǐhuān dǎ lánqiú kěshì wǒ bǐ xǐhuān kàn lánqiúsài. (bǐjiào); **D 1** Lily is happier than Cathy. **2** Lily is taller than Cathy. **3** Lily is thinner than Cathy. **4** Lily's earrings are bigger than Cathy's. **5** Lily's hair is longer than Cathy's. **6** Lily's shoes are newer than Cathy's. **7** Lily's dress is prettier than Cathy's.

105 **Recap: 1** Wǒ hěn huì shuō Zhōngwén. (I can really speak Chinese well.) **2** Tā mán xǐhuān zhǔfàn. (He / She likes cooking quite a bit.) **3** Tāmen fēicháng xǐhuān dǎ lánqiú. (They REALLY like playing basketball.) **4** Wǒ mèimei hěn xiǎng qù kàn yǎnchànghuì. (My younger sister would really like to go see the concert.)

Get to work: A 1 Wǒ xǐhuān kàn diànyǐng dànshì wǒ zuì xǐhuān kàn Měiguó diànyǐng. **2** Tā zuì xǐhuān chàng kǎlāOK. **3** Nǐmen bǐjiào xǐhuān shàngwǎng háishì kàn diànshì? OR Nǐmen bǐjiào xǐhuān kàn diànshì háishì shàngwǎng? **4** Wǒ bàba xǐhuān hē píjiǔ dànshì ō bǐjiào xǐhuān hē hóngpútáojiǔ. OR Wǒ xǐhuān hē píjiǔ dànshì wǒ bàba bǐjiào xǐhuān hē hóngpútáojiǔ. **B** xiǎng; Wèishénme? bǐ; Zhēnde ma? **C 1** Wǒ zuì xǐhuān tán gāngqín. **2** Wǒmen bǐjiào xǐhuān shùxué kè. **3** Jīnnián xiàtiān wǒ bǐjiào xiǎng qù Àozhōu hé Niǔ Xīlán. **4** Tāmen zuì xǐhuān zài jiā (lǐ) chī zǎocān.

106 **Recap: 1** Zhèzhāng yǐzi bǐ nàzhāng yǐzi shūfú. (This chair is more comfortable than that chair.) **2** Zhèxiē yīngtáo bǐ nàxiē yīngtáo tián. (These cherries are sweeter than those cherries.) **3** Zhètái píngbǎn diànnǎo bǐ nàtái píngbǎn diànnǎo guì. (This tablet is more expensive than that tablet.) **4** Zhèpíng niúnǎi bǐ nàpíng niúnǎi bīng. (This bottle of milk is colder than that bottle of milk.)

Get to work: A 1 Wǒde xiōngdi hé wǒ dōu hěn è, dànshì wǒde péngyǒu gèng è. **2** Wǒmen dōu hěn qiángzhuàng, dànshì wǒmende tóngxué gèng qiángzhuàng. **3** Nǐmende nǚpéngyǒu dōu hěn piàoliàng, dànshì Mike Lǎoshīde nǚpéngyǒu gèng piàoliàng. **4** Wǒde chēzi dōu hěn jiù, dànshì wǒde nánpéngyǒude chēzi gèng jiù. **B 1** Nǐde xiǎogǒu bǐ nǐde xiǎomāo gèng xiǎo. **2** Zhuōqiú bǐ bǎolíngqiú gèng hǎowán. **3** Zhōngwén kè bǐ Yīngwén kè gèng nán. **4** Wǒde bǐjìběn diànnǎo bǐ wǒde píngbǎn diànnǎo gèng guì. **C** Note: Subjects in bǐ comparisons could be reversed. **1** Zhèbēi kāfēi bǐ nàbēi kāfēi gèng tàng. **2** Zhèzhāng yǐzi bǐ nàzhāng yǐzi gèng yìng. **3** Nàběn shū gèng hǎokàn. **4** Wǒ érzide fángjiān bǐ wǒ nǚ'érde fángjiān gèng gānjìng. **D 1** diànshì; diànyǐng, **2** niúròu; chī yángròu, **3** niúnǎi; hē chéngzhī, **4** lánqiú; dǎ bàngqiú

107 **Recap: 1** Yes, **2** No, **3** No, **4** Yes

Patterns: 1 Wǒ gēge hé wǒ yīyàng cōngmíng. (My older brother and I are equally intelligent.) **2** Wǒ gēn nǐ yīyàng pàng. (You and I are equally fat.) **3** Nǐ hé nǐ jiějie yīyàng piàoliàng. (You and your older sister are equally beautiful.) **4** Tā gēn tāde tóngxué yīyàng lǎnduò. (He / She and his classmate(s) are equally lazy.) **5** Nàgè yīshēng hé nàgè yáyī yīyàng yǒuqián. (That doctor and that dentist are equally rich.)

Get to work: A 1 Tāde nánpéngyǒu gēn tā yīyàng dà. (Her boyfriend is as old as she is.) **2** Nàzhāng yǐzi hé zhèzhāng yǐzi yīyàng xiǎo. (That chair and this chair are equally small.) **3** Zhèliǎnggè chéngshì yīyàng dà. (These two cities are the same size.) **4** Zhèxiē chuáng yīyàng xiǎo. (These beds are equally small.) **B 1** Nǐde kè gēn / hé tāde kè yīyàng jiǎndān. **2** Wǒde shǒujī gēn / hé wǒde nǚpéngyǒude shǒujī yīyàng xiǎo. **3** Zhègè jīròu gēn / hé nàgè niúròu yīyàng hǎochī. **4** Zhètiáo lǜsède yǔ gēn / hé nàtiáo lánsède yǔ yīyàng cháng. **5** Zhètiáo lù gēn / hé nàtiáo lù yīyàng hǎo. **C 1** Nàliǎngtái chēzi . . . **2** Zhèwǔzhī gǒu . . . **3** Zhèshígè rén . . . y, **4** Nàbāgè xuéshēng . . . **D 1** Tā gēn wǒ yīyàng gāo. **2** Tāde tóufǎ hé wǒde tóufǎ yīyàng cháng. **3** Tāde yángzhuāng gēn wǒde yīyàng piàoliàng. **4** Lilide jièzhi hé Pèishānde jièzhi yīyàng guì.

108 **Recap:** If you answered "21" and "185 cm (6'1")" respectively, then we're on the same page.
Patterns: 1 e, **2** b, **3** d, **4** c, **5** a
Get to work: A 1 nǎ(yī), **2** bǐ; gèng, **3** gèng; zuì, **4** bǐjiào; **B1** Kàn zúqiúsài bǐ kàn lánqiúsài hǎowán. **2** Bàba hé māma yīyàng dà. **3** Wǒde péngyǒu bǐjiào xǐhuān chuān hēisède xīzhuāng. **4** Pèishān bǐ tāde tóngxué cōngmíng. **C 1** Gēge bǐ dìdi gāo. **2** Jiějie bǐ mèimei gèng piàoliàng. **3** Wǒde nánpéngyǒu bǐ wǒde jiějie cōngmíng dànshì wǒ zuì cōngmíng. **4** Bàba hé māma yīyàng lèi.

109 **Recap: 1** question particle, **2** comparative particle, **3** question particle (often used to ask "And you?"), **4** possessive particle
Get to work: A 1 ba, **2** a, **3** a, **4** ba; **B 1** b, **2** a, **3** e, **4** c, **5** d; **C** Answers will vary. Example given. **D 1** Morning, **2** Dàwèi, **3** She suggests that they go eat breakfast, **4** bacon and eggs, **5** He thinks pancakes are too sweet. **E 1** Hǎo a! (if you're cool); hǎo ba (if you're not), **2** Hǎo a!, **3** Hǎo a!, **4** Hǎo ba

110 **Get to work: A** Answers will vary; **B 1** Huì. Tā xiàgèyuè huì kāishǐ gōngzuò. **2** Huì. Míngtiān huì xiàyǔ. **3** Huì. Tāmen jīntiān wǎnshàng huì zài diànyǐngyuàn kàn diànyǐng. **4** Bú huì. Xiàgèxīngqīyī bú huì xiàxuě. **C 1** can, **2** can, **3** will, **4** will; **D** Dàwèi will . . . **1** go to a concert tomorrow evening, **2** go abroad next week, **3** will graduate next summer; Dàwèi will not . . . **1** take the bus to work the day after tomorrow, **2** review (his) Japanese on Friday night, **3** travel next month

111 **Recap: 1** Jīntiān wǒ yào kāiche qù gōngzuò / shàngbān. OR Wǒ jīntiān yào kāichē qù gōngzuò / shàngbān. **2** Xīngqīyī wǎnshàng wǒ tī zúqiú. OR Wǒ xīngqīyī wǎnshàng tī zúqiú. **3** Míngnián tā huì chūguó. OR Tā míngnián huì chūguó. **4** Míngtiān tā yào qù yínháng. OR Tā míngtiān yào qù yínháng. **5** Měitiān zǎoshàng tāmen děng gōnggòng qìchē / gōngchē. Tāmen měitiān zǎoshàng děng gōnggòng qìchē / gōngchē. **6** Xiàgèyuè wǒmen yào qù hūnlǐ. OR Wǒmen xiàgèyuè yào qù hūnlǐ.
Get to work: A 1 Yǐqián, **2** Yǐqián, **3** Hòutiān, **4** yǐqián; **B** Answers will vary. Example provided. **C 1** Tā yǐqián xǐhuān kàn diànshì ma? OR Tā yǐqián xǐ bù xǐhuān kàn diànshì? **2** Nàgè nǚrén yǐqián hěn piàoliàng ma? **3** Nǐ bàba yǐqián xiǎng qù Bālí ma? OR Nǐ bàba yǐqián xiǎng bù xiǎng qù Bālí? **4** Nǐmen yǐqián huì tiàowǔ ma? OR Nǐmen yǐqián huì bú huì tiàowǔ? **D 1** Pèishān **2** Pèishān played violin; Dàwèi played the drums. **3** Pèishān lived with her parents; Dàwèi lived with his (maternal) grandmother.

112 **Recap: 1** Yǐqián wǒ bù chī ròu. (I didn't eat meat in the past.) **2** Tā yǐqián yǒu lǎopó. (He had a wife before.) **3** Yǐqián tāmen zhù zài Zhījiāgē. (They used to live in Chicago.) **4** Wǒmen yǐqián bù xiǎng bānjiā. (We didn't want to move (house) before.)
Get to work: A 1 yǐqián, **2** yǐhòu, **3** yǐqián, **4** yǐqián; **B** Answers will vary. Example given.
C 1 Yǐhòu tāmen xiǎng shàng dàxué ma? OR Yǐhòu tāmen xiǎng bù xiǎng shàng dàxué?
2 Nǐ érzi yǐhòu yào zhǎo xīnde gōngzuò ma? OR Nǐ érzi yǐhòu yào bú yào zhǎo xīnde gōngzuò?
3 Yǐhòu nǐ yéye xiǎng zhù zài Zhōngguó ma? OR Yǐhòu nǐ yéye xiǎng bù xiǎng zhù zài Zhōngguó?
4 Dàwèi hé Pèishān yǐhòu huì líhūn ma? OR Dàwèi hé Pèishān yǐhòu huì bú huì líhūn?
D 1 a firefighter, **2** an English teacher, **3** a doctor, **4** a lawyer, **5** a chef, **6** an engineer, **7** a police officer, **8** Mike Lǎoshī

113 **Recap: 1** Correct, **2** Incorrect (Would you guys like to live in Shanghai in the future?), **3** Incorrect (In the past, I didn't like living here.), **4** Correct

Get to work: A 1 Tā shuìjiàode shíhòu . . . (When he / she was / is sleeping), **2** Bàba dào bàngōngshìde shíhòu . . . (When Dad arrives at the office), **3** Wǒ lǎogōng gōngzuòde shíhòu . . . (When my husband was / is working), **4** Tā māma zuòfànde shíhòu . . . (When his / her mom was / is cooking); **B** Answers will vary. Example given. **C 1** Xiǎopéngyǒu kàn diànyǐngde shíhòu xǐhuān chī tángguǒ. **2** Dàwèi kāichēde shíhòu xǐhuān tīng yīnyuè. **3** Jiéhūnde shíhòu gēge huì chuān xīzhuāng. **4** Bìyède shíhòu jiějie huì hěn gāoxìng. **D 1** d, **2** a, **3** e, **4** c, **5** b

114 **Recap: 1** zài, **2** shàng fēijī, **3** chī wǔcān, **4** dào

Get to work: A 1 Wǒde xiǎohái shuìjiào yǐqián (Before my child / children go(es) to sleep) **2** Tā rènshì tā lǎopó yǐqián (Before he met his wife) **3** Wǒmen bānjiā yǐqián (Before we move (house)) **4** Nǐ bàba chūmén yǐqián (Before your dad leaves the house) **5** Tāmen huíguó yǐqián (Before they return to the country); **B 1** e, **2** b, **3** a, **4** f, **5** c, **6** d; **C** Answers will vary. Example provided. **D** Answer will vary. Example provided.

115 **Recap: A 1** Tā shuìjiào yǐqián xǐhuān hē niúnǎi. **2** Chīfàn yǐqián nǐ yào xǐ shǒu. **3** Shàngkè yǐqián wǒ yào zuò zuòyè. **4** Tāmen shàngbān yǐqián yào děng gōnggòng qìchē / gōngchē.

Get to work: A 1 After he / she eats dinner, **2** After we get out of class, **3** After Sarah graduates, **4** After my older sister arrives home, **B 1** c, **2** e, **3** f, **4** a, **5** d, **6** b, **C** Answers will vary. Example given. **D** Answers will vary. Example given. **E 1** Wǒ huíjiā yǐhòu yào huàn yīfú. **2** Tāmen dàojiā yǐhòu ài dǎ zhuōqiú. **3** Mike Lǎoshī xiàkè yǐhòu xǐhuān hē yībēi báipútáojiǔ. **4** Lili qǐchuáng yǐhòu yào shuā yá. **5** Nǐ nǚ'ér kāixué yǐhòu huì bǐjiào máng.

116 **Recap: 1** yǐhòu, **2** yǐqián, **3** yǐhòu, **4** yǐqián

Get to work: A 1 Tā zěnme qù Zhījiāgē? **2** Nǐmen zěnme chī chǎofàn? **3** Tā jiějie zěnme gēn tāde péngyǒu liánluò? **4** Nǐ māma zěnme xǐ yīfú? **B 1** Tā zěnme qù túshūguǎn? (How does he / she go to the library?), **2** Nàgè rén zěnme hē tāng? (How does that person eat soup?), **3** Tāmen zěnme chī hànbǎo? (How do they eat hamburgers?), **4** Nǐmen zěnme mǎi yīfú? (How you do you guys buy clothing?); **C 1** Nǐ zěnme qí mótuōchē? **2** Nǐmen zěnme dǎ májiàng? **3** Tāmen zěnme yòng tāmende gānyījī? **4** Nǐ māma zěnme zhǔ lóngxiā? **D 1** Tā yòng chāzi chī niúpái. **2** Tā yòng xǐwǎnjī xǐ wǎn. **3** Tā qí zìxíngchē (jiǎotàchē) qù xuéxiào. **4** Tā yòng tāngchí hē tāng.

117 **Recap: 1** How do you get to the bowling alley? **2** How do you use this tablet (computer)? **3** How do you play ping-pong / pool? **4** How do you grill hamburgers?

Get to work: A Answers will vary. Example given. **B 1** c, **2** d, **3** a, **4** b; **C 1** Yīnwèi kāfēi tài kǔ. **2** Yīnwèi tángguǒ tài tián. **3** Yīnwèi zhèbēi níngméngzhī tài suān. **4** Yīnwèi nàbēi chá tài tàng. **D 1** Q: Why don't they like attending math class? A: Because math is too hard. **2** Q: Why isn't your husband going to work? A: Because he has a headache. **3** Q: Why don't you want to listen to my CD? A: Because I don't like listening to English songs. **4** Q: Why doesn't your friend have money? A: Because he / she doesn't have a job.

118 **Recap: 1** Why, **2** How, **3** How, **4** Why

Get to work: A Answers will vary. Example given. **B 1** Why is your dog so loud? **2** How could the child(ren) be so cute? **3** Why does he / she love to talk on the phone so much? **4** How could they like playing video games this much?; **C 1** b, **2** d, **3** a, **4** c; **D 1** zhème kě'ài, **2** nàme guāi, **3** zhème kuài, **4** nàme duō

119 **Recap: 1** b, **2** a, **3** d, **4** c

Get to work: A 1 How is that movie theater's popcorn? **2** How is this coffee shop's coffee? **3** How do you feel about English (black) tea? **4** What is American food like? (How's American food?); **B 1** Zhètái xǐwǎnjī hěn hǎoyòng. **2** Wǒde mótuōchē hěn hǎoqí. **3** Tā bàbade pútáojiǔ hěn hǎohē. **4** Zhèjiā cāntīngde shuǐ jiǎo hěn hǎochī. **C 1** Nǐmen juéde Wáng Lǎoshīde Zhōngwén kè zěnmeyàng? **2** Tāmen juéde nàgè diànshì jiémù zěnmeyàng? **3** Nǐ érzi juéde zhèshǒu gē zěnmeyàng? **4** Pèishān juéde *Chinese with Mike* zěnmeyàng? **D 1** c, **2** d, **3** a, **4** b

120 **Recap: 1** b, **2** c, **3** f, **4** e, **5** d, **6** a

Get to work: A 1 Měitiān tā xiān pǎobù zài qù gōngzuò / shàngbān. **2** Měigèxīngqīsān tā xiān dài tāde xiǎohái qù xuéxiào zài gēn péngyǒu qù kāfēitīng. **3** Měitiān xiàwǔ Dàwèi xiān xǐ yīfú zài zuòfàn/ zhǔfàn. **4** Měitiān wǎnshàng tā xiān xǐzǎo zài kàn diànshì. **B 1** Wǒ bàba xiān qù yínháng, zài dǎ wǎngqiú, ránhòu tā huíjiā zuòfàn. **2** Wǒ gēge xiān qǐchuáng, zài hē kāfēi, ránhòu kàn bàozhǐ. **3** Wǒ jiějie xiān xǐzǎo, zài chuān yīfú, ránhòu shū tóufǎ. **4** Wǒ dìdi xiān tī zúqiú, zài hē shuǐ, ránhòu qí zìxíngchē huí jiā. **C 1** Wǒmen zěnme qù diànyǐngyuàn? Diànyǐngyuán zěnme qù / zǒu? **2** Wǒ zěnme qù nǐ jiā? Nǐ jiā zěnme qù / zǒu? **3** Wǒ zěnme qù yóujú? Yóujú zěnme qù / zǒu? **4** Wǒmen zěnme qù gāo'ěrfūqiúchǎng? Gāo'ěrfūqiúchǎng zěnme qù / zǒu? **D 1** Nǐ xiān zhízǒu, zài zuǒzhuǎn, ránhòu yòuzhuǎn. **2** Nǐ xiān yòuzhuǎn, zài zuǒzhuǎn, ránhòu zhízǒu. **3** Nǐ xiān zuǒzhuǎn, zài zhízǒu, ránhòu zuǒzhuǎn. **4** Nǐ xiān zhízǒu, zài yòuzhuǎn, ránhòu zuǒzhuǎn.

Chinese–English Glossary

a / ā	*particle expressing exclamation / surprise*
ǎi	*short*
ài	*to love*
Ài'ěrlán	*Ireland*
Āijí	*Egypt*
Ālābówén	*Arabic (language)*
Àozhōu	*Australia*
āyí	*aunt (M's sis)*
ba	*particle expressing a suggestion / command*
bā	*8, eight;* **bā diǎn** *8:00, eight o'clock;* **bāshí** *80, eighty;* **bāyuè** *August*
bàba	*father, dad*
bàbamāma; fùmǔ	*mom and dad; parents*
bàibài	*goodbye (inf)*
báibǎn(bǐ)	*whiteboard (marker)*
báifàn	*white rice*
báipútáojiǔ	*white wine*
báisè	*white*
Bālí	*Paris*
bàn	*half (i.e. half-past an hour)*
bāng	*to help*
bàngōngshì	*office*
bàngqiú	*baseball*
bàngqiúchǎng	*baseball field*
bānjí	*a class*
bānjiā	*to move (house)*
bānmǎ	*zebra*
bānshǒu	*wrench*
bāo	*MW for packs / packages*
bàomǐhuā	*popcorn*
bàozhǐ	*newspaper*
bāshì	*a bus*
Bāxī	*Brazil*
bēi	*MW for cups, glasses, drinks, beverages;* **bēizi** *a cup, a glass*
Běi Měizhōu	*North America*
Běijīng	*Beijing*
bēizi	*cup*
bèn	*stupid*
běn	*MW for books, magazines, book-like objects*
bǐ	*a comparative particle (used to form -er; more . . . comparatives)*
bǐ	*pen*
biànlì shāngdiàn	*convenience store*
biǎo	*cousin;* **biǎogē** *M's older male cousin*
bǐjiào	*to compare / contrast; relatively*
bǐjiào xǐhuān	*to prefer; to like more*
bǐjìběn	*notebook;* **bǐjìběn diànnǎo** *laptop computer*
bīng	*cold (for objects)*
bīngxiāng	*refrigerator*
bǐsài	*a match; competition*
bìyè	*to graduate*
bízi	*nose*
bóbo	*uncle (F's older bro)*
bōcài	*spinach*
Bōlán	*Poland*
bówùguǎn	*museum*
bózi	*neck*
bú / bù	*no, not*
bù	*MW for movies, films*
bú cuò	*not bad; pretty good*
bú yào	*don't (when it's a command)*
Bú yào hē jiǔ (kāichē)	*Don't drink (and drive);* **Bú yào kāi mén** *Don't open the door;* **Bú yào kū** *Don't cry;* **Bú yào zǒu** *Don't go*
cài	*food*
cānguǎn	*restaurant*
cāntīng	*restaurant*
cǎoméi	*strawberry*
cèsuǒ	*restroom; bathroom*
chá	*tea*
cháguǎn	*teahouse*
cháng	*long (length)*
chàng(gē)	*to sing (a song)*
chàng(gē)	*to sing (a song)*
chāo	*super*
chǎo	*to fry, fried*
chǎofàn	*fried rice*
chāojí shìchǎng	*supermarket*

chāzi *fork*
chēkù *garage*
chénggōng *to succeed*
chéngsè *orange (color);* **chéngzhī** *orange juice;* **chéngzi** *orange (fruit)*
chéngshì *a city*
chènshān *shirts*
chēpiào *a bus / train ticket*
chēzi *car*
chī *to eat*
chōngdiànqì *battery charger (for phones, computers, etc.)*
chǒngwù *a house pet*
chǒngwùdiàn *a pet store*
chǒu *ugly*
chuān *to wear (clothing)*
chuáng *bed*
chuānghu *window*
chūfā *to start out; to begin a journey*
chúfáng *kitchen*
chūguó *to leave the country; go abroad*
chuī *to blow; (to play a wind instrument)*
chuízi *hammer*
chūmén *to leave the house; (lit. "to go out the door")*
Chūnjié *Chinese New Year*
chūnjuǎn *spring roll*
chūntiān *spring*
chūqù *to go out*
chūshēng *to be born*
chúshī *chef*
chūzūchē / jìchéngchē *taxi*
cí *a word made up of more than one character*
cì *a time (in order) (e.g. the first time to do something; I've done that ten times)*
cōngmíng *intelligent, smart*

dà *big; large; old*
dǎ *to hit; to play a sport, to beat; to strike (to play a percussion instrument)*
dǎ bǎolíngqiú *to go bowling*
dǎ májiàng *to play mahjong*
dàfāng *generous*
dàhòutiān *three days from now*
dài *to wear (accessories)*
dài *to bring; to carry*
dàjiā *everybody, everyone*
dàn *egg*
dāng *to become*
dànshì *but (more formal)*
dào *to arrive*
dàojiā *to arrive home*
dāozi *knife*
dàxiàng *elephant*
dàxuè *a university*
dàxué *college, university;* **dàxuéshēng** *college / university student*

de *a particle*
de shíhòu *when; at / during the time when . . .*
Déguó *Germany;* **Déwén** *German (language)*

dēng *light*
děng *to wait (for)*
dì *prefix for ordinal numbers*
diǎn *an hour of the day*
diǎn (cài) *to order (food)*
diànhuà *telephone;* **diànhuà hàomǎ** *telephone number;* **diànnǎo** *computer;*
diànzishū *eBook*
diànzishū yuèdúqì *eBook reader*
diànnǎo kè *computer class*
diànshì *television;* **diànyǐng** *movie;* **diànyǐngyuàn** *movie theater*
diànzuān *drill*
diàoyú *to go fishing; to fish*
dìbǎn *the floor*
dìdi *younger brother*
dìlǐkè *geography class*
dìtǎn *the carpet / rug*
dìxí *sister-in-law (younger brother's wife)*
dìxiàshì *basement*
dōngtiān *winter*
dòngwùyuán *zoo*
dōngxī *stuff, things*
dōu *both; all*
dòufǔ *tofu*
dòuzi *bean(s)*
dǔchǎng *casino*
duì *yes; right; correct*
duìmiàn *across from, opposite of; face to face*
duō *many, much, a lot of*
duōshǎo *how much; how many (used for money)*
dùzi *stomach*
DVD *DVD*

è *hungry*
Éguó *Russia;* **Éwén** *Russian (language)*

èr	*2, two;* **èrshí** *20, twenty;* **èryuè** *February*
ěrduō	*ear(s)*
ěrhuán	*earrings*
érzi	*son*
Fǎguó	*France;* **Fǎwén** *French (language)*
fàn	*food, a meal; lit. cooked rice;*
fàndiàn	*hotel*
fàng	*to release; to let out; set off*
fángdōng	*a landlord*
fàngjià	*to have a vacation / holiday*
fángjiān	*a room*
fángzi	*home, house*
fānqié	*tomato*
fàntīng	*dining room*
fēijī	*airplane*
(fēi)jīchǎng	*airport*
Fēizhōu	*Africa*
fēn	*a minute; a cent, cents*
fèn	*a portion, a share, an order of something*
fěnbǐ	*chalk*
fēng	*crazy; wind*
fènglí	*pineapple*
fěnhóngsè	*pink*
Fēnlán	*Finland*
fùqián	*to pay money*
fùqīn	*father (fml);* **Fùqīnjié** *Father's Day*
fùxí	*to review*
gān	*dry*
Gǎnēnjié	*Thanksgiving*
gǎnlǎnqiú	*American football; rugby*
gānyījī	*dryer (clothes)*
gāo	*tall, high*
gāo'ěrfūqiúchǎng	*a golf course*
gāoěrfūqiú	*golf*
gāoxìng	*happy*
gāozhōng	*high school;* **gāozhōngshēng** *high school student*
gè	*MW mainly for people and general objects*
gēge	*older brother*
gěi	*to give*
gējù	*(Western) opera*
gēn	*and; with*
gèng	*even more*
gōngchǎng	*a factory*
gōngchéngshī	*engineer*
gōnggong	*father-in-law (H's father)*
gōnggòng qìchē / gōngchē	*bus*
gōngjù	*tools*
gōngjùxiāng	*toolbox*
gōngxǐ	*congratulations*
gōngyù	*an apartment building, a block of flats*
gōngyuán	*park*
gōngzuò	*a job; to work (v)*
gǒu	*dog*
gǔ	*drum*
guā (húzi)	*to shave (beard)*
Guāngmíngjié	*Hanukkah*
gūgu	*aunt (F's sister)*
guì	*expensive*
guójí	*nationality*
guójiā	*a nation; a country*
guǒzhī	*juice*
hái	*still, yet*
hái méi	*not yet*
hǎibiān	*the seaside*
háishì	*or; still*
hǎitān	*beach*
hǎixiān	*seafood*
háiyǒu	*in addition; furthermore; also*
hànbǎo	*hamburger*
Hánguó	*Korea; Hánwén Korean (language)*
hánjià	*winter vacation*
hǎo	*good, well, fine*
hào(mǎ)	*a number*
hǎochī	*tasty (food) (lit., "good eat")*
hǎohē	*tasty (beverages) (lit., "good drink")*
hǎokāi	*"good drive" (a car that drives well)*
hǎokàn	*(lit., "good read / see / watch") (depends on context)*
hǎoqí	*"good ride" (a bike / motorcycle that drives well)*
hǎotīng	*(lit., "good listen," "good-sounding")*
hǎowán	*fun*
hǎoyòng	*useful (lit., "good use")*
hé (hàn)	*and*
hē	*to drink*
hēibǎn	*blackboard, chalkboard*
hēisè	*black*
hémǎ	*hippopotamus*
hěn	*very*
hěn duō	*a lot*
hóngchá	*black tea*
hóngpútáojiǔ	*red wine*
hóngsè	*red*
hòumiàn	*behind, in back of*

hòunián	*year after next*
hòutiān	*the day after tomorrow*
hòuyuàn	*backyard*
hóuzi	*monkey*
huā	*flowers*
huàn yīfú	*to change (clothes)*
huángsè	*yellow*
huānyíng	*to welcome*
huáxuě	*to ski; skiing*
huāyuán	*garden*
huì	*to know how (be able to), can; will (future tense)*
huí	*to return; to go back*
huíguó	*to return to one's home country*
huí jiā	*to return home; go home*
huílái	*to come back; to return*
huīsè	*grey*
hūnlǐ	*wedding*
huǒchē	*a train*
huǒchēzhàn	*train station*
hùshì	*nurse*
húzi	*beard*
jī	*chicken;* **jīròu** *chicken (meat)*
jǐ	*how many;* **jǐgè** *how many (people)*
jiǎ	*fake*
jiā	*home, house; MW for stores; shops*
jiàn	*MW for items of clothing*
jiǎn (tóufa)	*to cut / trim (hair)*
jiān	*MW for rooms; spaces*
Jiānádà	*Canada*
jiǎndān	*easy*
jiǎng	*to speak; to say*
jiànmiàn	*to meet*
jiànshēn	*to work out*
jiànshēnfáng	*the gym*
jiǎo	*foot (feet)*
jiào	*to call; to be called (a name)*
jiàoliàn	*coach (sports)*
jiàoshì	*classroom*
jiǎotàchē (zìxíngchē)	*bicycle*
jiàotáng	*church*
jiàrì	*a day off; a non-working day*
jiāyóu	*to get gas; an expression meaning "Go for it!"*
jiāyóuzhàn	*gas station*
Jiāzhōu	*California*
jīchǎng	*airport*
jǐdiǎn	*(lit. how many hours . . .)*
jiéhūn	*to marry; to get married*
jiějie	*older sister;* **jiěmèi** *sisters (coll);* **jiěfu** *brother-in-law (older sis's husband)*
jiémù	*a program; (e.g. a television program / show)*
jiérì	*a holiday; festival*
jièzi	*ring*
jǐfēn	*(lit. how many minutes . . .)*
Jìfù	*stepfather*
jǐgè	*how many (people)*
jìgōng	*mechanic*
Jìmǔ	*stepmother*
jǐngchá	*police officer*
jìngzi	*mirror*
jīnnián	*this year*
jīntiān	*today*
Jìnǚ	*stepdaughter*
jīpiào	*airplane ticket*
jítā	*guitar*
jiǔ	*9, nine;* **jiǔ diǎn** *9:00; nine o'clock;* **jiǔshí** *90, ninety;* **jiǔyuè** *September*
jiù	*old (for things)*
jiǔbā	*a bar*
Jiùjīnshān	*San Francisco*
jiùjiu	*uncle (M's brother)*
jǐyuè	*(lit. how many months . . .)*
Jìzǐ	*stepson*
juéde	*to think; to feel*
jūnrén	*soldier*
jùzi	*saw*
kāfēi	*coffee*
kāfēisè	*brown*
kāfēitīng	*coffee shop; café*
kāfēiyīn	*caffeine*
kāi(chē)	*to drive (a car)*
kāihuì	*(to attend) a meeting*
kāishǐ	*to begin; to start*
kāixué	*to begin school*
kǎlāOK	*karaoke*
kàn	*to read, to watch, to look at, to see*
kǎoròu	*to grill; to barbeque*
kǎoshì	*to take a test; a test; an exam*
kǎoxiāng	*oven*
kè	*class; course; lesson*
kě	*thirsty*
kē	*MW for small, round objects*
kě'ài	*cute*
kèběn	*textbook*

kělè	*pop, soda, cola*
kěshì	*but (less formal)*
kètīng	*living room*
kěyǐ	*may, could*
kǒnglóng	*dinosaur*
kǒu	*MW for people (fml)*
kǒuqín	*harmonica*
kǔ	*bitter*
kuài	*bucks (inf)*
kuài	*fast*
kuàizi	*chopsticks*
kùzi	*pants, trousers (Br)*
kètīng	*living room*
lā	*to pull; (to play a bowed instrument)*
là	*spicy*
lǎba	*horn (trumpet)*
làbǐ	*crayon*
lǎnduò	*lazy*
làngmàn	*romantic*
lánqiú	*basketball*
lánqiúchǎng	*basketball court*
lánsè	*blue (color);* **lánméi** *blueberry*
lǎo	*old*
lǎobǎn	*boss*
lǎogōng	*husband (inf);* **lǎopó** *wife (inf)*
lǎohǔ	*tiger*
lǎoshī	*teacher*
lǎoshǔ	*mouse*
lèi	*tired*
lěng	*cold*
liǎn	*face*
liàng	*bright*
liǎng	*two (for most things but counting);* **liǎng diǎn** *2:00; two o'clock*
liánluò	*to get in touch with; to contact*
liànxí	*to practice*
liànxíběn	*workbook*
liàolǐ	*food; cuisine (esp. for Japanese cooking)*
liáotiān	*to chat*
líhūn	*to get divorced*
lǐmiàn	*inside*
lǐmiàn	*inside, within*
líng	*zero*
lìshǐ kè	*history class*
liù	*6, six;* **liù diǎn** *6:00, six o'clock;* **liùshí** *60, sixty;* **liùyuè** *June*
lízi	*pear*
lóngxiā	*lobster*
lóushàng	*upstairs*
lóutī	*stairs*
lóuxià	*downstairs*
lù	*road*
Lúndūn	*London*
Luómǎ	*Rome*
Luòshānjī	*Los Angeles*
luósīdāo	*screwdriver*
lǜchá	*green tea*
lǚguǎn	*motel*
lǜsè	*green*
lǜshī	*lawyer*
lǚxíng	*to travel*
ma	*a question particle*
mǎ	*horse*
mà(rén)	*to scold; yell at; curse (someone)*
mǎi	*to buy*
mài	*to sell*
mǎi cài	*buy groceries*
mǎi dōngxī	*go shopping*
mǎkèbǐ	*marker, marker pen*
māma	*mother, mom, mum*
mán	*pretty, quite*
màn	*slow*
máng	*busy*
mángguǒ	*mango*
Màngǔ	*Bangkok*
máo	*1/10 of a* **yuán**
māo	*cat*
máobǐ	*brush pen*
máoyī	*sweater*
màozi	*hat*
měi	*each; every*
méi	*not*
měigèxīngqī	*every week*
měigèyuè	*every month*
Měiguó	*America (US)*
mèimei	*younger sister;* **mèifù** *brother in-law (younger sister's husband)*
měinián	*every year*
měishùguǎn	*art gallery / museum*
měitiān	*every day*
mén	*door*
miàn	*noodles*
miànbāodiàn	*bakery*
míngnián	*next year*
míngtiān	*tomorrow*
míngzi	*name*
mìshū	*secretary*
mógu	*mushroom(s)*
Mòsīkē	*Moscow*

mótuōchē	*motorcycle*
Mòxīgē	*Mexico*
mùgōng	*carpenter*
mǔqīn	*mother (fml);* **Mǔqīnjié** *Mother's Day*
nà	*that;* **nà lǐ** *there;* **nǎ lǐ** *where*
nàgè	*that, that one*
nǎguó	*which country?*
nǎinai	*grandma (F's mom)*
nàme	*so*
nán	*difficult*
nán	*(male)*
Nán Fēi	*South Africa*
Nán Měizhōu	*South America*
nánguā	*pumpkin*
nánguādēng	*jack-o'-lantern*
nánguò	*sad*
nánhái(zi)	*little boy*
nánrén	*man*
nánshēng	*a young man*
ne	*a question particle*
néng	*can, be physically able to do something*
nǐ	*you (sing)*
nián	*a year*
niánqīng	*young*
niǎo	*bird*
nǐmen	*you (pl), you guys (inf)*
nín	*you (sing) (fml)*
níngméng	*lemon;* **níngméngzhī** *lemonade*
niú	*cow;* **niúnǎi** *milk;* **niúròu** *beef*
niúpái	*steak*
Niǔyuē(shì)	*New York City*
nóngchǎng	*a farm*
nóngmín	*farmer*
nǜ	*(female);* **nǚ'ér** *daughter*
nǚhái(zi)	*little girl*
Nuówēi	*Norway*
nǚrén	*woman*
nǚshēng	*a young woman*
Ōuzhōu	*Europe*
pàiduì	*a party*
páiqiú	*volleyball*
pàng	*fat*
pángbiān	*next to, beside*
pángxiè	*crab*
pánzi	*plate*
pǎo(bù)	*to run*
pàochá	*to make tea; to bubble*
péigēn	*bacon*
péngyǒu	*friend;* **nánpéngyǒu** *boyfriend;* **nǚpéngyǒu** *girlfriend*
piányí	*cheap*
piàoliàng	*pretty, beautiful*
píjiǔ	*beer*
píng	*MW for bottles*
píngbǎn diànnǎo	*tablet (computer)*
píngguǒ	*apple;* **píngguǒzhī** *apple juice*
pīngpāngqiú	*ping pong*
píngzi	*a bottle*
pīnyīn	*a romanization system that changes characters into words in an ABC alphabet*
pīsà	*pizza*
pópo	*mother-in-law (H's mother)*
pūkèpái	*poker; playing cards*
pútáo	*grape(s)*
pútáojiǔ	*wine*
qī	*7, seven;* **qī diǎn** *7:00, seven o'clock;* **qīshí** *70, seventy;* **qīyuè** *July*
qí	*to ride*
qián	*money*
qiānbǐ	*pencil*
(qiáng) zhuàng	*strong; powerful*
qiángbì	*wall*
qiánmiàn	*in front of*
qiánnián	*two years ago*
qiántiān	*the day before yesterday*
qiánzi	*pliers*
qiǎokèlì niúnǎi	*chocolate milk;* **rè qiǎokèlì** *hot chocolate*
qǐchuáng	*to wake up; get out of bed*
qīn	*to kiss*
qǐng	*please (do something)*
qīngjiāo	*green pepper(s)*
Qíngrénjié	*Valentine's Day*
qīngwā	*frog*
qìngzhù	*to celebrate*
qínláo	*hardworking*
qióng	*poor*
qiú	*ball;* **qìqiú** *balloon*
qiúchǎng	*stadium;* **qiúsài** *sports match*
qiūtiān	*fall, autumn*
qù	*to go*
qùnián	*last year*
ránhòu	*then; after that*
rè	*hot*
règǒu	*hot dog*

rén *person; people*
rènshì *to meet; to know*
Rìběn *Japan;* **Rìwén** *Japanese (language)*
ròu *meat*
ruǎn *soft*
Ruìdiǎn *Sweden*

sān *3, three;* **sān diǎn** *3:00, three o'clock;* **sānshí** *30, thirty;* **sānyuè** *March*
sānmíngzhì *sandwich*
sànbù *to go for a walk; to take a walk*
sǎosao *sister-in-law (older brother's wife)*
shāfā *sofa*
shàng *to get on / in (a train, plane, bus, etc.)*
shàng *to go to; to use (the bathroom)*
shàngbān *to go to / start work / be at work*
shànggèxīngqī *last week*
shànggèyuè *last month*
Shànghǎi *Shanghai*
shàngkè *to go to / attend class*
shàngmiàn *on top of, above*
shāngrén *businessman / woman*
shàngwǎng *to go online; to use the Internet*
shàngxué *to attend school*
shānyáng *goat*
shéi *who;* **shéide** *whose*
shēng *tone*
shēng *to give birth; to have a baby*
shēngcài *lettuce*
shěng *a province (part of a country)*
Shèngdànjié *Christmas*
Shèngdànjié Kuàilè! *Merry Christmas!*
Shèngdànshù *Christmas tree*
shēngrì *birthday (birth year)*
shēngwùxué *biology*
shénme *what*
shénme shíhòu *when?*
shēntǐ *the body*
shī *wet*
shí *10, ten;* **shí diǎn** *10:00, ten o'clock;* **shíyuè** *October*
shì *to be (am, is, are)*
shì *things, matters, items, work*
shí'èr diǎn *12:00, twelve o'clock;* **shí'èryuè** *December*
shìchǎng *market*
shíwù *Western-style food; cuisine*
shíyī diǎn *11:00, eleven o'clock;* **shíyīyuè** *November*
shízhōng *a clock*
shīzi *lion*
shǒu *hand;* **shǒubì** *arm;* **shǒubiǎo** *watch;* **shǒutào** *gloves*
shǒu *MW for songs*
shòu *thin*
(shòu) ruò *thin and weak*
shǒujī *cellular phone;* **shǒujīké** *cell phone case*
shù *tree*
shū (tóufa) *to comb (hair)*
shū *book;* **shūjià** *bookcase*
shuā (yá) *to brush (teeth)*
shuài *handsome*
shuāng *MW for a pair of something*
shūbāo *bookbag;* **shūguì** *bookcase;* **shūjià** *bookshelf*
shūcài *vegetable(s)*
shūdiàn *bookstore*
shūfáng *study (n) (U.K., also, sitting room)*
shūfú *comfortable*
shuǐ *water*
shuǐ jiǎo *Chinese dumplings (food)*
shuìjiào *to sleep (fml)*
shǔjià *summer vacation*
shuō *to speak; to say*
shūshu *uncle (F's younger brother)*
shǔtiáo *french fries*
shùxué kè *mathematics class*
sì *4, four;* **sì diǎn** *4:00, four o'clock;* **sìshí** *40, forty;* **sìyuè** *April*
suān *sour*
suì *year of age (years old)*
suǒyǐ *so, therefore*

T-xù *T-shirt*
tā *he, him; she, her; it;* **tāmen** *they, them*
tái *MW for vehicles, machines, electronic objects*
tài *too (much)*
Táiběi *Taipei*
Tàiguó *Thailand*
tàijí *taiji (tai chi), the martial art*
tàitai *Mrs*
tàiyáng *the sun*
tàiyáng yǎnjìng *sunglasses*
tán *to play (a stringed instrument like piano / guitar)*
táng *cousin;* **tángdì** *F's younger male cousin*
tàng *hot, burning*

táng	*MW for classes; lessons*
tāng	*soup*
tāngchí	*spoon*
tángguǒ	*candy*
tānxīn	*greedy*
tǎoyàn	*disagreeable*
táozi	*peach*
tī	*to kick; to play a sport*
tián	*sweet*
tiānhuābǎn	*the ceiling*
tiānqì	*the weather*
tiáo	*MW for long, thin objects; (e.g., fish, road)*
tiào	*to jump;* **tiàowǔ** *to dance*
tīng	*to hear; to listen to*
tíngchēchǎng	*parking lot*
tǐyù kè	*physical education class*
tǐyùguǎn	*gymnasium*
tòng	*painful, hurts*
tōngcháng	*usually*
tóngshì	*colleague; co-worker*
tóu	*head;* **tóufǎ** *hair*
tóufǎ	*hair*
tǔdòu (mǎlíngshǔ)	*potato(es)*
tuǐ	*leg*
tuī	*to push*
túshūguǎn	*library*
tùzi	*rabbit*
wā	*particle meaning "Wow"*
wàigōng	*grandpa (M's dad);* **wàipó** *grandma (M's mom)*
wàiguó	*foreigner*
wàiguórén	*foreigner*
wàimiàn	*outside*
wàimiàn	*outside, on the outer side of*
wàitào	*coat*
wǎn	*bowl*
wǎn ān	*goodnight;* **wǎnshàng hǎo** *good evening*
wǎn	*bowl; MW for bowls*
wán	*to play*
wǎncān	*dinner*
wǎnfàn	*dinner*
wǎnglù	*the Internet; a network*
wǎngqiú	*tennis*
wángù	*stubborn*
wánjù	*toy*
wánpí	*naughty*
Wànshèngjié	*Halloween; All Saints' Day*
wàzi	*socks*
wéi	*hello (for phone only)*
wēibōlú	*microwave*
wéijīn	*scarf*
wèilái	*the future*
wèishénme	*why*
wēnnuǎn	*warm*
wǒ	*me;* **wǒmen** *we, us*
wòshì	*bedroom*
wǔ	*5, five;* **wǔ diǎn** *5:00, five o'clock;* **wǔshí** *50, fifty;* **wǔyuè** *May*
wǔcān	*lunch*
wǔfàn	*lunch*
wūguī	*turtle*
xǐ (zǎo)	*to wash (to take a shower)*
xǐ yīfú	*to wash clothes (do laundry);* **xǐ wǎn** *to wash dishes*
xià	*to get off / out of (a train, plane, bus, etc.)*
xiàbān	*to finish work; get off work*
xiàgèxīngqī	*next week*
xiàgèyuè	*next month*
xiàkè	*to finish class / school*
xiàmiàn	*under, below*
xiān	*first*
xiǎng	*to want, would like to; to think about; to miss*
xiāngbīnjiǔ	*champagne*
Xiānggǎng	*Hong Kong*
xiāngjiāo	*banana*
xiàngqí	*Chess*
xiānshēng	*Mr*
xiànzài	*now; at the present*
xiǎo	*small; little; young*
(xiǎo) háizi	*child; children*
xiǎo(de) shíhòu	*childhood*
xiāofángyuán	*firefighter*
xiǎogǒu	*puppy*
xiǎomāo	*kitten*
xiǎoshí	*an hour*
xiǎotíqín	*violin*
xiǎoxīn	*to be careful; Be careful!*
xiàtiān	*summer*
xiàwǔ hǎo	*good afternoon*
xiàxuě	*to snow*
xiàyǔ	*to rain*
Xībānyá	*Spain;* **Xībānyáwén** *Spanish (language)*
xiě gōngkè	*(to write / do) homework*
xiě(zì)	*to write (words)*
xièxiè	*thank you*

xiézi *shoe*
xīguā *watermelon*
xīguǎn *straw*
xǐhuān *to like*
xīn *new (for things)*
xīngqī *a week;* **xīngqīyī** *Monday;* **xīngqīèr** *Tuesday;* **xīngqīsān** *Wednesday;* **xīngqīsì** *Thursday;* **xīngqīwǔ** *Friday;* **xīngqīliù** *Saturday;* **xīngqīrì** *Sunday*
xīngxīng *star(s)*
Xīnjiāpō *Singapore*
xīnlǐ yīshēng *psychologist*
xīnnián *new year*
xīnwén *the news*
xióng *bear*
xiōngdì *brothers (coll)*
xiōngdì jiěmèi *brothers and sisters (coll)*
xióngmāo *panda*
xiūchē *to repair a car*
xiūxi *to rest*
xǐwǎnjī *dishwasher*
xǐyīdiàn *cleaners*
xǐyīfáng *laundry room*
xǐyījī *washing machine*
xīzhuāng *suit*
xué(xí) *to learn, to study;* **xuéshēng** *student;* **xuéxí** *to learn / study;* **xuéxiào** *school*

yáchǐ *tooth (teeth)*
yǎnchànghuì *a concert*
yángcōng *onion(s)*
yángé *strict*
yángròu *lamb*
yángwáwa *doll*
yángzhuāng *dress*
yǎnjīng *eye(s)*
yǎnjìng *glasses*
yánsè *color(s)*
yǎnyuán *actor, actress*
yǎnzòuhuì *a classical music concert*
yào *to want something immediately available; to be going to do something; to be about to*
yào *to want; to be going to; must*
yàofáng *pharmacy*
yáokòngqì *a remote control*
Yàzhōu *Asia*
yě *also; too; and*
yèdiàn *nightclub*
yéye *grandpa (F's dad)*
yī *1, one;* **yī diǎn** *1:00, one o'clock;* **yìbǎi** *100, one hundred;* **yīyuè** *January*
Yìdàlì *Italy*
yīfú *clothes*
yīgè *one (of them); a*
yǐhòu *in the future; after (a specific event)*
Yìndù *India*
yìng *hard, firm (physically)*
Yīngguó *England (UK);* **Yīngwén** *English (language)*
yīngtáo *cherry*
Yīngwén kè *English class*
yínháng *bank*
yǐnliào *a beverage; a drink*
yīnwèi *because*
yīnyuè *music*
yìqǐ *together*
yǐqián *before; in the past; before (a specific event); ago*
yīshēng *doctor, Dr*
yīyàng *the same*
yīyuàn *hospital*
yǐzi *chair*
yǒng *always (the character that illustrates eight basic strokes)*
yòng *to use*
yǒu *there is / are; to have*
yòubiān *right, to the right of*
yóujú *post office*
yóulèchǎng *amusement park*
yōupán *USB flash drive*
yǒuqián *rich*
yǒuqù *interesting*
yóuxì *a game*
yóuyǒng *to swim*
yóuyǒngchí *swimming pool*
yòuzhuǎn *to turn right*
yú *fish*
yuán *Chinese currency (dollars)*
yuè *a month*
yuèfù *father-in-law (W's father);* **yuèmǔ** *mother-in-law (W's mother)*
yuèlì *monthly calendar*
yuèliàng *the moon*
Yuènán *Vietnam*
yǔmáoqiú *badminton*
yùmǐ *corn*
yún *cloud(s)*
yùndòng *sports, exercises*
yùshì *bathroom*

zài *again*
zài *in, at, on; indicates an action is in progress; then; again*
zàijiàn *goodbye*
zāng *dirty, filthy*
zǎocān *breakfast*
zǎofàn *breakfast*
zǎoshàng hǎo *good morning*
zázhì *magazine*
zěnme *how; why*
zěnmeyàng *how; how is it?; how about it?*
Zhāiyuè *Ramadan*
zhāng *MW for sheets of paper; tickets; flat objects*
zhǎo *to look for*
(zhào) xiàngjī *a camera*
zhè *this;* **zhè lǐ** *here*
zhé (yīfú) *to fold (clothes)*
zhègè *this, this one*
zhègèxīngqī *this week*
zhègèyuè *this month*
zhème *this much; so much*
zhēn(de) *really, truly*
zhèng zài *to be in the process of doing something (emphatic)*
zhī *MW for stick-like objects;* **zhī** *MW for animals*
Zhījiāgē *Chicago*
zhīzhū *spider*
zhízǒu *to walk (go) straight*
zhōng *(used in formal expressions of clock time)*
zhòng *heavy*
zhòng huā *to plant; grow flowers*
Zhōngguó *China;* **Zhōngwén** *Chinese (language)*
Zhōngguóchéng *Chinatown*
zhōngjiān *in the middle of, between*
Zhōngwén kè *Chinese class*
zhōu *a state (part of a country)*
zhōumò *the weekend*
zhū *pig;* **zhūròu** *pork*
zhù *to live*
zhǔ(fàn) *to cook (rice; a meal)*
zhuǎn *to turn*
zhuànqián *to earn money*
zhuō mí cáng *to play hide-and-seek*
zhuōqiú *table tennis; ping-pong; billiards (in mainland China)*
zhuōzi *table*
zì *a single word, one single character*
zìdiǎn *dictionary*
zǐsè *purple*
zǒu ba *Let's go!*
zǒu *to walk; to go*
zǒu(lù) *to walk*
zū *to rent*
zuì *the most; (used to form –est; most . . . superlatives)*
zuì xǐhuān *to like the most*
zuǐba *mouth*
zuìjìn *recently; in the near future*
zuò *to make, to do; to sit; to take (a plane, a train, etc.); to become*
zuò mèng *to dream; to have a dream*
(zuò) zuòyè *(to do) homework*
zuǒbiān *left, to the left of*
zuótiān *yesterday*
zuǒzhuǎn *to turn left*
zúqiú *soccer (football)*
zúqiúchǎng *soccer field*
zúqiúsài *soccer game; soccer match*

Voice credits:

Recorded at Alchemy Studios, London.

Cast: Sarah Cole, Xiaoyun Yao, Qiang Wu

Photos

100472092 © Shutterstock.com p. 9
92852914 © Shutterstock.com p. 28
115406227 © Shutterstock.com p. 28
12474675 © michaelztong/istockphoto.com p. 28
42-26911097 © IMAGEMORE CO., LTD/Imagemore Co., Ltd p. 33
189218858 © Shutterstock.com p. 53
143825479 © Shutterstock.com p. 72
29091658 © Shutterstock.com p. 72
179773268 © Shutterstock.com p. 72
130223891 © Shutterstock.com p. 76
102853205 © Shutterstock.com p. 76
97779629 © Shutterstock.com p. 76
45683650 © Shutterstock.com p. 76
139115975 © Shutterstock.com p. 86
54350242 © Shutterstock.com p. 86
72004336 © Shutterstock.com p. 86
73658080 © Shutterstock.com p. 86
149029946 © Shutterstock.com p. 86
193158353 © Shutterstock.com p. 86
61824715 © Shutterstock.com p. 117
114702394 © Shutterstock.com p. 160
111949736 © Shutterstock.com p. 160
178655171 © Shutterstock.com p. 160
231455866 © Shutterstock.com p. 160
92284378 © Shutterstock.com p. 160
80636173 © Kamira/Shutterstock.com p. 160
15065554 © Shutterstock.com p. 160
193904369 © Shutterstock.com p. 202
183395042 © Shutterstock.com p. 202
140502955 © Shutterstock.com p. 202
132400127 © Shutterstock.com p. 202
102414559 © Shutterstock.com p. 208
1440232 © Shutterstock.com p. 208
157359311 © Shutterstock.com p. 208
82838443 © Shutterstock.com p. 208
93283711 © Shutterstock.com p. 208
224331265 © Shutterstock.com p. 211
142785145 © Shutterstock.com p. 211
103969298 © Shutterstock.com p. 211
107475737 © Shutterstock.com p. 211

Illustrations

Barking Dog p. 45, 49 and 53

DVD build

Jon Stone Video